major label madness: lee, thurston, steve, and
kim. (1990 ©MICHAEL LAVINE)

kim gordon,
italy,
summer 1992.
(STEFANO GIOVANNINI)

glenn branca
conducting at
st. mark's church,
new york,
may 13, 1982.
(CATHERINE CERESOLE / BACHMANN)

a contemplative thurston on the streets of
germany, 1983. (LEE RANALDO)

shonen knife greets thurston in tokyo on the
DIRTY tour. (COURTESY SONIC YOUTH)

NEW YEARS
EVE
330 Broome

MUSIC

at ♥'s

FREE CHAMPAGNE

BY

The Coachmen
Harry Toledo
Liquid Idiot
Alan Suicide

FOOD

BY U + $4 OR $6 ADM.

ie. CHILI
LAZAGNA
COQ AU VIN
SALAD
LO MEIN etc.

XEROX

SCIENCE—A PROCESS APPROACH

9 PM 12/31/79 →
'80

THE ARCADIANS
+ DOG EAT DOG
WED. MAR. 11
CBGB

a rare arcadians flier. a photocopy of kim's
drawing later graced the cover of CONFUSION IS
SEX.

a poster from the night lee and david linton
joined the arcadians onstage.

SONIC
NEEDS A

lee, richard edson, thurston, and kim in the
band's first promotional photo, taken for the
NEW YORK ROCKER review. (LEE RANALDO)

TEENAGE MEN
TEENAGE MEN (6 times)
WALKING DOWN THE STREET
PLAYING LOUD GUITARS
IN NO MOOD FOR WOMEN
PLAYING LOUD GUITARS
TALKING ON THE TELEPHONE
PLAYING LOUD GUITARS
LOCKER ROOM AND ATTITUDES (← repeat bunch of times)
TEENAGE MEN (6 times)

YOUTH DRUMMER

CALL:
26-5258
OR
25-3757

live at new york's pyramid club, october 27,
1983. (CATHERINE CERESOLE / BACHMANN)

CONFUSION IS SEX
+ CONQUEST FOR DEATH

SONIC YOUTH
NECROS

LIVE AT DANCETERIA - FRIDAY FEB. 1st

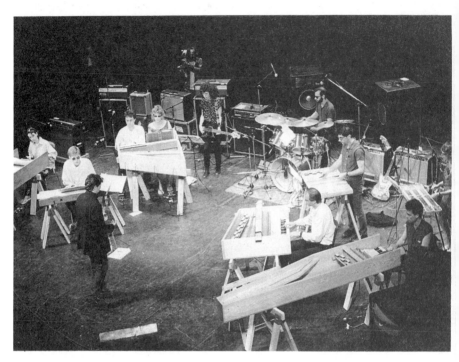

performing SYMPHONY NO. 4 in poitiers, france,
june 4, 1983. thurston is second from left; lee,
third from the right. (CATHERINE CERESOLE / BACHMANN)

cbgb, december 17, 1983. (CATHERINE CERESOLE / BACHMANN)

killer #2
$1.00

THIS ISSUE:

SONIC-YOUTH
CONFUSION IS SEX

I MAINTAIN THAT:
CHAOS is the future
AND BEYOND it is freedom
ConFusion is NEXT
AND NEXT AFTER THAT
IS THE TRUTH
YOU'VE GOT TO
CULTIVATE WHAT YOU
NEED TO NEED:
SONIC TOOTH

STICK YOUR FINGERS
IN YOUR MOUTH
SQUEEZE YOUR TONGUE
AND WRENCH IT OUT
FROM ITS UGLY
FUCKING CANCER
ROOT — YOU GOT TO
CULTIVATE WHAT YOU
NEED TO NEED:
SONIC-TOOTH

KILL YR IDOLS
W/ SONIC DEATH

KonFusion is NEXT
Sonic-Youth
N.Y.C. 1983

WIG-
HEIST

BLACK
FLAG

MINUTE-
MEN

DNA

HEART
ATTACK

FLIPPER

WHITE-
HOUSE

CAUSE
FOR
ALARM

RUDOLPH
GREY

VIRGIN
PRUNES

AND SOME
OTHER
JERKS

sonic youth received a warm reception at the gila
monster jamboree, despite the chilly desert
temperatures. (A. PEAK 85)

an outtake from BAD MOON RISING's back-cover shoot.

(JAMES WELLING)

gunning for the big time: kim in the video for
"death valley '69." (©R. KERN)

Treachery
Pays

RISK YOUR LIFE

SONIC FRI.
YOUTH JULY
+UT 22

YOU MAY be mugged,
Knifed, Slashed, robbed,
raped, buried, killed,
murdered, beaten, shot,
etc.
BUT it's WORTH it

SIN CLUB
272 E. 3rd + AVE. C
10:30 pm — $3.00

X X
SONIC
DEATH

BE YOUR
Brother's
KEEPER

DEUTSCHE BUNDESPOST
EDITH STEIN
†1942 IN AUSCHWITZ

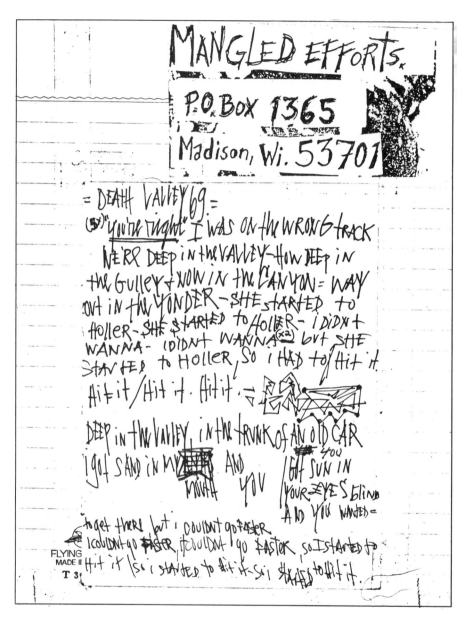

lydia lunch's handwritten contribution to
"death valley '69."

ALt. DV69 tuning
Good for something...

Low F# A Ā F# F# F#

y'have to live w/ waves of fear
we're gonna kill CAlifornia girls
the exploding load
and the milkmaid maidenhead

WE'RE Gonna Kill the CALIFORNIA Girls
WE'RE Gonna fire the exploding load
in the milkmaid maidenhead
WE'RE Gonna find the meaning of feeling good
And WE'RE Gonna STAY there as long as we think we should
the mystery train is a two way plane
one way is the expressway to your skull

VI 7.9/V2-7/M-7/T-5/B-6/T-5/HM-10/LM-3.5/B-6.7

MARILYN MOORE

Sound asleep till night until day
frustrated desire turns you away
and turns you insane
over and over
you get to a point
to make it dissappear
~~and you're always~~ believing and believing in fear

over and over ~

NECROS
THE MIRROVR which Flatters not.

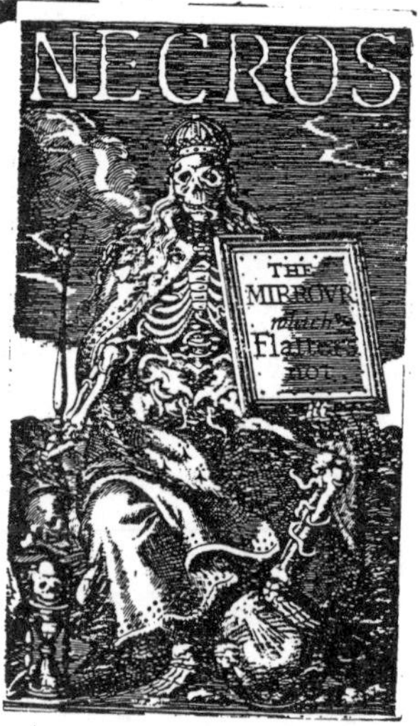

VI - 7
V2 - 7
M - 6
T - 8
B - 8
T - 7
HM - 7
LM - 4
B - 8
R - 3

EVOL

madonna, Sean + me
piano tape
Death to our Friends
Green Lights
?

Lee Part

I
12-4 w shimmer

13-4

II Crashes,
? 5-8 w distort

7 clean

III open distort
clean up to 5,
hi up + end slide

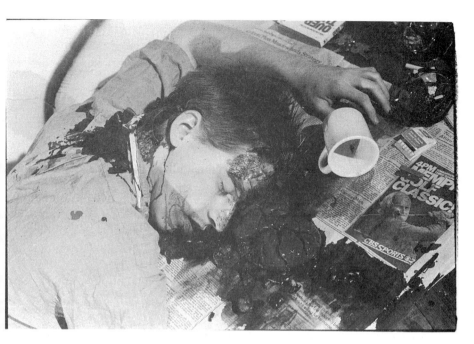

above: richard kern flaunted his low-budget, yet convincing, gore effects in the "death valley '69" video, displayed here on steve. (©R. KERN)

left: eyes without a face: thurston mugs for the cover of the "starpower" single. (LEE RANALDO)

ciccone youth unmasked: steve, mike watt, kim, lee, and thurston. (©1994 IAN HARPER)

the band chose the snapshot on this "dunceteria"
flier--of kim, age 10, and her older brother
keller in hawaii--for its creepy aura.

iggy pop first joined sonic youth onstage for "i wanna be your dog" in london during the 1987 SISTER tour; and again (this photo), in australia, early 1993. (TONY MOTT)

SEA SIK SMART AND FAST

1 HE'S RUNNING ON A TUFF GNARL IN HIS HEAD HE'S GOT A FATAL ERECTION HOME IN BED
2 HE'S REALLY SMART AND HE'S REALLY FAST THERE'S A HARD TIT KILLER FUCK IN HIS PAST
3 SAINTS PRESERVE US IN HOT YOUNG STUFF THE SAVING GRACE IS A SONIC PIG PILE
6 AN ADRENAL MENTAL MAN-TOOL BOX EXPLODES IN MUSIC CREATES UTOPIA
4 AMAZING GRAZING STRANGE AND RAGING FLIES ARE FLARING THRU YOUR BRAINS
5 SPASTIC FLAILING LITERALLY RAISING MY ROOF (MY ROOF AT LEAST)
7 YOU GNARL OUT ON MY NERVES YOU WEIRD AND CRUSH THE CRANKING RAUNCH
  FLESH DIRT FORCEFIELD LOST AND FOUND LET'S BURN YOUR BROKEN HEART
  SET OUR SIGHTS ON SIGHTS NOT YET SET
  LET'S SCORCH YOUR FRAZZLED BRAINWAVE WIG
  LET'S POKE YOUR EYES OUT
  OK OK YOU READY? YOU READY?
  THE WRENCH IS SET.

V1 - 7.5
V2 - "
m - 6.5
T - 8
B - 8.2
T - 8
HM - 7
LM - "
D - 7
R - 10

THUR.
AMP
SET
FOR
FEEDBACK

GHOST BITCH

an early draft of "tuff gnarl."

(COURTESY SONIC YOUTH)

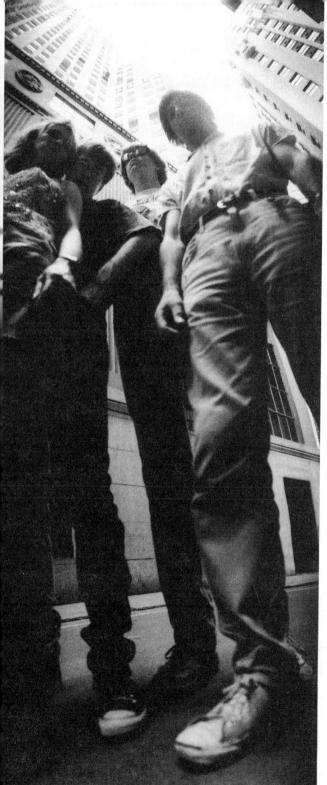

walking tall,
circa
**DAYDREAM
NATION.**

(1988 ©MICHAEL
LAVINE)

sonic youth, 1993. (CLAIRE TUCKLEY, MELBOURNE, AUSTRALIA)

lee and thurston frequently hammer new sounds
out of their guitars, often mid-concert.
(CATHERINE CERESOLE / BACHMANN)

thurston and a
wide-eyed kurt
cobain in los
angeles, 1992.
(COURTESY SONIC YOUTH)

(TONY MOTT)

yoshimi and kim with some stiff, old rock star.

dim stars: thurston, don fleming, steve, and
richard hell. (LARRY BUSACCA)

thurston, kim, australian rocker kim salmon (the scientists, the surrealists), nick cave, and mudhoney's mark arm at the big day out festival, adelaide, australia, 1993. (TONY MOTT)

Confusion
Is
Next

Confusion Is Next

THE SONIC YOUTH STORY

Alec Foege

ST. MARTIN'S PRESS
NEW YORK

FOR SONG PERMISSIONS, SEE PAGE 275.

DESIGN BY SARA STEMEN

LIBRARY OF CONGRESS
CATALOGING-IN-PUBLICATION DATA

FOEGE, ALEC.
  CONFUSION IS NEXT : THE SONIC YOUTH
STORY / ALEC FOEGE.
    P. CM.
  ISBN 0-312-11369-2
  1. SONIC YOUTH (MUSICAL GROUP)
2. ROCK MUSICIANS—UNITED STATES-
  -BIOGRAPHY. I. TITLE.
  ML421.S615F6 1994
  782.42166'092'2—DC20   94-12768
[B]   CIP
                                MN

10 9 8 7 6

for Erica

Contents

Acknowledgments

Because so much of the territory covered in this book remains at best haphazardly documented, those who granted me interviews provided valuable, one-of-a-kind source material.

Thanks are due to the following people, who all took time out of busy schedules to recollect events, major and minute: Bob Bert, Martin Bisi, Glenn Branca, Tim Carr, Robert Christgau, Gerard Cosloy, Mike Diamond, Richard Edson, Ray Farrell, Don Fleming, Gary Gersh, Kim Gordon, Mark Ibold, Marc Jacobs, Mike Kelley, Richard Kern, Lydia Lunch, Greil Marcus, Susan Martin, Thurston Moore, Lee Ranaldo, Christian Francis Roth, Ron Saint Germain, Nicholas Sansano, Arleen Schloss, Jim Sclavunos, Steve Shelley, Leah Singer, Paul Smith, Epic Soundtracks, Jim Testa, Butch Vig, and Mike Watt.

I also owe thanks to Jim Fitzgerald at St. Martin's Press for being enthusiastic about a book on Sonic Youth from the start; and to Faith Hamlin for her valuable advice and reassurances.

Others who provided vital contacts and/or assistance include Jon Silva, Mike Meisel, and Janet Billig at Gold Mountain, Jim Merlis at

Geffen, Spencer Gates and Johan Kugelberg at Matador, Evie Greenbaum at St. Martin's Press, Ally Finkel at Sanford J. Greenburger, Amy Aronson, Steve Bodow, Sheenah Fair, Jane Friedman, Steven Huvane, Danny Kahn, Miriam Lockshin, Craig Marks, Anne Milburn, Elaine Pfefferblit, Michael Pietsch, Jill Richmond, Michael Sanders, Barbara Shelley, Janet Siroto, Ken Weinstein, and Howard Wuelfing. Special thanks to Brian Keizer, who first convinced me of this book's merits.

Additional gratitude is due to the members of Sonic Youth—Lee Ranaldo, Thurston Moore, Kim Gordon, and Steve Shelley—who graciously opened their homes and their memory banks to me (and even provided the photos and documents to prove it all happened just the way they said).

Lastly, I'd like to thank to my parents, Kenneth and Norma Foege; my sister Andrea, transcriber extraordinaire; and Erica Sanders, who lived with this book as long as I did and whose constant love and support helped make it a reality.

Foreword

Sonic Youth started out just as any band starts out—four people fresh into their twenties wanting to make music to explore and experss their feelings. As a history this book pretty much has all the facts and scenarios in order. It's funny—and somewhat disturbing—to read about yourself. There are no rock and roll incidents à la Led Zeppelin. Nor are there any major catastrophes. Boring? Yeh, maybe—but some people like Mr. Foege seem to think we're important within the scheme of rock and roll. Whatever that may be. The personal life and secret side of each member is really not too revealed here. The band comes across as conceptual, forced, pretentious, and materialistic, but also friendly, smart, happy, and diligent. I'm displayed as a total freak—obsessive to the point of inanity. But where's the sadness and soul-searching which, like anyone, we all experience?

I can only say it's undercover

And it's in the music.

And like The Beatles said before us

(lest we forget):

All

you

need

is

love.

-------thurston

Prologue | Kill Yr. Idols

''ELECTRICITY COMES FROM OTHER PLANETS.''
—FROM ''TEMPTATION INSIDE YOUR HEART,''
BY THE VELVET UNDERGROUND

Imagine a world without rock bands. It isn't hard to do.

A little more than thirty years ago, rock and roll—a new hybrid music riven from country and blues, largely based around the amplified sounds of an electrified guitar—had little or no impact on most Americans. Today, of course, its influences can be seen and heard everywhere. And yet, fresh forms of rock and roll—music defined in its narrowest sense by drums played with a backbeat—are virtually nowhere to be found.

The effects of the media and recording-industry frenzies that darkened Seattle in 1991 have already begun to recede into the past. The massive success of Nevermind—the major-label debut of a now-famous punk-inspired trio named Nirvana—convinced big recording conglomerates that they could co-opt a certain style of rock music and make money off it.

But Nevermind's success didn't much change the way the industry does business. Labels still labor to sign the sure thing—that's just good business, after all. So while guitar-based rock music dominated the charts in 1992 for the first time in over a decade, the names at the front lines of the skirmish—Pearl Jam, Stone Temple Pilots, Blind Melon, the Spin Doctors, the Black Crowes, and Lenny Kravitz—were either second-rate imitators, nostalgia acts, or some combination of the two. The status quo. (Want proof? Nirvana's 1993 follow-up to Nevermind, titled In Utero, made a showy debut at number one on Billboard's album chart, but was quickly supplanted by a new album from a suitably bloated seventies artifact, Meat Loaf. A few weeks later, In Utero dropped from the Top Ten.)

Rock is dead. And Sonic Youth helped kill it.

For the past thirteen years, a tight group of New York transplants questioned and ever so slightly altered rock music's most basic tenets—and by doing so, succeeded in separating flesh from bone. Rock music was born out of the starkly anti-entertainment notion that raw emotion was more affecting than whimsically wrought craft. From Jerry Lee Lewis to Keith Richards to Sid Vicious to Darby Crash, you had to live it to lasso it. No more.

Not that people don't still kill themselves trying. It's simply that in the wake of a career as varied, as ground-breaking, as invigorating, and as ironic in tone as Sonic Youth's, why bother?

The story of Sonic Youth is the tale of what many believed to be the post-rock era, an era fraught with unchecked corporatism and conservativism. Surprisingly, the 1980s proved to be rock music's most fertile decade. In 1990, Thurston Moore, Sonic Youth's tendentious lead singer, talked of producing a follow-up edition of Killer, a music fanzine he published via photocopier over a decade ago, listing the best 10,000 records of the 1980s. He never produced the issue, but he meant the part about the 10,000 records.

"There was a huge number of records made independently, but the mainstream was so horrible during the eighties that people look back on it as this very bad period of music," Moore observes. "It'll go down in history as a very bad period of music, until people realize how prolific it was underground." While a lot of people, including much of the recording industry, weren't paying attention, an itinerant bunch of idea-fueled musicians and artists devised a new popular vocabulary.

These days, however, an awful lot of people are speaking the new mother tongue. "Alternative"—the term the mainstream recording industry devised to describe hip music that got played on college radio stations throughout the 1980s but didn't quite match the sales figures of older acts—looks like its going to fade from use any day now. "Alternative"? one wonders. Alternative to what?

More than one subject I interviewed for this book suggested that if the thousands of great independent releases that came out on hard-to-find labels in the early eighties were rereleased today under different band names, they'd all have a chance at Nirvana's success. While the music industry didn't change much, listeners' tastes certainly have.

Sonic Youth, too young to be punk and too old to be alternative, is the key to understanding and appreciating what happened between then and now. In 1981 Sonic Youth formed amid the burnt embers of punk's explosion and No Wave's fizzle. In 1990 the band enjoined Geffen, its current label, with Nirvana, the group who changed it all. This book is an attempt to tell the story of the last fifteen or so years in rock-music history through a band that, although it has yet to sell a million albums or become an MTV or commercial-radio mainstay, somehow embodies a sea change in American popular-culture tastes.

Over the past thirteen years, Sonic Youth has made some of the most enduring, innovative pop product—all the while teetering on the line between the serious and the sublime. Chances are the band's work won't be widely appreciated till it can be observed with a bit of chronological perspective, from a point where its hair-thin irony will seem a little less intimidating. Only then will the circle be broken.

In October 1993 Time magazine slapped a photo of Pearl Jam's Eddie Vedder on its cover and ran a story titled "Rock's Anxious

Rebels.'' The article quickly cut to the striking similarities figures like Vedder share with their forebears: "Does he refuse to adopt the trappings of a rock star, thus demonstrating that he's such a genuine article that he doesn't need stardom? Absolutely.''

Once an underground movement's diverse gestures can be reduced to an act guaranteed to evoke familiar responses from a rapt audience, anyone can duplicate them. Kurt Cobain's well-publicized dalliance with heroin, his quibbles with the press, his painfully wrought songs that chronicle the tribulations of instant stardom, seemed woefully cliché to anyone familiar with his antecedents. Even Cobain himself admitted that Nirvana was, in essence, a nostalgia show for kids who missed the original punk movement. Then he shot himself to death. Which leads one to wonder: Is that all there is?

MTV, the world's most influential all-music cable television channel, long ago committed itself to pop stars: Michael Jackson, Janet Jackson, George Michael, U2, Madonna, Guns N' Roses, Prince—artists whose larger-than-life images were established early on in their careers and thus were well-suited to the medium's cinematic properties. With the occasional exception made for an act with possible mega-hit potential, anything less than hugely popular—that is, multi-platinum sales—is banished either to "120 Minutes," MTV's late-night "alternative" ghetto, or one of a few other off-hour specialty slots designed to keep genuinely antiauthoritarian alternative, hip hop, and heavy metal away from the big-money advertisers.

Perhaps, one day soon, No Wave will get its due. An extremely brief period in rock's development, No Wave explored rock's true extremes in a pre-MTV world. An exclusively New York scene, lodged right in between punk and new wave (1978 to 1979), No Wave happened at loft parties and in the tiny clubs of downtown Manhattan. Few of the acts ever recorded and few lasted more than a year. Most recorded documents were released on obscure labels and are long out of print.

Unlike MTV, No Wave imagined a future. A future where electric guitars no longer ruffled feathers—unless of course you literally banged people over the head with them. A future where noisy guitar solos no longer elicited appreciative sighs—unless those noisy guitar solos amounted to pure noise. A future where rock music meant absolutely nothing to the masses, where it existed primarily as a homegrown folk music prepared and performed for the very few. A future very much like today.

From the start, Sonic Youth understood and appreciated No Wave's mission. Punk was revolutionary and exciting, but its scope was too narrow. The establishment New York art world was too elitist. Shorn of its artlike pretension, popular music's ties to the so-called legitimate art world have always been tenuous at best. Art, in the traditional sense, is difficult, deep, for a rarefied few; popular culture is frivolous, easy, pointless.

Rock music's conspicuous quest for material gain and abstruse meanings for many years easily ensured it, in the minds of the art world, from being mistaken for anything consciously artful. Conversely, most rock musicians gleefully characterized their work as ''anti-art''; those who presented themselves as aspiring to anything higher than commercial gain were categorized derisively as ''art rockers.''

John Cage, the late avant-garde composer, is perhaps the patron saint of art rock. In the 1950s, Cage sought to apply the ideas of Marcel Duchamp—the French artist best known for displaying factory-rendered urinals as finished artwork—to music. In 1952, Cage birthed ''4'33'' ''—in essence, four minutes and thirty-three seconds of silence. Determined to further dissolve the line between art and everyday existence, Cage set out to produce randomly determined ''chance'' music. When his precepts were rejected by his music colleagues, Cage turned to artists in other fields for support. A generation of visual artists, beginning with the likes of Claes Oldenberg and Jasper Johns and culminating with Andy Warhol, were liberated by Cage's taboo-testing discovery: There cannot, and ought not, be any line drawn between popular art and high art. Sonic Youth continues in that tradition.

"Indeterminacy is not an invitation to anarchy," warned Margaret Leng Tan, a pianist and protégée of Cage's, in a tribute to her late mentor published in the New York Times on August 1, 1993. "Only through knowing the material so well that it has become reflex does one produce a responsible indeterminate performance. As John said, his biggest problem was finding 'a way to let people be free without their becoming foolish.' " Judging from the scolding, remonstrative tone of Tan's words, it's easy to appreciate why rock musicians to this day remain wary of the art establishment.

Whatever the case, the effects of rock music on modern-day American culture are largely incalculable. Its basic components—screaming guitars, pounding drums, four-four rhythms—are everywhere; yet in more than one sense, its effects have been negligible.

This is not to say that one can't see the wrinkles the rock culture has left in our society's cultural fabric. The more casual, less rigid settings in which we interact today are a lasting result of a music that said, in the words of John Lennon, that things would be alright. So, too, is the omnipresent recreational drug culture that few American adolescents pass by en route to adulthood. The average citizen's notions of hipdom—the way people dress up, converse, make love—are another effect. It's just that they're hard to filter out of a culture that's changed more in the past thirty years than it did in the previous hundred.

From the wizened perspective of the mid-1990s, it is difficult to recall the heady mix of hope and cynicism that clouded the American psyche at the end of 1980. On November 4, 1980, a majority of voters registered their approval of Ronald Wilson Reagan, who on that day was elected fortieth President of the United States. And on December 8, 1980, thirty-four days later, John Lennon—the former Beatle who represented more than any other performer of his generation the effect rock music could have on real life—was gunned down in front of his New York City apartment building by a fan, one Mark David Chapman. The relatively coincidental occurrence of these two events might as well have set the tenor for the decade of pop culture to come.

For backers of the status quo, Reagan's election proved what they in their hearts already knew to be the case: The counterculture forged in the 1960s had run its course. Rock music, arguably the soundtrack for the counterculture movement, had also changed. Thrust into the forefront of American culture in the late sixties by arresting performers such as Bob Dylan, Jimi Hendrix, Janis Joplin, Mick Jagger, and Pete Townshend, rock music had been the first popular cultural force purporting to represent goals other than those that were entertainment-related. But the voters who put Ronald Reagan into office had forged a fundamental opposition to the dwindling ranks of the sixties counterculture. Big fish swallows little fish; case closed.

For those set on change, Lennon's murder sent a more poignant message: Believing in change is not change itself. Furthermore, the rock culture, freshly minted only a decade or so earlier, could no longer even be considered a tool in implementing proposed change.

In 1983 Kim Gordon, the 30-year-old bassist for what was then a virtually unknown downtown band called Sonic Youth, wrote in *Artforum*: "People pay to see others believe in themselves. . . . On stage, in the midst of rock'n'roll, many things happen and anything can happen, whether people come as voyeurs or come to submit to the moment." Gordon went on to describe the awesome power acquired by performers who appear to be in total submission to their audiences—and how, inevitably, that intensity becomes "mannered and dishonest."

As Greil Marcus aptly commented, in response to Gordon's dictum, in his 1989 book *Lipstick Traces*: "Such words would not have been written in the mid-1970s, when people paid to see others believe that others believed in them."

* * *

In the world in which Sonic Youth was formed, hit singles—the cornerstone of the old-school rock-and-roll mentality—are irrelevant. Not because these bands didn't want to be successful for fear of losing their hip credentials, but simply because that notion of success was initially so far beyond their scope and abilities.

The network of independent rock-and-roll labels that cropped up in the early 1980s was the collective response of a generation of young musicians and fans who had been systematically ignored by the major labels. According to Hit Men, Frederick Dannen's insider account of corruption at the major labels during the 1980s, these young bands never even had a chance anyway. Institutionalized payola kept many big-league music corporation executives in the early eighties so busy deciding which singles merited a payoff to the Network—a group of all-powerful independent promoters that determined who got Top 40 radio play—that there was little time spent scouting new talent.

Furthermore, Sonic Youth took the punk ethos to heart. Kim Gordon, Thurston Moore, and Lee Ranaldo were all drawn to downtown Manhattan by verdant tales of punk's glory. Kim to this day will not admit herself a musician; but punk taught her that that was just fine as long as your ideas were fresh. Thurston is constantly apologizing for his rudimentary guitar playing. "Lee's the real musician in the group," he'll say. And yet Lee is the member of Sonic Youth most likely to be found coaxing white noise out of his guitar. Steve Shelley, of course, is too young to remember having to take the above sentiments as anything but a given.

Whether by coincidence or on purpose, Sonic Youth warranted not even a mention in Time's detailed 1993 cover story. ("In a way I'm almost happy," Kim Gordon says. "Because alternative music is really just heavy rock.") No hit singles, no gold albums, little MTV airplay, no drug habits—why should that be surprising? And yet few bands mentioned in the piece—the Breeders, Nirvana, Mudhoney, Babes in Toyland—can claim to be wholly uninfluenced, either directly or indirectly, by Sonic Youth.

Rock music has changed an awful lot in the last decade and a half—for one, it seems a lot closer to an imminent wane. Never again will sounds emanating from an electric guitar provoke terror.

My hope for this book is to excite and encourage exploration down unpaved creative avenues, even those that appear especially rocky. *Confusion is next*, as Sonic Youth once wrote. But it ought to be a happy confusion. *And after that is the truth.* Well, maybe.

For right now, I'm convinced that Sonic Youth is as good and confusing as this stuff gets. The Velvet Underground, New York's last momentous sonic blast, had to re-form twenty years after the fact to get its proper due. So why not celebrate Sonic Youth now, some thirteen years into its original journey?

Sonic Youth detractors frequently argue that the band's consistent inability to produce even one hit single that captures everything it's about—its own "Smells Like Teen Spirit"—is evidence of failure. This book seeks to dispel that notion, but if that's one's belief, there's a more compelling reason to read on: You're not likely to have heard the story that follows—unless, of course, you're already a part of it.

1 | Total Trash

Sear Sound doesn't look like the future. The Times Square studio where Sonic Youth is recording its new album looks more like a bowling alley cocktail lounge.

On a rare crisp day in early October 1993, Sonic Youth is laying down the basic tracks for *Experimental Jet Set, Trash and No Star*, the band's eighth album. At work, the members of Sonic Youth act essentially the same way they do onstage—they're irksomely relaxed, almost somnambulant at times.

Butch Vig, the disc's producer and a proto-legend in his own right, is working behind a sixteen-track Neve console that is primitive by today's digital standards but has played home to the warm sounds of countless jazz acts as well as John Lennon's last efforts. (Sear Sound—formerly the Hit Factory—just happens to be the studio Lennon was returning from the night he was shot.)

For a band so bent on innovation, Sonic Youth remains surprisingly attached to spaces and equipment with histories. The band nearly traveled all the way to Valdosta, Georgia, a nowhere town in the middle of nowhere (the band has recorded all its albums in

New York) for a chance to play through the same board on which the Beach Boys' *Pet Sounds* album took shape. Walter Sear, the studio's namesake and proprietor, has a collection of two hundred vintage microphones from which the band selects a few with which to record. Thurston marvels to one visitor that Sun Ra once graced the smallish wood-paneled studio with his presence.

When I arrive, on the final day of basic-track recording, things seem well-ordered in an extremely low-key kind of way. Kim Gordon and Steve Shelley are in the back corner of the narrow recording room; Kim is facing Steve, with her back to the window that separates the recording space from the mixing booth. They are running through the primordially basic riff for an unfinished Gordon track, which she titles on the spot: "Quest for the Cup"— "That's what it's called in golf, right?" Kim asks in mock precision to no one in particular.

After Kim plays her simple, textured part on a six-string guitar rigged through her bass amplifier, Butch Vig expresses concern that the first section sounds too much like the two-chord stomp that opens Led Zeppelin's "Whole Lotta Love"—enough so that the legendarily litigious supergroup might officially protest. Kim counters that the homage is intentional but that she'll alter it if he likes.

Dressed in what looks to be a rather particular pair of Levi's boot-cut corduroys, circa 1975, and a sweatshirt tattooed with a Playboy insignia, Gordon plays her guitar part with intensity, her dirty-blonde hair tossing back and forth with each jerk at the guitar.

Steve Shelley, a hipster nerd in a short-sleeve plaid shirt, wire-rims, and light brown bangs that meet his glasses frames at the top, is tossing around rhythm combinations that run slightly against Gordon's. At first listen, the result doesn't sound like much of anything, what pickup musicians might play after learning a few chords. But one comes to suspect grand things hatched from simple beginnings with this bunch.

Thurston Moore (at six and a half feet, he's towering at close proximity) certainly isn't worrying. His long figure—clad in unfaded blue jeans, a red T-shirt that reads TWISTED VILLAGE (an obscure Connecticut independent label) on the back, and large-looking basketball shoes—lies prone (he's dead asleep) on a black leather sofa directly in front of the console. Kim and Thurston rarely exchange the in-public glances and touches of most married couples, but their complementary wardrobes make their closeness apparent.

Lee Ranaldo, who from certain angles looks like a more sallow version of the actor James Woods, is dressed in the jeans-and-a-rumpled-button-down uniform of a former Deadhead (which he is). He wanders around from room to room of the studio, making small talk with the session's few guests, reading the New York Times, offering a sixth cup of coffee to everyone.

Butch Vig, carefully accoutered in what is best described as "grunge chic" (expensive-looking flannel shirt, gray pressed pants, desert boots), and engineer John Siket diligently preserve each take on wide tape running at a slower-than-normal 15 ips (inches per second), a high-fidelity trick used for additional "warmth" on the bottom end. Vig and Siket offer support, mentioning takes they prefer and offering to edit out stray bars that seem uneven. Otherwise, Gordon and Shelley are left on their own, trusting that everything Sonic Youth does, it does with purpose.

A couple hours later, all four members step into the recording chamber together. The basic tracks are always done this way—live in the studio. For this album, thirteen tracks were put to tape in four days; the most productive day yielded the groundwork for four songs. The band is ahead of schedule.

Again Gordon stands, facing Shelley. Moore and Ranaldo sit in chairs lined up behind her, both facing the same way. Their equipment—a few amps, a rack of guitars, a few old-fashioned ribbon microphones—is clustered around them, giving the overall effect of bomb makers at work in a bunker.

They're recording another Gordon number, "Bone," which features a typically asymmetrical Sonic Youth song structure: It begins with a fast part, this time led by Steve's military-precise drum roll, leads into a slower, prettier segment, during which Gordon half-sings her lyrics, and falls back into the spaceship-with-a-couple-bolts-loose mode of the first section.

Independently, none of the band members seems a virtuoso. Kim is slapping out a repetitive two-note pattern on her guitar. Thurston occasionally slashes at his guitar, producing a harsh, tinny sound that ignites the song's quick parts like a motorcycle kickstart. Lee furiously strums his guitar with his right hand while running his left up and down its metal neck, eliciting an unearthly chatter that perfectly complements the videotape of *Blade Runner* that runs throughout the evening with the sound off in the control booth. Only Steve performs in a style easily defined as rock. Together, the four members of Sonic Youth—even live through the studio's monitors—sound like no other group around.

Later, a quick in-studio photo session turns into an impromptu twenty-minute improvisation that sounds closer to free jazz or the bombastic progressive rock of the mid-seventies than to Sonic Youth's "polished" numbers. ("That was called jamming on a riff—isn't that what rock bands do?" Moore says archly as the band finishes up.)

A jam session, the bane of most musicians raised in the wake of punk rock's aesthetic downsizing (Sonic Youth included), reveals where Sonic Youth finds musical roads less traveled. Any member of the group can change the vibe; Lee even switches guitars midway to explore some spur-of-the-moment idea. But unlike its forebears, this band doesn't take its incantatory powers for granted. Newfound grooves or sounds are remembered or recorded, and frequently find perfect homes as jewels in other, more complementary settings.

A few nights later, Moore spends a solitary evening in the darkened studio recording his vocal tracks. Reading fresh lyrics scrawled in felt-tip pen off a jumble of sheets propped on a music stand, Moore runs through each song a number of times before he loosens up.

Moore's voice, neither a classical instrument nor the standard rock belt, becomes more supple after a few takes and a couple drops of licorice oil swallowed with hot water.

For "Waist," a wry look at consumerism in some futuristic metropolis, Moore at first sneers through the verses, a strategy he then abandons as "too punk." He then crosses out the end of a line on the sheet, in which the protagonist catches his friend "slipping into Burger King," and changes it to "slipping into Agnes B." The change appears to drastically alter the verse's meaning—then again, it may just be an oblique reference to X-Girl, the ultra-hip fashion concern co-operated by Kim and Daisy Von Furth.

Moore's lyrics frequently manage to be meaningful without retaining one exact meaning. Thurston himself is quick to point out that although his lyrics often refer to aspects of his daily life, they are purposely rendered ambiguous for popular consumption.

By the third and fourth takes, Moore's voice has become elastic, as if trying to twist out of a plastic bag. "Self-Obsessed and Sexxee" ends with the refrain "Party, party, party / Party all the time"—not one of the more distinguished Sonic Youth lines, but one that sounds increasingly bizarre with each successive run.

Moore now sits on a stool, having removed the microphone from behind its filter circle, and cups it in his hands as he sings. On the playback, his singing sounds electronically treated. Of course, it's not. One of Sonic Youth's main feats is delivering arrestingly unique music with the same basic tools used by every other home-grown four-piece rock band in the world.

On the albums Sonic Youth recorded in the mid-eighties, such as 1986's EVOL and 1987's Sister, Thurston's vocals usually take the background to the guitar fireworks. So it comes as a surprise—as much to him as anyone, judging from his enthusiasm and persistence—that sometime between then and now, Thurston Moore devised a brand-new vocal style. Somewhere in the deep chasm between a hardcore whine and a balladeer's whisper lies Moore's expressive range.

For "Tokyo Eye," another song set in a space-age consumer

culture, Moore sings the chorus in a hushed, melismatic falsetto that proves difficult for him to master. Despite the multiple takes afforded by a major-label contract and a perfectionist producer, Moore is largely the same person that ten years ago sang lines like "Chaos is the future," and "Society is a hole." With his heavy flannel shirt and his tousled blond hair, Thurston belies his thirty-six years. Except for the thick horn-rimmed glasses he now wears offstage, he could easily be mistaken for his former self—a gawky, impressionable seventeen-year-old from Bethel, Connecticut, come to New York in search of the underground's fast lane. (His left upper arm still bears a tattoo of a star-cross emblazoned with the words Sonic Life, an early Sonic Youth emblem.)

Intense yet funny, anarchic yet articulate, cutting-edge yet ineffably in awe of the past, Thurston Moore is about as intelligent a rock star as one is likely to find. The mere fact that he can be described as such and still be considered the real thing holds him a place in the pantheon. A more evolved rock star, one for whom raw power and sexism don't come hand in hand, for whom ribald humor and rock-and-roll abandon do. A rock star who will never really be a rock star, simply because he forever chooses self-deflating wit over ritualistic rock puffery.

The same guy who sings, "Doe, a deer, a female deer," to loosen up his throat, stays till two-thirty one night to record an alternate version of "Screaming Skull," an uproarious gibe at the corporate-like superstore recently opened in Los Angeles by SST, Sonic Youth's former employer and the top independent rock label of the eighties. (An unreleased alternate version features a raunchy rap courtesy of Moore, which jokingly accuses SST of "sucking on the big D," in Thurston's best John Wayne voice.)

"That song is different from the others because it's more comical," Thurston says. "I wrote it while I was hanging out at Dave Markey's house in L.A., sitting on his couch, playing his acoustic guitar. We were just sort of talking about the SST superstore and the fact that [that] existed on Sunset Strip. We'd gone by there and Pat Smear was working there. And Pat Smear was guitar player with the

Germs, a big deal. It's really funny because now he's back in action, playing with Nirvana. So the song is really topical, but it wasn't meant to be.''

One night in the studio, Don Fleming, a longtime Sonic Youth cohort, holds court, sitting quietly in a dark corner, listening, smiling and puffing on a mammoth joint like a caterpillar with his hookah.

Fleming, a successful producer, former member of the Velvet Monkeys and Half Japanese, and currently leader of Gumball, typifies the sort of figures that populate Sonic Youth's world. As tall and gawky as Thurston, but with shoulder-length reddish brown hair and Coke-bottle-thick glasses, Fleming looks like a famous big-time rock star. And with a contract with Sony for Gumball and recent production credits on albums by Teenage Fan Club, Shonen Knife, and the Posies, he may soon qualify as one. But one suspects he's always looked like one.

In the ''alternative'' world—a world circumscribed by college- and post-college-age music fans who can afford to spend a good portion of their time and money following a mostly American rock scene that was built up from the basics—Sonic Youth is a supergroup.

Mind you, not like Nirvana. Nirvana's Geffen debut, Nevermind, sold in excess of nine million copies worldwide. Sonic Youth, the group largely responsible for Nirvana's signing to Geffen, has never even gone gold (500,000 copies)—not in its whole decade-plus history. But rest assured, Sonic Youth is the band that has cool cornered. Nirvana's Kurt Cobain admitted to more than one interviewer that his band's original goal was ''to be one of the most popular alternative-rock bands, like Sonic Youth.''

Yet Sonic Youth and Nirvana have little in common. The members of Sonic Youth aren't rich rock stars living in media-made plastic bubbles while writing catchy pop songs about the fury fame hath wrought.

''For us, we're doing really well, we're selling the most records we've ever sold," says Kim. "But unless you make a gold record, it's like, 'You're not a Foreigner. You don't count. You're not going to be on the cover of Rolling Stone or Spin.' Major labels have a different mentality. And now that there are alternative bands who are getting signed—like Smashing Pumpkins—who do get in the Top Ten, they expect everybody else to be like that, too. Basically, we're just carving out our niche."

Kim and Thurston, married since 1984, only recently moved from a cramped tenement apartment on Manhattan's Lower East Side to a bright, spacious but sparsely furnished loft just below Houston Street, in SoHo. Lee lives in a ramshackle duplex in the city's financial district, decorated in late-style dorm room (artwork tacked to the walls, industrial-quality carpet). Steve remains ensconced across the river in Hoboken, New Jersey, college rock's equivalent of Mecca.

Neither did the members of Sonic Youth start a rock band because they were bored and had nothing better to do. Nor to "get chicks." Not even to develop drug habits.

("We're not really a very druggy band," Lee admits. "I think Thurston has made the first overt drug reference on our new record. There's a line from 'In the Mind of the Bourgeois Reader' about 'Pass it around or stick it on a pin,' which is the way we always smoked hash when we were in Europe. You'd get a badge off your shirt and bend up the pin and stick the hash on it and a glass over it. And then just lift up the glass and inhale the smoke. We always think of it as a really good, pure way to smoke hash because there's no paper or cigarettes or tobacco or anything. And people in Europe just think we're totally bonkers, sitting there with a glass.")

They did it because they couldn't imagine doing anything else. And thirteen years after first playing together (Steve Shelley joined in 1985), the band's members are as immersed in the cutting edge of pop culture as ever. Both Kim and Lee have played producer on seminal post–Sonic Youth releases. (She coproduced Pretty on the Inside, the first album from Gordon manquée Courtney Love's band,

Hole; he coproduced *Fontanelle*, the Warner Bros. debut of Babes in Toyland, an influential, superloud all-woman trio from Minneapolis.)

These days, Sonic Youth's members are so frequently called away from their music-related tasks that it's a wonder they were able to spare the time required to record *Experimental Jet Set*. That's why it may come as a surprise to some that this album's songs are among the most daring the band has ever recorded.

"I noticed a while back when we were playing a lot with Mudhoney and Nirvana—*real* rock bands—because we had to put out so much in order not to be blown off the stage by them, that it started gradually altering our songwriting," says Kim. "I think *Dirty* [Sonic Youth's previous album] was a product of that. I don't want to say negatively, because there are a lot of songs I like on it. But it was leading us astray from our more poetical side."

The band again chose the services of Butch Vig (he also produced 1992's *Dirty*), not because the Wisconsin native has two platinum-selling "grunge" efforts under his belt (Nirvana's *Nevermind* and Smashing Pumpkins' *Siamese Dream*), but because Vig learned his craft recording albums by legendary but obscure mid-eighties independent rock acts such as Killdozer and Tar Babies, frequently only in a couple days' time.

' ' I think it's a reaction to a spate of short titles," Thurston says in an effort to explain the surreal name of the new album. "It's something that I wrote down and sort of sprung on everybody on tour." ("Lee is experimental, Kim is jet-set, Thurston is trash, and I'm no star," says Steve jokingly.)

A bit more prodding gets Thurston to explain that the *No Star* part was provided by Yoshimi, the slightly built drummer from the Boredoms, the noise band Sonic Youth befriended while touring Japan, who also drums for Free Kitten, Kim's current side project. "We were in a car on Broadway and some kid came up to the car and asked Yoshimi for her autograph, and we were making fun of her like, 'Oh, you're a rock-and-roll superstar,' " he says. "And she was like, 'No! No star. No star.' "

Upon further reflection, one realizes *Experimental Jet Set, Trash and No Star* perfectly encapsulates the current Sonic Youth state of mind.

From the earliest songs that the band hurriedly pulled for its very first live performances, Sonic Youth engaged in a Cage-ian kind of songwriting process. Now that they're a bunch of experimental jet-setters, they can see that; back then, they just called it punk rock. "I wasn't aware of the true existence of improvisational music until later," says Thurston. "I think that's why I've become so interested in instant songwriting. Anybody can make noise, but can anybody do instant composition?"

Sonic Youth scheduled a tour of festival dates in Europe which began with two late-June shows with the Breeders and St. Johnny at New York's Academy club. Rather than sticking to old favorites, the band performed a set half-comprised of brand-new material, songs the audience had never heard before. "The band got to a certain point with *Dirty*," Thurston says. "We were in the big league of alternative rock, and I really wanted to do something away from the norm." Sonic Youth considered the tactic a way of putting itself in the place of a new band.

"It was great doing the new songs in the festivals," Thurston says, "because we'd be on these massive bills with Metallica, Neil Young, Lenny Kravitz, and Faith No More. So a large percent of these 60,000-plus audiences weren't aware of Sonic Youth's music to begin with. And a lot of these songs were decidedly less bombastic and crazoid and noise-rocking. They're a little more introspective."

"Bull in the Heather," "Skink," "Tokyo Eye," "Starfield Road," "In the Mind of the Bourgeois Reader," and "Self-Obsessed and Sexxee" are a few of the songs the band spent the summer of 1993 performing live which ended up on *Experimental Jet Set, Trash and No Star*.

Some were half-written right in the studio. " 'Waist' was a song that I just came in with a melody idea for and didn't tell anybody how it went," Thurston explains. "I just said play whatever you want. Then I just counted to four and Steve started playing and I started singing and playing. We were like, 'That sounds cool, let's keep it like that.' "

Other songs were finished before the band entered the studio. "Androgynous Mind," another Moore-penned ditty, mines territory not so far removed from the goofy but brilliant songs that kept the Beatles' *Abbey Road* glued together—lyrically it falls somewhere between "Polythene Pam" and "Maxwell's Silver Hammer." ("Everything is alright / God is gay / You were right," goes one peculiar exchange.) The music is all Sonic Youth's, though; it starts, stops, and turns around like a crab navigating its way across a seastrand.

"Self-Obsessed and Sexxee" is the album's tribute to alternative rock's new breed. "It's not about Courtney Love, it's not about Kathleen Hanna from [riot-grrrl group] Bikini Kill," Thurston assures. "It's just sort of about being attracted to somebody who's obviously out of control with self-obsession in the high-profile alternative-rock world."

For many of Sonic Youth's more recent converts, Kim Gordon is the draw. Dubbed high priestess of "grunge" fashion—a dubious school of style pioneered in 1992 by young designers like Christian Francis Roth and Marc Jacobs—Kim has appeared on the pages of *Vogue, Harper's Bazaar, Elle,* and *Vanity Fair* draped in everything from star-spangled flairs to satin pajamas. (Though Kim avers, "*Vogue* has gotten it all wrong, because this stuff is so old.") Now with X-Girl in operation, one wonders whether she expects to trade the music world for fashion in the future.

"My friend Daisy Von Furth works at X-Large [a hip-hop clothing store owned by friends of the Beastie Boys], and I know those guys," Kim says. "Eric, one of the brothers, asked us if we wanted to design a clothing line. We're committed for a year. I like the idea. If I was a male I could never do this. It would be too weird, it would be unacceptable. I think for women, in a way, there are fewer rules about what you can and can't do, because there's less history. Maybe the riot grrrls won't think it's very cool."

Kim clearly has plans to continue pursuing both. On Sonic Youth's recent albums, the songs she sings stand out as the most radical. Previous to the latest album, most of the songs Kim wrote lyrics to and sang, originated in musical ideas devised by Thurston (two notable exceptions are "Flower" and "My Friend Goo"), a circumstance that drastically affected their outcome. "For Kim, if they're songs that already exist, unless she writes them herself, they're going to be songs that don't have singing ideas going for them," Thurston says.

"Bull in the Heather," "Bone," and "Quest for the Cup" are all songs Kim conceived from the ground up.

"Skink" is named after a popular character from *Double Whammy* and *Native Tongue* by Florida novelist Carl Hiaasen. In Hiassen's books, Skink is the nickname of a former Florida governor who escaped to the swamps where he lives alone and dines on roadkill. The music bobs and weaves as if the band were trying to play fast underwater, and thus communicates a comical yet dignified grace.

"Bull in the Heather" is as close to a single as Sonic Youth is likely to get this time around. Its appealing melody is only enhanced by the carefully orchestrated cacophony that accompanies it.

Sonic Youth circa 1994 occupies the unenviable position of being simultaneously in and out of vogue. "Sonic" and "youth"— neither word alone does justice to a pair that together seem to perfectly suit a band which has spent its history teetering between the modern-art continuum and the adolescent, ahistorical fury of the underground music scene. Steve Shelley—at thirty the group's youngest member—was already in his mid-twenties when he first joined, hardly young enough to mask as a "youth." And "sonic" was a word made redundant amid the early-eighties New York scene in which the band first appeared, one so caught up in the multifarious bewitching powers of sound.

But much has changed since then: Today's Sonic Youth easily stands out from the pack. On the last night of mixing the new album, the band decided to write five new songs and record them on the spot. "We needed a song for this DGC compilation that's coming out, and we didn't have any B sides," Thurston explains. "So we decided, Why not just do 'em now?" Using a drum kit and a few acoustic guitars—the only equipment lying around—the band created a whole new sound for itself almost instantaneously. "I wrote a couple, Lee wrote one, and Kim wrote one, and then me and Steve did a piano-drums thing," he says. "And then we all overdubbed on top of each other's things." From start to finish, the process took four hours.

For *Experimental Jet Set*, the band spent even less money than it did recording each of its two previous major-label efforts. "You don't want the mix to sound like you're selling it," Kim adds. "There's a whole vocabulary of mixing that doesn't even enter major-label records at all."

And at the very point when more-demanding denizens of the rock underground were prepared to excommunicate Sonic Youth for sins of commercial acceptance, the band released an album without any singles. "We never really wrote singles," says Steve, "but it was always sort of easy to pick out a song for radio. But for this record I have no idea; they're all so peculiar."

The members of Sonic Youth are usually so busy creating that they just don't have time to worry about their work's consequences. The band's certainly not going to sweat it if the new album doesn't do any better than the previous one, even if it means getting dropped from Geffen.

Kim, for one, sees the band's 1990 move to Geffen (its first album for the Geffen's DGC sublabel was *Goo*) as an inevitable one that to this day still harbors both advantages and disadvantages. "If you're not on a major label it's like you don't exist," she says. "But once you're on a major label, suddenly you're all supposed to be competing for the brass ring."

2 | New York Noise

''I don't even know what the term *underground* means, unless it means that you don't want anyone to find out about you or bother you, the way it did under Stalin or Hitler. But if that's the case, I can't see how I was ever 'underground,' since I've always wanted people to notice me.''

—Andy Warhol, in *Popism: The Warhol '60s*

He was too late. Much like everybody else who arrived in New York in late 1976 to experience firsthand this legendary loud, fast, anarchic music, Glenn Branca—a twenty-seven-year-old theater major from Harrisburg, Pennsylvania—had missed the boat.

In 1976, the nation's young, hip, and creatively inclined were all flocking to New York. Punk rock had exploded and the word was out. CBGBs, a former Hell's Angels hangout on Manhattan's Bowery, had been showcasing acts with names like the Ramones, Television, Blondie, and Richard Hell and the Voidoids for nearly three years.

The Ramones, the quintessential New York punk band, signed to Sire Records in January 1976. A month later, the band recorded its debut album and thereby signaled the end of that brief but wildly influential period. Talking Heads signed with Sire later that spring. By the end of 1976, virtually every one of the original CBGBs bands had secured a recording contract. August found Blondie at Plaza Sound, putting together its first album. *Marquee Moon*, Television's stellar debut, was recorded in November 1976. Richard Hell and the Voidoids made a deal in January 1977 to cut *Blank Generation* for Sire.

Branca, a graduate of Emerson College in Boston, says that at that time he had no intention of pursuing music as a career. "I had started acting when I was eleven—and that's all I ever thought I was going to do," he says, "although I had started playing the guitar when I was about fifteen and I was very into rock. I had done a band when I was in college; it was called the Crystal Ship and we mainly just did cover songs of various good psychedelic songs of the time: We did Stones, and we did the Doors. We did 'You Baby' by the Turtles, for chrissakes."

Although he loved rock music, Branca also listened to plenty of other kinds of music. But he was much more interested in theater. Wild theater. Furthermore, Branca had become possessed by the powers of experimental drama. "To me, people like Beckett and Pinter and Ionesco were straight. The kind of theater I was doing was on the far, deepest edge."

While in Boston, Branca founded the Bastard Theater. Today, Branca describes the Bastard's work as "music theater"—not *Oklahoma!*—due to the fact that all the actors also played instruments. The usual Bastard Theater production incorporated elements of Dadaism, performance art, rock music, and experimental music. There were never any characters or a plot.

"One of the plays," says Branca, "would start off with an attack on the audience, in which the actors would create a kind of vocal piece that would be intended to intimidate and offend the audience in the most extreme possible way you could imagine. The actor would be asking, 'Why the fuck did you bother to come here? This is garbage. You're garbage.' Of course, it was a little more poetic than that." What made the work all the more powerful and jarring was that the company would spend six or seven months devising and rehearsing each piece, often on a budget of around fifty dollars.

Branca and his cohorts were developing a kind of punk theater. Finding himself increasingly bored with the standard rock fare of the mid-seventies, Branca had begun to explore the outer limits of "serious" music. The works of Polish composer Krzysztof Penderecki and French composer and organist Olivier Messiaen were early inspirations. "It wasn't that we were trying to imitate anything," Branca says, "it's just that we knew what was going on and we were working within that context."

Penderecki, born in 1933, had developed his own system of musical notation to accommodate the unusual sonorities he desired. Messiaen's work is characterized by his interests in religious mysticism and mammoth crescendos. (A 1935 piece was titled L'Ascension, no doubt inspiring the title of Branca's first solo recording, The Ascension.) The work of German composer Karlheinz Stockhausen, too, provided impetus to explore dissonance, improvisation, and free rhythms in a formal setting. Gruppen für Drei Orchester, a piece Stockhausen wrote in the mid-1950s, requires the efforts of three independent orchestras led by three different conductors, surrounding a concert-hall audience on three sides. Very loud and seemingly chaotic, Gruppen is grand spectacle, momentous music that demands firsthand appraisal.

Having found a way to simultaneously engage his interests in rock music and the more academic avant-garde, Branca ought to have been content. Yet no amount of creative energy could bring him what the ambitious performer most desired: a decent-sized audience. In the mid-seventies, few people associated rock music with intellectual pursuits.

Tired of oscillating between the esoteric anarchy of his avant-garde roots and the adrenaline rush of rock, Branca left for New York. The exported musings of his New York punk heroes, performers such as Patti Smith and Richard Hell, convinced Branca that success lay on Manhattan Island.

"Part of the reason I came to New York was because the punk scene was so cool," Branca says. "Although Boston definitely had its own scene, it was nothing like what was going on here." Branca arrived in New York, confident that the scene collecting in Manhattan's East Village would be predisposed to his unique brand of drama. But what Branca arrived to find was not exactly what he had expected. Punk was pretty much dead; all the key bands had already been signed and were off on tour.

What did exist was the beginnings of the post–Studio 54 after-hours culture. Studio 54 had defined the mid-seventies New York disco culture by giving trend-setters a place to congregate after two in the morning. By the late seventies, Studio 54's hip quotient had ebbed. Its would-be patrons soon began checking out the downtown punk clubs.

Straight-ahead punk venues such as the Mudd Club (the dingy room at 77 White Street made world-famous by the line "This ain't no disco," from the 1979 Talking Heads song "Life During Wartime") were not as appealing to the high-profile, Warhol-inspired glamour crowd as were multilevel clubs like Danceteria, which had different music and a different environment on every floor. The original Danceteria, which opened at the start of 1980, was located on West 37th Street and featured dance floors, live rock performances, video lounges, and quiet conversation nooks—all under one roof. Danceteria brokered a less rigorous "door policy" than the beauty-blinded Studio 54, setting the stage for a brief period in New York when club-goers, visual artists, underground filmmakers, and rock musicians saw themselves as creative equals with a common purpose. (Later, at a new location on West 21st Street, Danceteria featured an "Art Attack" night every other Wednesday, at which "serious" artists like composer Philip Glass and performance artist Diamanda Galas strutted their stuff in the "vulgar" nightclub setting. Although Branca and Sonic Youth later both played Danceteria, neither ever did so on "Art Attack" night.)

Undeterred, Branca set out to start a theater group with one of his New York friends, Jeffrey Lohn, who had a loft in SoHo the pair planned to use as their theater. According to Branca, he and Lohn had expected to generate productions similar in scope and tone to those of the Bastard Theater's. Like Branca, Lohn was something of a musician himself, also interested in the outer limits of twentieth-century composition. But one day, Branca had an epiphany.

"I just said to myself—I mean, just out of the blue—'I'm gonna start a fucking band. I just have to. I'm just gonna do it. I don't give a shit.' I didn't even tell Jeffrey," Branca says. "I put up some posters for musicians. I wanted to call the band the Static at the time. And Jeffrey saw one of the posters, and said, 'What the fuck are you doing? You're starting a band and you haven't even talked to me about this? I definitely want to do it.' So immediately we decided we were going to do it."

Remarkably, Branca and Lohn didn't own instruments at the time. They borrowed equipment, they even borrowed a drummer; Branca played guitar, and Lohn, keyboards. A young drummer named Wharton Tiers, and bassist and keyboard player Margaret DeWys (who became Joan Tower's protégée and currently enjoys a successful career as a classical composer) completed the lineup.

Almost immediately, a performance-artist friend, Dan Graham, invited the band, wittily dubbed Theoretical Girls, to open for his performance at Franklin Furnace, a downtown theater space. In three weeks the band wrote some songs, rehearsed them, and performed them at the Furnace. The show was a rousing success.

From here Branca found it easy to make the transition into a rock format after having established his interests in art and experimental music. (He claims to have not seen a connection between the two previously.) Early Theoretical Girls songs were relatively straight-ahead punk fare with a few noise breaks, but soon enough the outfit began to test its limits.

"Theoretical Girls was truly an experimental band," says Branca, "because every song was different. We were just trying every possible idea that came to our minds. We really didn't care at all what the fucking audience thought. And all of a sudden we had this incredible audience that was coming from the art world. When we played audition night at CBGBs, the place was totally packed. And although [CBGB owner] Hilly [Kristal] hated us, he had to book us because we packed the place."

Unbeknownst to Theoretical Girls, a bunch of other bands were trawling downtown Manhattan for stray bits of punk energy. Teenage Jesus and the Jerks, DNA, Mars, Red Transistor, Terminal, Tone Death, the Gynecologists, and the Contortions were some of the best known. Roy Trakin, then a writer for *New York Rocker*, is often credited with labeling the scene "No Wave," a name meant to convey both the new directions and the negation implied by the music's determinedly clangorous approach.

The Contortions were No Wave's archetypal act. Fronted by a small, scrawny pale character named James Chance, the Contortions used a funk groove as a canvas for Chance's confrontational rants. "They were just really scary," says Thurston, who saw the band a number of times upon first arriving in New York. "I wasn't really interested in the funk element or the jazz element. But Chance was really twisted—he was like a little cockroach, he was superjittery. He'd play his saxophone and scream and then just do this hyper James Brown move and twirl around and jump on somebody and push 'em really hard. Or hit somebody or kick somebody."

Jim Sclavunos, who later played for a spell with Sonic Youth, began his career as the teenage drummer for Red Transistor. "These guys claimed they were from outer space," says Sclavunos. "They had me play drums while they executed various maneuvers on their instruments. Rudolph Grey used take a power drill and drill into his guitar right next to the pickups. And Von Lmo would destroy my drums with a chain and a fireman's axe while I was playing them."

Around this time, Brian Eno, a founding member of Roxy Music and self-described "non-musician," began attending No Wave performances. He had recently collaborated with David Bowie on *Low* and *"Heroes"* and went on to produce three Talking Heads albums. Although Eno had recently moved to New York from his native England and was well-informed about the No Wave scene (he even attended Lohn's loft for an evening's performances), he is generally credited with having ended the scene.

Eno originally intended to record ten bands for a No Wave compilation; somewhere along the line, he decided to record only four: DNA, the Contortions, Mars, and Teenage Jesus and the

Jerks—those situated in the East Village, both literally and musically. Legend has it that Lydia Lunch of Teenage Jesus and the Jerks and Arto Lindsay of DNA convinced Eno that four bands were enough.

"Those guys really hated our guts," Branca says. "They thought we were the SoHo bands. That we were, to be very explicit, 'art fags.' They really thought that we were not part of what they considered to be their scene. And they obviously convinced Eno of that." No New York, the resultant album, was recorded soon after a festival held at SoHo's Artists Space from May 2 to May 6, 1978.

Very quickly the rift between the SoHo camp and the East Village camp widened. Theoretical Girls, along with a few of the other so-called SoHo bands (the Gynecologists, Red Transistor), decided to start boycotting the downtown rock clubs, in protest of unfair booking and paying policies; instead, pursuing gigs at performance spaces, galleries, and private lofts. The East Village bands continued playing the clubs.

The divergent approaches of these two distinct No Wave factions were to have a dramatic effect on what was to come. As late as November 1981, Andy Schwartz, editor of New York Rocker, one of the original rock gazettes spawned by the mid-seventies punk scene, was blaming the SoHo crowd for killing the muse.

In an article grandiosely titled "The State of New York," Schwartz warned that "there's something very wrong with the current new music/new wave/whatchamacallit scene in New York City," and went on to cite two small sub-scenes that had left the fold. One was a tiny hardcore scene, including bands such as the Undead and False Prophets, which only played at tiny clubs like A-7 on the far seedier Lower East Side; the other was a group of "experimental" bands (Schwartz listed Sonic Youth, Mofungo, V-Effect, and the Avant Squares, among others). Schwartz took both scenes to task for marginalizing the music, and the latter especially, for being "difficult": "They don't grin like Adam Ant or dress like Joan Jett. They don't have managers or booking agents, and are unwilling to indulge in the haggling and ass-kissing required to land a paying gig, even at CBGBs.''

For all the excitement the first and second generations of New York punk bands delivered, the lasting effects were difficult to gauge. ''Punk rockers talked a good game, all about reenergizing rock, deprofessionalizing it, giving it a shot of rude noise,'' Jon Pareles reflected in Mother Jones in 1981. ''Unfortunately, punk's front line turned out to be virtual nostalgia acts: Who reruns from the Ramones and the Sex Pistols; Mersey retreads from the Clash; Brill Building updates from Blondie.''

''We all pretty much held punk in contempt,'' Jim Sclavunos says of the No Wave crowd. ''For its self-satisfaction, for its self-indulgence and various nostalgic trends. It just seemed like a very easy scene for a bunch of losers. And we were determined to be bigger losers, I guess.''

Of course, what East Village punk-rock audiences perceived as No Wave's self-conscious artiness was just that. In fact, the average Theoretical Girls audience included as many visual artists as it did standard-issue rock fans. ''It was Robert Longo and Cindy Sherman and Julian Schnabel, and all these people who were just young kids at the time—they were the ones who were coming to our shows,'' says Branca. ''It was Expressionist rock music, basically, I think, from their point of view. And I don't think it's coincidental that the first visual-art scene of the eighties that exploded really big was so-called neo-Expressionism.''

And so began an unlikely but reasonably cozy relationship between young SoHo artists and the disenfranchised No Wavers. In the spirit of breaking boundaries artistically, Theoretical Girls would attempt to play differently for different pieces. Although the band was set up like a traditional four-piece rock-and-roll outfit, its members were determined to play any kind of non-blues-based music they could think of. ''One of many ideas I had was to do a piece with a lot of guitars using unusual guitar tunings,'' Branca says.

After the gigs at clubs such as CBGBs and Max's Kansas City dried up, Theoretical Girls were left playing the downtown art spaces—the Kitchen, Rhys Chatham's center for video and music (then located at 484 Broome Street), and Artists Space.

"The actual No Wave scene died very quickly," says Branca, "because what happened was [that] there was so much interest, that everybody who ever had even thought about playing guitar decided to start a band."

In 1978, spurred by the unexpected success of Theoretical Girls, Branca formed the band he'd originally dreamt of—the Static. The Static featured Barbara Ess (Branca's girlfriend at the time) on bass and Christine Hahn (later of the German band Malaria) on drums. This band stood out even more: Women rock musicians playing instruments were still something of a rarity, though the Static could hardly be called a rock band in the most parochial sense.

Kim Gordon, in a piece titled " 'I'm Really Scared When I Kill in My Dreams,' " published in *Artforum* in January 1983, quoted from her own notes taken during a typical Static performance. Her notes describe the two women playing while staring at Branca, who took off his guitar and began writhing on the floor. As they continued to play, Branca headed for a mirror wherein he began popping his zits. Lines of dialogue such as "Breathe in, breathe out" were repeated in both English and French. Throughout, the music continued and culminated with Branca forming a cross by placing his guitar against Ess's. Gordon interpreted this unique theatrical display as deliberately confronting rock's stereotypical sexual postures. "The abrupt starts and stops and up-and-down interweaving speed of Branca's guitar and Ess's bass characterized the music," concluded Gordon, "creating an atmosphere of high sexual tension, of frenzied contact and momentary withdrawal inducing a state of sustained expectancy."

Ironically, Branca and his cohorts' willful immersion in the downtown art scene proved apocryphal. It was Max's Kansas City—the club where "Pop Art and pop life came together in New York in the sixties," as Andy Warhol put it in *Popism*; by then predisposed to booking primarily major-label acts with national name recognition—that ended up changing the music's course. In the spring of 1979, Max's contacted the band about playing with the Contortions and the Model Citizens, another happening New York band. When Max's called, Branca was out of town, touring with the Static; Jeffrey Lohn decided to perform solo and got his friend Rhys Chatham a slot as well.

Branca returned to town and demanded his own solo set on the bill. In typical Branca fashion, the fiercely competitive impresario manqué whipped up a piece called Instrumental for Six Guitars and corralled some of his visual-artist friends to play with him. The band consisted of six electric guitarists, a bassist, and a drummer. In its first incarnation, Barbara Ess played bass, and Christine Hahn played guitar. Steve Harvey, a visual artist, also played guitar. Stephen Wischerth was the drummer.

Branca began devoting the bulk of time to writing instrumental works. "That year, I wrote a number of pieces very quickly," he recalls. And while Branca had clearly made a commitment to non-rock composition formats, his work, by dint of the fact that it continued to be performed on electric guitars in a particularly loud fashion, continued to address rock-music concerns, albeit in a far more attenuated manner than most rock audiences were comfortable with. "I wrote a piece called Dissonance, which was meant to be a prototypical idea of rock music as dissonant. And I wrote a piece called Lesson No. 1, which was very clearly a very easy piece that was meant to be kind of rock minimalism. I wrote another piece called The Spectacular Commodity, that was intended to be a kind of nineteenth-century classical music played by a rock band."

From the start, Branca's machinations were the nexus of these performances. The first thing that stood out about him was his "look": jeans, scuffed boots, and a black shirt. At the time, his dark curly hair was twisted into a mussed-up pompadour. His bands seemed similarly influenced by his proto-grunge apparel, wearing "shabby mismatched garments of somber hue that seemed to say 'I was too busy thinking about that fourth cadenza in the third movement to notice the huge stain on my shirt,' '' in the words of one downtown critic. Then there was his performance demeanor, a trancelike state during which Branca seemed as transfixed by the holy racket as his audiences were. By the time each piece reached peak volume, Branca would be twitching and thrashing, his shirt sleeves fluttering with his wild gestures. By 1979, Branca represented a major link between the avant-garde and the pop-music sides of downtown New York culture.

As band leader, Branca not only provided cheap guitars, each tuned for a particular purpose, but also taught each performer his or her fairly repetitive part and conducted the proceedings, frequently with a guitar strapped around his neck. Due perhaps to the minimal role each guitarist played in each performance, Branca found himself replacing guitarists on a regular basis.

It was by this rotisserie approach that Branca met a musician named Anthony Coleman. Coleman shared a floor of loft space in downtown Brooklyn with two members of a second-generation No Wave band called the Flucts; all, at one time or another, performed with Branca. One day Coleman brought in one of the Flucts, a young guitarist named Lee Ranaldo. Ranaldo began playing with Branca and subsequently introduced Branca to other guitarists interested in expanding their repertoire.

Branca eventually pared down his ''guitar army'' to a semi-constant touring group of six (Lee Ranaldo, Ned Sublette, David Rosenbloom, and Branca on guitars; Jeffrey Glenn on bass, and Stephen Wischerth on drums).

Around the same time, Dan Graham, the visual artist who had given Theoretical Girls their first break at Franklin Furnace in 1977, introduced Branca to an eager art-school graduate, fresh from Los Angeles, named Kim Gordon. Gordon and Graham lived in the same building, 84 Eldridge Street; she had attended some Theoretical Girls gigs and counted herself a fan. It was through Graham that Branca and Gordon became friends.

Branca recalls that even early on, Gordon was interested in starting a band of her own—clearly sparked by the scene, since she didn't know how to play an instrument. "At one point I remember her telling me that she had come across these two fabulous, beautiful young boys that she was going to start a band with," says Branca. "Later she met Thurston and some other guy, J.D. King, who were from a band called the Coachmen, whom the Static had played on a bill with one time. I remember hearing them and I thought they were quite good—they sort of sounded a little bit like Television. They were a good band. It was fairly straight punk stuff and more, for my taste, in the area of art rock than No Wave."

By 1980, the do-it-yourself ethic plagued the New York scene; more than two hundred local bands were laying claim to creative liberation à la No Wave. Inspired perhaps by seminal No Wave figures such as DNA's Arto Lindsay (who to this day refuses to play a single chord on the guitar, preferring rather to thrash at it rhythmically, treating it as a noisemaker rather than a melodic instrument) countless rock wastrels sought to find fans and fame under the rubric of "noise rock." While the first generation of No Wavers was essentially cynical, lampooning the notion of rock music having integrity, the second generation lapsed back into less ironic and less provocative formulas. "They were Talking Heads imitations," says Branca. "They were doing boring kind of nebbishy, kooky . . . you know, this idea of art having to be kooky and not being intense. And that kind of killed the whole thing."

Furthermore, major record labels were no longer interested in plundering the East Village for new acts to sign. It was easier to look much farther east, to England, where radio-ready synth pop— embodied by groups like Duran Duran, A Flock of Seagulls, and Depeche Mode—had begun its meteoric rise; or toward the New York disco scene, which had built its own distribution network already. Later shake-ups at the major labels would reveal rampant industry payola scandals. Too much seed money was left mired in the labyrinthine coffers of commercial radio to allow for any wagering on fresh talent. The East Village scene was left to its own resources.

* * *

In 1978 Susan Martin, a California native who ran Some Serious Business, an organization that produced exhibits by avant-garde visual artists, was living in Los Angeles. Representative if not typical of the kind of exhibit Martin promoted, was the work of the Viennese artist Hermann Nitsch.

One Nitsch installment, *Orgies Mysteries Theatre*, involved "two dead lambs and gallons and gallons of lamb's blood." In another, Nitsch would train an orchestra of volunteers to play classical instruments in two days, using hand signals. Many such events were staged at the Otis College of Art and Design, a downtown art school that, at that time, "was basically a rehearsal hall for post-punk bands," according to Martin. The volunteers that showed up for events were usually half local punks and half students from Otis. It was at one of these events that Martin met up with Michael Gira, an Otis student with a penchant for the macabre. Gira had been publishing a magazine with a couple friends called *No*; one cover featured authentically graphic autopsy photos.

Early in 1979 Susan Martin, who was now living with Gira, made a trip to New York alone. "In one weekend, I saw Teenage Jesus and the Jerks, Suicide, and the Contortions," she says. "I was living with a guy who wanted to be a rock-and-roller and I was in the art world. And I went to galleries and museums, and I had never seen—*never* seen—so many people looking at art in my life." The couple moved to New York at the end of 1979.

Within a year, Martin had hooked up with Heiner Stadler, the former head of an eclectic label known as Tomato Records. Stadler had recently licensed the rights to a blues catalog, Blue Labor, from a friend, and was looking for an outlet through which to release it. In December 1980, the two business partners started up an independent label on their own, called Labor Records. Labor's first release was *Alone*, John Lee Hooker's first solo LP in twenty years. Its second release was an EP by Circus Mort, Gira's first New York band. Other early releases included contemporary composer Peter Kotik's *Many, Many Women*, a five-LP set.

Glenn Branca, too, was making do on his own. That same year, Branca had convinced Ed Bahlman, the owner of 99 Records, a small collector's record store at 99 MacDougal Street, to release *Lesson No. 1* as an EP. Soon after, Bahlman began signing other acts, based on Branca's recommendations, and selling the records out of the store. Among other, later 99 signees were the Bush Tetras, whose "Too Many Creeps" became an instant and influential club disco hit; ESG, five black women from the South Bronx, a funk-rock anomaly; and Liquid Liquid, leaders of the New York mini-malist funk movement. Due to his "disco mafia" contacts, Bahlman was able to push a surprising number of units. Branca went on to release the *Ascension* LP through 99, and sold upward of 10,000 copies out of the one store.

In December 1980 Minneapolis's Walker Art Center, one of the few federally assisted performance spaces willing to pay top dollar for Branca's services, did so. A year earlier the enterprising Tim Carr, Walker's twenty-five-year-old assistant director, had orga-nized M-80, the nation's first new-wave festival, thus putting to-gether on the same stage diverse New York acts such as the Contortions, the Fleshtones, Judy Nylon, and Robin Crutchfield for the first time. "Any presenting organization in the country could have been doing it," says Carr, today an A&R (artists and repertory) representative at Warner Bros. "Most of them chose not to. Most of the people who ran those things would just get the string quartet from the local college." The Walker date, Branca and crew's first venture outside of New York, brought in approximately $2,500 plus round-trip plane fare—a killing for a group lucky to make $500 a show. Branca subsequently arranged a tour of the Midwest around that one lucrative Walker gig.

Encouraged by enthusiastic audiences (made up mostly of young intellectuals) numbering in the hundreds, Branca took his act on the road again. For the next two and a half years, Branca's ensemble toured the country in any way it could manage. Outside of New York, the group usually played rock clubs; few avant-garde per-formance spaces existed. The fact that Branca composed four symphonies for the ensemble during this period had little real effect on the number of venues willing to host a performance by his group.

"In those days you could get an unlimited mileage pass on one of the airlines," Branca says. "So for $350 each we could go anywhere we wanted for three weeks. We would actually do fifteen-city tours, flying back and forth, from San Francisco to Denver, from Denver to Houston. Suddenly we could play the hipper clubs in the bigger cities—but of course we had to do it in a very short period of time."

3 | Melt Down

One Tuesday evening in July 1979, two young college graduates were looking for something to do in New York. They had just moved to town, armed only with the idea of reviving a band the two had put together in their last years at college.

They riffled through the back pages of the *Village Voice*, the downtown weekly that—along with the rival *SoHo Weekly News*, and smaller music publications like the *East Village Eye* and *New York Rocker*—had chronicled the doings of the punk era.

Melt Down. The display ad, one among many, for Max's Kansas City listed "Melt Down featuring Rhys Chatham." It had been only months since one of the worst nuclear-reactor accidents on record had occurred at Three Mile Island near Middletown, Pennsylvania. High noon in the nuclear era, and some band had called itself Melt Down.

Lee Ranaldo and his friend, David Linton, were so tickled they decided to go to Max's that night. What they saw there astonished them.

Three men with electric guitars standing in a row across the stage; behind them, at center stage, a drummer kept time on a lone high-hat cymbal. The man in the center began thrumming the low E-string of his guitar. Soon, the other two began doing the same on their instruments. For the next half hour, the sound grew as the performers began to add the other notes of an E-major chord. And then it was over.

The man in the center was Rhys Chatham. On the sides were Glenn Branca and David Rosenbloom. At the high hat, Wharton Tiers. The piece was Chatham's *Guitar Trio*.

Chatham, a New York–born classically trained musician and composer whose work had been monumentally influenced by John Cage's book *Silence*, was at the peak of his powers. Born in 1952, Chatham had become director of the Kitchen—New York's premier center of experimental music—in 1971, at the age of nineteen. But Chatham had lost his way artistically; by 1973 he had stepped down from his post to pursue the tenor saxophone, the instrument of his jazz idols, John Coltrane and Ornette Coleman.

An early Ramones concert again shifted Chatham's creative impulse. Chatham saw the precepts of minimalist "serious" music spark to life in the pared-down energy of early punk. These formative experiences led Chatham to study at the feet of New York's most-renowned minimalist composers: Steve Reich, Philip Glass, and LaMonte Young (who in the sixties acted as muse to the Velvet Underground).

In 1977 Chatham was renamed music director of the Kitchen (a post he held until 1980); he had also picked up the electric guitar and joined a rock band, Arsenal. (Tone Death, too, was a Chatham enterprise.) At first obsessed with calling himself a rock musician rather than a "composer," Chatham later decided that rock's provincial life-style no longer jibed with his needs, and contented himself with the loftier title. "Every artist after Cage has had to go through a process of reductionism," he told the *New York Times* in the early eighties, "and only then can they build themselves back up as artists on their own terms. Cage taught us that we can do anything we want. So the question becomes, What do we want?"

"People tend to lump Rhys Chatham and I together," Glenn Branca warned another journalist, "but our music isn't really that similar. My music is about extreme density while Rhys is working with ideas about harmonics. He uses tunings exclusively, while I'm trying to deal with a full range from bottom to top."

To Ranaldo and Linton, Melt Down's performance was nothing if not revelatory. "Rhys was a little drunk and he was standing in the center," recalls Lee. "He had these weird Roger McGuinn granny glasses on and he started moving out into the crowd. Max's was a long narrow place—the tables were all those long ones without a break that you just sit alongside of—and he started walking out between the tables and like, swinging his guitar absentmindedly, hitting people in the head and stuff. He was really out of it."

After the piece was over, Chatham announced that the band was going to perform another number, a surprise to most in attendance, considering that *Guitar Trio* was essentially one chord played for a full half hour. The group then proceeded to play the exact same thing again, for another half hour. This time, black-and-white slides of ambiguous, film-noirish scenes were faded in and out on a screen behind the band. The slides were provided by a then fledgling New York painter named Robert Longo. "I felt that night like something that I'd always heard in my head, I was finally hearing in real life," says Lee.

For Lee Ranaldo, born February 3, 1956, a suburban kid from East Norwich, a small fishing town on Long Island, the New York avant-garde was hardly his destiny. Having been taught a bit about guitar chords and open tunings in junior high by an older cousin, Lee had played in cover bands throughout high school. The Rolling Stones, the Beatles, the Kinks, Cream, and Led Zeppelin—via FM radio, virtually every white teenage boy in America had been inculcated by the first and second British Invasions of rock by 1975. Lee was no exception.

By the time Lee had decided to attend the State University of New York's giant-size campus in the sleepy city of Binghamton, his musical tastes had headed West—to San Francisco. The Jefferson Airplane, Hot Tuna, and the Grateful Dead wooed Lee with their psychedelic free-form improvisations. "At the time, the Dead were the band doing stuff in some odd ways very similar to what Sonic Youth ended up doing," says Lee. "Musical extrapolations that were about texture and getting into strange musical spaces with dissonance. Linking songs together in ways that we've explored, three singers. I would never liken Sonic Youth to the Dead stylistically. But in terms of the kind of thing they were doing with their live show—as far as looking at the music as something more than just songs that you're playing at a gig."

The first years of college Lee studied "music and drugs," by his own account, disenchanted with the impersonal size and approach of the math and science classes in which he was enrolled. Halfway through school, though, he met a new crowd: the art students. Lee had not previously perceived his creative interests as a career option, but nevertheless began taking studio-art and film courses. "When I first applied for studio-art classes they said, 'Well, bring some drawings in,' " he recalls. "So I went home and made some drawings, and they said okay." Lee soon flourished as an art student.

To Lee, the fine arts seemed a welcome refuge from his dour, impersonal science classes. His art studies also fed him new ideas about modern music which slowly trained his ear away from the same old tunes he was used to hearing on the radio. In 1975 rock music was at one of its least inspirational junctures: Psychedelia had given way to stadium and glam rock—Fleetwood Mac, Pink Floyd, Emerson, Lake and Palmer. Punk had yet to make its way outside of urban centers. But Lee had begun to develop more diverse tastes. He finished college with a major in studio art and minors in both film and philosophy.

For Lee and his art-student friends like David Linton ("David was a cinema person taking art courses and I was an art person taking cinema courses—that's how we met."), the first punk act to capture Lee's excitement was Talking Heads. A group of art grads from the Rhode Island School of Design, Talking Heads appealed to both Lee's music and art instincts. He saw the band in Binghamton on its very first tour.

"They were obviously not trendy people, dressed up in glam clothes or whatever," Lee remembers. "They looked like everyday people and they just happened to be making this music. The sound and the wordplay was really weird and quirky compared to music that was happening at the time. It seemed a lot more informed." He recalls that the band showed up at the tiny club in a station wagon, its only touring vehicle.

David and Lee frequently traveled to New York to see bands and began immersing themselves in the music of Talking Heads, Elvis Costello, and Television. Back in Binghamton, the pair started a band and began gigging around town with a repertoire that included new-wave hits mixed with a smattering of sixties favorites and a few originals. The band had two keyboard players, plus Linton on drums and Lee on guitar. They called themselves the Fluks—in part after Fluxus, the playful group of New York–based artists (including Nam June Paik and Yoko Ono) that challenged the establishment art world's stuffiness in the mid-sixties by constructing pun-riddled art and staging absurdist "happenings."

The band quickly garnered a following in the Binghamton area (a dubious distinction). Upon graduating, Ranaldo and Linton decided to move to New York. They reformed the band, occasionally calling it the Flucts (the German word for flight).

The Flucts were overtly influenced by Elvis Costello's Attractions, among other new-wave acts—"One guy on a Farfisa-type keyboard," says Lee, "another guy playing more of a Moog thing, like the bass parts Ray Manzarek played on keyboard in the Doors."— but also by the work of Philip Glass and Steven Reich. Already, unorthodox song structures and tape loops were a part of the band's act.

Holed up in an unfinished loft space in downtown Brooklyn, where they both lived and rehearsed, Ranaldo and Linton began to navigate the ins and outs of the New York club scene. They played gigs for free and sometimes didn't get to plug in until three in the morning. They became friendly with other bands similarly hobbled by the paucity of venues and desirable time slots, like the Coachmen. The Coachmen, a tallish foursome, regularly played a bar in Chelsea's flower district, called the Botany Talk House.

Living on the other half of the floor in their building was a keyboard player named Anthony Coleman, who had played with Branca on *Lesson No. 1*. Linton and Ranaldo had been to see Branca's ensemble play—they even got hired to join Rhys Chatham for a few shows. During one gig, at Tier 3 on Franklin Street at West Broadway, Lee spotted Branca in the audience. A week later, Lee called Branca up and introduced himself as "the guy who was playing with Rhys last week." Branca quickly hired him. Linton continued on as Chatham's drummer for the next three and half years.

Over the next year, Lee toured with Branca and his six-piece *Ascension* band twice, once in the U.S. and once in Europe. The first tour was three weeks in December 1980. Lee remembers playing a show in San Francisco the night John Lennon was murdered. The group would play California Institute of Arts one night and some rock dive the next night. "We did very often feel like we were aliens from another planet," says Branca. "We were coming to clubs where people were still wearing soccer shirts and drinking beers in mugs."

"Those tours were something to behold," confirms Lee. "They were unbelievable—unbelievably loud, unbelievably astounding— all across the country. No one had any inkling that shit like this was going on in New York." Lee soon became Branca's foil in the band, willing to "perform" as well as play. And the sound of Branca's ensemble had begun to evolve—imagine the full-orchestra coda of the Beatles' "A Day in the Life" sustained and jacked-up, climax upon climax.

"Lee was the most important musician that ever played in my group," says Branca. He and Lee soon devised visual images to accompany the aural onslaught. They would press their guitars together onstage, releasing the most excruciatingly loud feedback. Branca would push Lee to the floor; Lee would begin to convulse "like a cockroach being stabbed by a needle," according to Branca. Amps would topple, smoke would billow forth.

Some fifteen years earlier, Pete Townshend of the Who had made a habit of enacting similarly violent autodestruction mid-performance, but few of Branca's audiences, especially those at the more arty venues, had ever experienced this kind of performance havoc firsthand. "I remember one night where I laughed at Lee when he was down on the floor writhing around and he was very pissed about that," says Branca. "Because here I was doing all this ridiculous bullshit, and I'm laughing at him. He actually took it very seriously."

But Branca's work didn't fit the format of a rock band so much as it did that of a performance group. Touring was sporadic—he'd rehearse for two weeks, do a tour for three weeks, and then there'd be nothing for five months. And the Flucts broke up, not unusual considering the cost-of-living to price-per-gig ratio common among young bands in New York.

In the early months of 1981, Ranaldo and Linton formed a trio with a Dutch woman named Truss de Groot, who had performed in the Netherlands under the name Plus Instruments. In that brief period, the new group (under the same name) toured Europe and recorded a Europe-only album. Then Lee went back to Europe with Branca and the six-piece outfit.

For Kim Gordon, born in 1953 and raised in West Los Angeles, New York was far away only in terms of physical distance. Her head seemed destined for the lower-Manhattan art milieu long before she ever arrived.

After high school, Kim went to Santa Monica College, a local junior college, for two years. By her own account a poor student in high school, Kim dreamed of attending art school from the time she was a teenager. Convinced by her father, a professor of sociology and education at UCLA, that a university education would serve her better than an art-school degree, Kim eventually deferred her artistic dreams by following a friend to York University in Toronto.

Kim's mother was a seamstress who sold homemade fashions out of their home. "I remember her making crazy clothes in the sixties, long Abba dresses and caftans," she recalls. Kim and her older brother quickly became accustomed to spending their paltry clothing allowance on anything but clothes. "My parents grew up in the Depression, so the idea of buying clothes was really foreign, especially for kids."

Taking modern dance lessons rather than playing a musical instrument satisfied Kim's childhood creative impulses. It was only later, when Kim observed how many of her boyfriends were musicians, that it occurred to her that she might herself play an instrument.

Listening to her father's jazz records and her brother's rock collection growing up made her aware of a wide range of musical styles at an early age. "I would listen to Bob Dylan, and my brother would make fun of me because I didn't know what the words meant," Kim says.

When Kim was twelve, her father took the family along with a group of his students to Hong Kong for a year. Her first boyfriend was a fellow student, a British boy who played the drums. Kim looks back on that time with fondness, although she admits it was difficult for her to adjust at the time. "I was coming from an experimental laboratory elementary school that I'd gone to since kindergarten, to an English school and wearing uniforms and getting grades." Since she was held back a grade in the switch, she was also a year older than the rest of the students in her grade.

York University was largely a disappointment for Kim, with the exception of one professor, underground filmmaker George Manupelli (who founded the influential Ann Arbor Film Festival). It was for his media class that Kim formed a band with a few of her classmates. The band played once, at the Ann Arbor Film Festival—the plug was pulled on the band midway through its set in protest of the noise. By coincidence, a future friend saw the performance. "While I was going to school in Detroit, I'd gone to a show there," recalls Mike Kelley, then an undergraduate at the University of Michigan at Ann Arbor. "And I'd seen this really crude noise band from Canada. Later Kim and I talked about this, and I found out that Kim had been sort of a go-go dancer with them."

"I went there because I thought I could do art and take dance as an interdisciplinary program," recalls Kim. Her proudest achievement at York, however, was a film she made, with Manupelli's equipment, about Patty Hearst. Nevertheless, a disgruntled Kim soon returned to Los Angeles and graduated from Otis College of Art and Design a year later. At Otis—then at the fertile crossroads of the conceptual-art fringe and the burgeoning L.A. punk scene—Kim felt more comfortable and finally came to appreciate art history as a discipline. She also experienced firsthand the late-seventies phenomenon of visual artists, spurred by punk's cataclysmic arrival, starting rock bands. Around this time she met Mike Kelley, a young MFA candidate at the California Institute of the Arts (CalArts), at a lecture given by conceptual artist Dan Graham. After the lecture, she went up to Graham, a recent acquaintance, who was arguing over the finer points of punk rock with Kelley. (Kelley himself recalls first meeting Kim at the home of L.A. conceptual artist and Kelly collaborator David Askevold in 1979.)

While at Otis, Kim created what were to be her last visual-art projects. For a painting class, she collected automobile brochures from showrooms and rendered little paintings in the windows of the car photographs. Her teacher, an aging Abstract Expressionist, was outraged. For another, she cut personalized quotes written to accompany display ads out of newspapers, and signed her name to them.

In her final semester, she met Michael Gira, a long-haired Otis student with attitude. They became quick friends. Kim recalls being impressed by one Gira project that consisted of a naked woman lying on a table in a room rigged with a video camera. As viewers left the room, they would come upon a monitor screening their reactions to what they had just seen. At the time, though, Kim ribbed Gira about the sensational yet derivative nature of his exhibit.

Increasingly, Kim was more impressed by arty rock bands than by visual arts. "If you think of art in a linear way, like what's been done, it was like, This is really the next step," she says. "That was always in the back of my mind. I really felt like, Well, anything I do other than that is just going to be superfluous, that it would lack integrity." Taking to heart the edicts of Andy Warhol, the modern muse for so many art students of the era, Kim began to fully realize rock's potential. True popular art, as demonstrated by Warhol, required working in a form with real access to the popular culture.

Soon after finishing school, Kim visited New York for a few months, in anticipation of moving East. "I never really felt comfortable in L.A.," she says. "I always just felt I could never get anything done there. It's hard to feel like you have an identity there." Kim found New York's claustrophobic energy and high artist-per-square-inch density well-suited to her hybrid interests. On her first trip she saw Teenage Jesus and the Jerks and a few of the other No Wave bands perform. Kim saw an emotional, confrontational element present in the New York No Wave bands that was missing in the straight-ahead punk world.

Upon returning to Los Angeles to earn more savings for her move, Kim discovered her friend Mike Gira ensconced in the joys of New York punk rock and No Wave. Kim's interest was piqued— few people she knew in L.A., besides Gira, were listening to these bands. With the exception of the few local bands with combustible live shows, such as the Plugz and X, the Los Angeles punk scene seemed too conventional to Kim. Another noteworthy act that Kim saw perform was the earliest incarnation of Black Flag, featuring Keith Morris (later of the Circle Jerks) on vocals. "Morris looked like an ex–Vietnam vet, but younger—short hair, normal-looking, with an army coat," she says. "He was this weird sort of character who passed out fliers at the gig."

When Kim and Mike Kelley drove to New York in 1980, they

slept by the side of the road at night. Kim's first endeavor upon moving to New York was an operation she called Design Office. Best described as a fake interior-decorating firm, Design Office involved Kim "altering" living spaces. In the case of Dan Graham's Eldridge Street apartment, Kim removed his stove, which he never used, put down commercial-space tiles in his kitchen area, and painted a watercolor of Deborah Harry of Blondie on his wall. Then she wrote about what she had done and had her words printed with photos of her work in a Canadian art magazine. It played like a parody of traditional architecture-magazine spreads. Kim also curated an occasional gallery show: A new friend, Josh Baer, the son of minimalist artist Jo Baer, invited Kim to plan exhibits for his new gallery, White Columns, on Spring Street in SoHo. For one, Kim gathered chairs from different people's homes and exhibited them. For another, which ran in March 1982, she asked artists and musicians to design album covers, operating from the notion that graphic artists frequently ripped off gallery artists anyway. Mike Kelley, Tony Oursler, and Vito Acconci were some of the artists whose work was exhibited.

Immersed in the SoHo art world of the early eighties, Kim happened upon many of the artists who were soon to become the blue-chip darlings of the downtown gallery scene: Robert Longo, Cindy Sherman, Jenny Holzer (Kim stayed at Holzer's loft when she first arrived). Through meeting these artists and doing occasional work for gallery owners, Kim developed both a curiosity and a repulsion for the art of the high-stakes gallery gambit. To Kim's eyes, the art world had begun peddling pure elitism over aesthetics.

Not surprisingly, when Dan Graham asked her to participate in a performance he was organizing around all-female rock bands at the Massachusetts College of Art in Boston, Kim eagerly formed a group. (Graham proved to be an important influence on her: He introduced her to No Wave figures such as Glenn Branca, Barbara Ess, Wharton Tiers; he encouraged her to write songs; and his multimedia career as artist, critic, musician, lecturer, and performer provided her with an encouraging role model.)

Kim summoned her friends Christine Hahn (of the Static) and Stanton Miranda (better known as Miranda), a member of Rhys Chatham's Arsenal, who later recorded music as Thick Pigeon for the Belgian label Le Disques de Crepescule. The three women called themselves CKM, an acronym derived from their first names. Kim played guitar, Miranda played bass, and Christine played drums. Although the Boston gig was the band's sole public performance, Kim immediately discovered that performing engendered a raw emotional response that she had yet to experience via visual art. Also, in her mind, studying art had frozen her ability to create freely.

One song CKM performed was called "Cosmopolitan Girl," which featured both singing and talking, like an old Shangri-Las song. "They used to have an ad in Cosmopolitan on the back page, written in the first person," Kim recalls. " 'I love my Cosmopolitan . . .' The lyrics were literally those words." Another was titled "Soft Polish Separates," which again had lyrics culled from ad copy.

Kim began to imagine life as a musician. Then one night Miranda took Kim to see her friend's band, the Coachmen. To Kim, the band's boyish guitarist, Thurston Moore, stood out from the start. ("I thought he was cute.") Miranda suggested the two might get along, though Kim was sure he was too young for her (she was twenty-eight, he was twenty-three). Despite what proved to be dissimilar interests, the two young musicians hit it off from the start.

"Even though Thurston didn't go to college and he didn't really know about art, we both grew up in academic households," says Kim. "It's funny, when I first tried to play him jazz records, he wouldn't have anything to do with it. All he would listen to was hardcore."

4 | Thurston's Song

The summer of 1976, as immortalized in Richard Linklater's movie *Dazed and Confused*, found a generation of suburban white teens blissed out on pot and bored out of their skulls. For Thurston Moore, born July 25, 1958, the youngest of three children growing up in semirural Bethel, Connecticut, *Dazed and Confused*'s scenario of young high-schoolers getting knocked around by their older hippie siblings was the reality.

"I had a guitar but my brother took it over," says Thurston, "and he got really into playing lead guitar and got really good and jammed with his friends. But that was totally like, Hendrix or nothing." Moore's older brother would chain his equipment up in his closet; when his brother was out, Thurston would carefully remove the chains and play the guitar through the family stereo system, making sure to return it to its proper place before his brother came home.

In high school, Moore's favorite rock star was Alice Cooper, an allegiance that didn't exactly win the rangy teen many friends. His classmates were primarily interested in the popular British supergroups of the day: Yes, Pink Floyd, and Emerson, Lake and Palmer. "I remember sitting in the cafeteria and those kids came around me, the music kids, the Yes fans," he recalls. "They sort of wanted to find out where I was coming from, and I could tell that's what they were up to." They had seen Thurston wandering around the school halls with tattered issues of *Creem* magazine under his arm. So, they wondered, was Thurston into Flash, the new Yes spinoff group?

Moore told them he was more into "theater rock"—the term magazines like *Hit Parader* used then to describe freakish stage acts of the day like Alice Cooper. The music kids stifled laughs; Thurston immediately became aware that the music that he liked appeared, on the surface, less sophisticated than the so-called progressive rock of the day. Not that he wasn't used to standing by his preferences. "I knew these guys were jerks," he says. "I knew that I had an intellectual edge over them."

Thurston's father, George E. Moore, was a music and philosophy professor. He had been a band leader in the army as a young man. When Thurston was a child, the family moved from Tennessee to Florida, and finally settled in Connecticut when his father won a post at Western Connecticut State College in Danbury. An accomplished pianist as well as an unrecorded classical composer, George Moore exposed his youngest son to a wide range of music from an early age.

But the Moore family's otherwise typical suburban existence came to a tragic end in 1976. George Moore died of a brain tumor within months of Thurston's high-school graduation. The family's youngest, Thurston was most affected by his father's passing; he withdrew and became very close to his mother. The cataclysmic event forever left a small tear in his soul.

One day, on the way back from a visit to his father in the hospital, Thurston's mother took him to a department store and let him pick out a record. Thurston selected the Ramones' debut album, which he had read about in one of the music magazines he now scanned regularly with a keen eye. Concurrently, he had stumbled upon the darker-hued pleasures of Iggy Pop, Lou Reed, and Captain Beefheart.

Moore began driving in to Cutler's Records in New Haven, the closest metropolis, to satisfy his increasingly obscure tastes in rock. One day in Cutler's, late in December, 1976, he bumped into a tall dark-haired guy with glasses—"he looked like Buddy Holly"—at the Velvet Underground bin.

"Not much in the Velvets section these days," Thurston observed. The tall, geeky-looking guy, named J.D. King, asked Thurston if he knew where he could buy an issue of *Punk* magazine. King, a recent graduate of the Rhode Island School of Design (the Talking Heads' alma mater), was working in an art-supply store and trying to find work as a free-lance illustrator. "He was obviously older than I was," Thurston says. "He was a college kid." They spoke of the Velvets, the Flamin' Groovies, and the MC5; before they parted, they exchanged addresses.

That fall Moore enrolled in a few courses at Western Connecticut State. Deep down, he knew he wanted to move to New York; at school only a few months, he dropped out. With his leather jacket, punk T-shirt, and close-cropped bristle cut, Moore dressed for a different kind of success than that which college provided.

In high school, Thurston had one close friend, Harold Paris, who shared his tastes in rock music. Together the two saw their first punk show, Patti Smith at the Westport Playhouse in Westport, Connecticut, and would read through issues of *Creem* and *Rock Scene* from cover to cover. One day, while cutting out the photos of all their favorite New York punk celebrities—Nico, Patti Smith, Lance Loud, Joey Ramone, photographer Leee Black Childers—they decided to take a road trip to New York in Thurston's battered Volkswagen Bug.

"We had been there before on class trips or whatever and didn't really know our way around it," Thurston says, "but we actually drove and found Max's. Just looked for it, found it, and went in." The bill for the night listed Suicide, the Fuse Band, and the Cramps.

Later that evening the teenagers watched in horrific fascination as Cramps lead singer Lux Interior contorted his body to sing into a microphone that he refused to position higher than his waist. Then came punk's most perspicacious duo, Suicide.

"We thought Suicide was going to be like a really cool hard-rock thing," Thurston says. "But that was when Suicide was at their most diabolical—green light flooding the stage, and a superloud Martin Rev on keyboards. Just staring at the audience. You know, Max's was really tiny; he just stared with these big bug-eye glasses. Alan Vega was in an old-lady's wig with scars on his face that I guess were fake, but you didn't know." As Vega sang "Cherie, Cherie," Suicide's signature number, he dropped to his knees and tears began streaming down his face. Then he leapt off the stage and grabbed an audience member by the hair; he screamed in someone else's face; he wrapped the microphone cord around another person's neck and pulled it.

Thurston and Harold, really just out-of-town kids looking for a good time, left somewhere in the middle of all this. Vega had begun picking up drinks and smashing them to the floor, and licking people's faces. "The whole audience was freaked out," Thurston says. "It wasn't like they were jaded New Yorkers—they were barricading the front of the stage with chairs and tables. It was totally, totally freaky."

Despite their jarring introduction to the New York punk scene, Thurston and Harold began driving to the city as often as they could. And each weekend trip inevitably turned into another night to remember. One evening, late in 1977, taking in a show by Wayne County and the Sheriffs, led by the legendary Warhol trans-vestite-turned-punk-rocker (later to become transsexual Jayne County), Moore spotted Joey Ramone of the Ramones in the crowd. Girding himself, Moore approached Joey and introduced himself as a fan. The Ramones had just returned from London, where they had seen the Sex Pistols perform. Joey confessed to Moore that he thought more of County's performance than he had the Sex Pistols'.

After the show, the teens got into their car to head home. Moore spotted Joey Ramone again, on the street, and yelled out, "Where's CBGBs?" To Thurston's surprise, Joey responded, "Follow me." It was right down the road, just like it read in the club's advertisements, at "315 Bowery (at Bleecker)."

The tiny club was packed, and Blondie was onstage. Thurston already owned Live at CBGBs, the club's compilation album recorded during the summer of 1976; to his excitement, the real CBGBs looked just like the photo on the front of the album.

A beer bottle whistled by just as he and Harold entered the club, narrowly missing Thurston's head. "And like, nobody seemed to notice," Thurston recalls. The band was on. "I was like, Wow, this place is really fucked up. I thought it was a totally hardcore kind of atmosphere. Of course, that never happened again in my life."

Punk music, Thurston decided, was the avocation he had been looking for. "College always felt like a dead end," he says. Thurston's mother had always imagined her youngest son would grow up to become a writer. He himself had always been attracted to rock music, but hadn't really been able to picture himself as a performer.

Unlike hardcore bands later on, the original punk rockers weren't kids. Many figures on the scene had been to art school; the mere fact that they were surviving in New York implied adulthood to the small-town teenager. "The big revolutionary thing was that they were playing in places where they would hang out with the audience after the gig," Thurston says. "You'd read interviews with Joe Strummer of the Clash, and he'd be like, Yeah, you know I have a beer with me mates and then I go onstage and play. None of this rock-star shit."

Another trip prompted one of Thurston's few drug tales—what has become known to friends as the "Tad's Steaks acid story." New Year's Eve, 1976, Thurston and some pals were headed for the old

Palladium to witness a lineup consisting of John Cale, Television, and Patti Smith. Getting high before what promised to be a phenomenal show was a must. "We used to do blotter acid a lot, for a year or so," Thurston says. "I never really went out and bought it, but it was like, there'd be a couple of guys who would always have it."

This night, instead of smoking pot and and doing blotter acid, essentially cheap speed, he took a dose of powerful green mescaline at Tad's Steaks, right down the block from the club. "I started tripping out on it, and it was really weird. New York is the worst place to take acid, and it was the first time I did it. Tad's was really flipping me out and then we made it to the Palladium and sat down. John Cale was on first, and I sincerely thought I was losing it. I was really seeing extreme trails and stuff. I just tried to follow them, because that was the only logic I could follow. If I didn't follow them I was going to go into this black void and forever be gone. I was really flipping out. But I came out of it by the end of his set. Or at least the beginning of Television's set. I'll never forget that."

Strangely enough, Thurston's first, albeit brief moment of punk celebrity came via the post office.

Thurston made contact with Eddie Flowers, a writer for the West Coast punk fanzine *Search and Destroy*, through a classified ad in the back of a rock magazine. Flowers and Moore began corresponding—in one letter, Moore described a disappointing Dead Boys gig he had attended. Having gotten word of the legendary Cleveland band's confrontational live shows, Moore was dismayed to find a long-haired band playing Mott the Hoople covers. "We sat in back 'cause we didn't want to get hurt," says Moore. "But nothing happened, so we felt stupid. [Lead singer] Stiv [Bators] was really drunk, and I remember them carrying him off the stage." Flowers got the letter published in the debut issue of *Gulcher*, the successor to *Search and Destroy*, along with a threatening photo-booth mug shot of the prepubescent-looking Moore with a cigarette dangling from his lip.

Back in sleepy Bethel, nobody thought punk was cool. "It was this weird thing that was going on that nobody knew about," Moore says. A couple kids he knew had heard of punk rock, maybe through a record purchased by an older sibling. But there were few boosters. "The whole attitude was that you had to say punk rock sucked—because it was bad. It was not cool at all." Undeterred, Moore continued searching for soul mates through the network, keeping abreast of new punk developments by mailing away for single-issue fanzines and regional album releases.

He also struck up a correspondence with J.D. King. One letter from King, written in the fall of 1977, informed Moore that King and a few fellow RISD grads—John Miller, Randy Ludacer, and Danny Walworth—were moving from Providence to New York to try their luck in the Manhattan music scene. A couple months later, Moore got a call from King; the guys had rented a decrepit loft near South Street Seaport, then a desolate strip a few blocks above Manhattan's Wall Street area. King had written that they were planning to start a band and wanted Thurston to play bass. Having no other immediate plans, Thurston decided to go. Armed with a Stratocaster (a gift from his brother) and his mother's blessings, he drove off for New York.

At first, Thurston stayed at his friends' loft. King, Miller, and Moore began jamming together while King and Moore compared notes. "His songs were more sort of 'sophisto,' kind of more Modern Lovers, Velvetsy kinds of things," Moore says. "My shit was more Dictators." Art rock versus punk primitivism. The three asked Dan Walworth to play drums, because he was around. The four played at one loft party before Miller left for graduate school in Los Angeles. Bob Pullin, another Providence transplant, soon replaced Miller on bass.

Thurston found an apartment on 13th Street between Avenues B and C, a bleak block in the East Village, plagued to this day by a bustling heroin trade. "I would only leave during the daytime, because nighttime, forget it," he says. But rent was only $110 a month, allowing Thurston to get by for a while on his savings and a little help from his mother.

He first took a job with Design Research, a purveyor of postmodern furniture, in part because he had heard Chris Frantz of Talking Heads had held the position previously. When Design Research folded, he found a low-paying menial job at Masterdisk, a sound-mastering facility later used by Sonic Youth, through an ad in the *New York Post*. But even with his nominal rent, Moore had trouble keeping solvent. He also got fired.

One night King suggested calling their group the Coachmen, a name used by countless regional bands in the early sixties, as a joke. The name stuck.

The Coachmen immediately distinguished themselves by playing only originals, a strategy predetermined by the fact that the group found it impossible to learn the chord progressions to their favorite songs by the Modern Lovers and Tommy James and the Shondells. Randy Ludacer, too, had formed an art-rock band with his two younger brothers, called Ludacer. Thurston was excited by the prospect of performing, though at the time he expressed concern for his compatriots' rarefied leanings: Talking Heads had recently garnered national attention, and downtown was brimming with recent RISD grads bent on following in David Byrne's quirky footsteps.

Moore had always fantasized about being a member of a punk band: the Heartbreakers, formed by Johnny Thunders from the New York Dolls and Richard Hell from Television, were his favorite punk group. But the art-school crowd that Thurston was meeting in New York was already bad-mouthing punk.

"It was a very modern way to be," he says. "To them, punk rock was corny. I remember hanging out with them, and I had even bought a Johnny Thunders T-shirt. Artist friends would come to the CBGBs audition night to see us, and I was definitely like the punker kid in the band. They were like, 'Isn't that cute? They've got this eighteen-year-old kid, and he's a punker.' They thought that was kind of funny. They didn't take me seriously." Even while No Wave figures like Lydia Lunch were giving provocative interviews in which they slammed the work of punk icons like Patti Smith as "barefoot hippie shit," Moore remained a kid enamored with the promise of punk's new romanticism.

Thurston's friend Harold, upon seeing the Coachmen perform, confirmed what the lanky blond suspected: It was great to be in a band, but just imagine someday joining a real punk band. . . .

King and Walworth wrote most of the Coachmen's lyrics; King sang lead on songs with names like "Girls Are Short," "Household Word," and "Radical Lifestyle," written in homage to bands such as the Velvet Underground, Television, and the Modern Lovers. Judging from the few tracks released on *Failure to Thrive*, a posthumously released EP, the band largely succeeded in approximating the lean, rhythmic style of late-period Velvet Underground. One tune, titled simply "Thurston's Song," featured a smoothly appealing chord progression devised by Moore. On May 1, 1979, the Coachmen and Ludacer scored an off-night at CBGBs.

Moore still perceived himself as a punk. The Coachmen began playing parties at artists' lofts; and while Thurston remembers being excited upon spotting David Byrne at one such Coachmen gig, he remained constantly aware of the gap between his sensibilities and those of the older patrons—urbane artists with carefully reasoned opinions on virtually every topic, who observed new music from a decidedly detached perspective.

"They would play disco records and dance to them," he says, "and that was like a radical thing they were doing: 'Oh, we *like* to dance, we *like* rhythm. Disco's great.' It was this very cynical appreciation. I was like, man, disco sucks! I was still in that whole thing of 'Punk rocks, disco sucks,' et cetera. So I was kind of separate from them. I didn't really socialize with them that much."

Even as the Coachmen secured the occasional club gig or loft-party appearance, their brand of streamlined, melodic material seemed oddly out of synch with most of the downtown scene.

Moore began to take notice of the No Wave acts, some of whom the Coachmen appeared with on loft-party bills.

One night they shared the floor with the Static, Glenn Branca's group, at Jenny Holzer's loft. "I was totally unimpressed," Thurston says. "The gig they did with us was super-atonal. It was these long, fifteen-minute pieces—*nobody* liked it. I think they did some really interesting gigs, but this one was totally annoying." Still repelled by No Wave's anti-punk aesthetic, Moore nevertheless began to warm to the strangely reversed celebrity mystique brokered by these provocative artist folk. "I kind of got indoctrinated when I heard the first Mars single—I thought that was really good," he says.

He also became intrigued by the way the No Wavers looked— striking, disheveled, yet somehow ordinary people. A benefit concert for X magazine, an underground film journal, held at the Anthology Film Archives—which featured performances by Theoretical Girls, the Contortions, and DNA, among others—finally sold Thurston on the merits of the music. "I thought it was amazing," he says. "Theoretical Girls was just off the wall. And DNA was the fucking ugliest band in the world."

Through No Wave, Thurston began to appreciate the power culled from straying, even slightly, from the narrow strictures of punk. The two most immediate ways to tinker with the formula were sound and image.

The Feelies, based directly across the Hudson River from Manhattan, in Hoboken, New Jersey, were a frenetic Velvet Underground–influenced band in their earliest incarnation. And one night at Max's Kansas City, at a Feelies show, Thurston observed his future self.

"That was the first time I saw really geeky guys playing, without any kind of punk-rock attitude," he says. "Even Richard Hell and Patti Smith had this very classic kind of New York punk-rock vibe onstage. But the Feelies were the first band I saw onstage that were just sort of suburban noodniks."

After one song, Feelies lead singer Glenn Mercer kicked an

orange-juice carton across the stage. The angry gesture seemed so slight, almost comical, yet it perfectly expressed the quick fury inherent in the band's maniacally strummed guitar buzz. The Feelings were average-looking people playing extremely kinetic music based on the unusual sounds made by electric guitars.

While the Coachmen were able to secure the occasional gig at CBGBs and even played Max's Kansas City once, they most often played a loft space turned club called A Space, or A's. A's was run by Arleen Schloss and Todd Jorgensen, out of a loft owned by Schloss.

Schloss's loft is located between the Bowery and Christie Street, the virtual midpoint between the East Village and SoHo. Yet deep in the import-export heart of Chinatown—a produce distributor down the block is called Five Brothers Fat Enterprise, Inc.—A's was off the beaten paths of both SoHo and the East Village. Opening night at the loft featured, among other acts, a band fronted by Jean-Michel Basquiat—the renowned enfant terrible and early tragedy of the eighties' commercially revitalized New York art scene—and a performance by Schloss.

Schloss herself was typical, in her atypicality, of the kind of artists that scurried about the garbage-strewn streets of lower Manhattan in the early eighties. A Brooklyn-born "multimedia artist," educated at Parsons School of Design and New York University, Schloss decided in October 1979 to open her second-floor loft to performances. Having moved on from painting to, in the late seventies, experimenting with such diverse forms as Xerox art and Super-8 filmmaking, Schloss built the A's roster out of and around her interests and those of her friends. And for much of the first year, according to Schloss, the creative mood at A's remained relatively untouched by outside forces such as careerism and greed.

Schloss and Jorgensen (whose photocopy business later provided Kim Gordon with some part-time work) would book a night's worth of events a week in advance and plaster the neighborhood with advertising fliers of their own crude design. For three or four dollars, one was treated to a night-long extravaganza that began at seven-thirty and ran till midnight, and might include an art exhibit, a few video projections, a string of art performances (Schloss began one night by reciting a monologue consisting solely of the letters of the alphabet), and end up with a string of bands. (Red Milk, an early Moore-Gordon collaboration, also played the space.)

"They played one New Year's Eve, and they were fabulous," says Schloss, recalling a standout Coachmen performance from a night that also featured Alan Suicide (a.k.a. Vega) and Harry Toledo. "They were developing a sound. A lot of people were interested in what they were doing, and a lot people thought they were really good." Toledo's drummer, David Keay, soon replaced Dan Walworth, who left the Coachmen to pursue filmmaking.

Up until then, Moore was still taking the train back to Bethel many weekends to visit his mother and listen to his record collection, most of which he still hadn't brought into the city. It was only after Sex Pistols bassist Sid Vicious died of a heroin overdose at the Chelsea Hotel in October 1979, a New York event that many perceived as the passing of an era, that Thurston decided to stay in Manhattan for good.

Lee Ranaldo remembers seeing the Coachmen a number of times at the Botany Talk House, a tiny bar in Chelsea's floral district. "For some reason, the Coachmen used to play there a lot," he says. "So we went and saw them play—I guess they'd seen us play. We were actually starting to get somewhere a little bit, both of these bands. CBGBs finally decided that we all warranted a reasonable night, and we got a Sunday night." On January 27, 1980, the Flucts [sic], the Coachmen, and A Band (another Wharton Tiers project) all played on the same bill. By the fall of 1980, the Coachmen had broken up.

Thurston first saw the earliest version of Glenn Branca's six-guitar ensemble at A's. "It was a real revelation," he says. "The thought of doing anything with guitars as far as different tunings had never occurred to me, and the No Wave bands didn't seem to be doing different tunings—they just didn't know how to play."

The buzzing, chordal intensity of Branca's music struck Thurston like a tidal wave. Suddenly, being in a punk band wasn't a necessity anymore. Branca's group was louder and more intense than any punk outfit Thurston had ever heard.

In an effort to distance himself from the Coachmen's relatively staid sound, he searched for playing partners as far apart from what he had already experienced as possible. A friend told Thurston about his girlfriend, Miranda, a keyboard player. "When I went to play with her, I said to myself, I'm just going to throw away everything that I did with Coachmen—I just didn't want to play D to C to G anymore," says Thurston. "So one day I just started playing really fast all over the neck, jumping around but playing very rhythmically." He quickly realized that no matter what he'd attempt on his guitar, Miranda's keyboard parts still sounded good.

Miranda brought her best friend Kim Gordon to one of the Coachmen's last gigs, at the Plugg Club, a venue on West 24th Street run by the Rolling Stones' former manager, Georgio Gomelski. After the show, Kim and Thurston met for the first time. "She was cool, although I couldn't really get a sense of what was going on there," Thurston says, "because she had these flip-ups on her glasses, so I just sort of saw that and her hair."

Ann DeMarinis and Thurston first met at the Brooklyn loft she shared with her companion, the visual artist Vito Acconci. Thurston remembers Ann as a thin girl with peroxide blonde hair, a striking art-school punk with almost translucent pale skin. As soon as the two got talking about music, Ann revealed that she, too, played keyboards. Within days, Ann, Thurston, and Miranda (who had switched to playing bass) were jamming together at the loft. Kim and Ann got along from the first time they met; Thurston and Kim began dating. When Miranda lost interest in the group, Kim took her place.

"I thought Thurston was really inventive," says Kim. "I didn't know he didn't know how to play guitar—to me, he was really impressive. Ann had the opposite problem: Because she was musically trained, she couldn't invent anything. She was too neurotic."

Yearning to perform again in public, Thurston excitedly answered a classified ad Glenn Branca had placed in search of new
guitarists to play "weird music." Kim had met Branca through Dan
Graham and put in a good word for Thurston. But after Thurston
auditioned, Branca decided he no longer needed another guitarist.
Kim got the word back from Glenn: The composer was also con-
cerned that Thurston was "too wild."

Disappointed, Thurston called up Dave Keay, the Coachmen's
last drummer, and invited him to join the new group with Ann and
Kim. They even had a band name, Male Bonding. (One Male
Bonding song, called "Teenage Men," had the chorus "Teenage
men playing loud guitars.") They changed the name to Red Milk
for their first show, on December 17, 1980, at A's. Everyone
present, except Dave Keay, acknowledged the noisy show as a total
disaster. Fortunately, very few people saw the performance. In a
brisk effort to start anew, Thurston came up with another new
name, the Arcadians, taken from the peaceful tribe in ancient
Greece that used music to communicate. Then he stomped into
CBGBs and demanded a gig; to Thurston's surprise, Hilly Kristal
agreed to give the Arcadians a January 14 slot.

One night, when the Arcadians performed at Inroads, a small
club in SoHo, David Linton and Lee Ranaldo jammed with band.
The members of Plus Instruments and Sonic Youth had become
familiar faces to each other. "We got up on one song, and I played
half of Ann's keyboard," says Ranaldo. "And David was banging
some percussion stuff."

Only a few gigs later, Ann announced she was leaving the
Arcadians to pursue more promising projects. "To lose Ann was to
lose this real appealing factor in the band," says Thurston, "because she was hot: She was this peroxided girl who played keyboards really fluently."

5 | Crosstown Traffic

''I'm just walking around / Your city is a wonder town.''

—from ''The Wonder,'' *Daydream Nation*

Like most genuine pop-music scenes, No Wave relied heavily on an exchange of ideas. That No Wave's milieu, lower Manhattan, deteriorates on its edges into a jumble of ramshackle tenements and boarded-up warehouses only made creative cross-pollination easier.

For the No Wavers especially—few of whom were aptly compensated for their creative experimentation—checking out the competition was as much a professional necessity as it was an aesthetic one. No Wave musicians frequently played in more than one band just to make ends meet. The noisier ones, for the most part performance artists and untrained musicians, were forever sniffing out new sounds and techniques to add to their generally narrow repertoires.

By the beginning of 1981, downtown musicians far outnumbered spots to play. In response to the sheer volume of eager but underemployed performers they knew between them, Kim and her friend Josh Baer convinced Thurston to organize a nine-day music festival to be held at White Columns.

"I called up anybody I knew," says Thurston. "I called up Glenn Branca and he said, 'You should call up Mark Cunningham from Mars, because Mars isn't together anymore but I hear he has something new. . . .' " Before long, word of the festival spread, and acts began calling Thurston. (The late Lester Bangs even phoned in asking to perform one evening, although the legendary rock critic showed up late, having missed the whole night's proceedings.)

The Noise Festival took place at White Columns from June 16 through June 24 of 1981. Named in response to a disparaging comment made by Robert Boykin, proprietor of the rock club Hurrah, that most newer bands sounded like noise, the "Noisefest" provided a sense of community among performers who couldn't get dates at the more established rock clubs.

Each night three to five acts performed in the cramped gallery space (60 people was capacity). Glenn Branca, Rhys Chatham, Jeffrey Lohn, Dog Eat Dog, Built on Guilt (artist Robert Longo's band), Rudolph Grey, the Avant Squares, Mofungo, Red Decade, Robin Crutchfield's Dark Day, and Ad Hoc Rock were among the names on the bill. David Linton played both with Elliot Sharp's Carbon and Rhys Chatham's band; Lee played with Branca. Lee and David Linton performed a piece called *Avoidance Behavior*, which consisted of Ranaldo playing an electric guitar strung with steel wire (a Branca trick) while Linton recorded him from the back of the room and then, seconds later, mixed the tape loop with Ranaldo's live playing. Then they switched positions and Ranaldo did the same with Linton's drumming. A third section mixed both tape loops with a series of slides projected on a screen.

The Noisefest lineup for the night of June 18 was Rhys Chatham, Sonic Youth, Smoking Section, and Chinese Puzzle. "I came up with the name Sonic Youth while Ann was still in the band but I didn't tell anybody," says Thurston. "I thought it was maybe a little too rock-and-roll for the art band that we were." Sonic Youth was an amalgam of Big Youth, a late-seventies reggae band, and Sonic's Rendezvous Band, the post-MC5 band that Fred "Sonic" Smith led from 1977 to 1979.

"As soon as we came up with the name Sonic Youth, we started getting a better idea of what direction to go in," says Kim.

Thurston called up Ann DeMarinis and cajoled her into playing in the group once more, this time under the name Sonic Youth, with a new drummer, Richard Edson. "Thurston and Richard were kind of secondary to Kim and Ann," Tim Carr, who had moved to New York and later managed Glenn Branca among other tasks, recalls of Sonic Youth's first performance. "But to me, that's what the Noisefest was all about: There were women in bands every single night."

"The room is tiny, the reverb is deadly, and the amplification so loud that it is all but impossible to stand inside for more than a minute," the SoHo News's Tim Page reported from the Noise Festival. "Every now and then the doorman will run outside, looking like a fugitive from the Dresden firestorm—'The Horror!'—shaking his head as if to spill out the surplus decibels and fragments of his eardrums, and then heading back inside."

"It was the place to be for those ten days," Ranaldo recalls. "Everyone in the music community who wasn't already on the level of Richard Hell and Television, all the next generation was there. All of sudden you met everybody. Everybody became friends and interrelated."

The Noisefest was the most energized kind of artistic events—a serious happening run by amateurs. "There was a place called Nino's across the street that sold sixteen-ounce beers," says Tim Carr, who attended every night of the festival. "So we'd all go over to Nino's and buy these beers, and then Josh and Thurston realized they were losing out to Nino's, so they started a beer concession and sold twelve-ounce Heinekens for a dollar."

The White Columns festival also proved to be a brief era's swan song. Little more than year later, critics were mourning the death of the New York underground. "No Wave was New York's last stylistically cohesive avant-rock movement," observed Steve Anderson in the Village Voice. "Its abrasive reductionism undermined the power and mystique of a rock vanguard by depriving it of a tradition to react against."

Richard Edson turned up in New York via San Francisco. Born in Manhattan and raised in New Rochelle, a suburb just north of New York, Edson had headed West after graduating from SUNY's Albany campus with a degree in English and music. Heeded, too, by punk's call to make it new, Edson was nevertheless drawn stylistically to funk and free jazz. "At that point, free jazz was the most radical, the most avant-garde, the most in-your-face type of music," says Edson. "Not that many of the players understood what the hell they were doing. And I must admit, I was one of the guilty ones—and unfortunately, because I think I robbed myself of a lot of the history of jazz by just trying to play the most avant-garde style."

Edson found a fertile music scene in San Francisco but returned to New York once he became frustrated with what he perceived as the city's state of voluntary musical segregation. He found a job as a darkroom printer with the *SoHo News* and began drumming with a seven-piece group called Konk, in the "dance, R&B, funk, Afro-percussive polyrhythmic realm." When the *SoHo News* folded in 1982, Edson joined a few other bands to make ends meet: One was called Body, a band that included Tom Paine and Mark C., later of Live Skull. The other was Sonic Youth.

"Between those bands, I was making enough money to get by," Edson recalls. "Every now and then, I'd take a painting job. I had some friends who had a painting company, so we'd take cocaine and paint for fourteen hours a day. Do these jobs and make five hundred bucks and with the rent in those times and living where we were living on five hundred bucks, we'd say okay that's two months I don't have to work."

Edson was living at 330 Broome Street in SoHo, upstairs from Arleen Schloss's club, A's. In the wake of a scene that had bifurcated on artistic grounds, A's was one of the few places where unrepentant music purists like Edson might run into what he calls "arty people who were very influenced by punk but weren't really a part of it." Every Wednesday and (sometimes) Saturday night for about a year, A's would host free-wheeling, open-ended performance parties. On a pleasant night, the crowd might spill out into Schloss's sculpture garden—in actuality a tarred rooftop appointed with serpentine metal sculptures and welded furniture. Beer was served.

Richard would wander downstairs, more out of convenience than anything else. "It was a little too conceptual, a little too smart for its own good," he says. "I was much more into music as music. This was music as performance and art as performance. Much more conceptual. I had what I considered a very healthy disregard for that stuff."

One night he saw the Coachmen play A's, but recalls little about the music. "The unique thing about the Coachmen was that three of the guys were like six feet four and over. And that's what impressed me about them more than anything else. The tallest band I'd ever seen."

According to Richard, when the Coachmen played A's again the two musicians got to talking. (Though Thurston doesn't recall meeting Richard at A's, he can't remember exactly where he did.) Moore invited Edson to play with the group he had been trying to start up. Taking what he today admits was the mercenary approach, Edson drummed in all three bands for a while.

Edson quickly became a grounding force in Sonic Youth. Not only was he an accomplished drummer, but he also provided a rehearsal room—Konk's rental space—a basement on Second Avenue between 4th and 5th streets in the East Village.

"What they loved to do was just crank up the amps and just play with sound," says Edson. "And for a drummer, it was like, 'Um, I don't have an amp.' So I'd have to play myself raw. I would always insist, 'We've got to have a form, we've got to have a form. Otherwise I'm going to die here.' So I kept forcing them: 'This isn't a song. I just played twenty minutes without a break.' "

In order to attend Noisefest, Linton and Ranaldo had reneged on an agreement to tour Europe with Truss de Groot, their partner in Plus Instruments; and Sonic Youth, whose Noisefest gig was the first under the new name, had fallen apart almost immediately. Edson announced his departure after the White Columns show, having decided to devote his efforts to the jazzier rhythms of Konk. The Noisefest conveniently coincided with the demise of both bands.

Kim approached Lee at White Columns one night during the festival and expressed her disappointment in her nascent group's dissolution. "Why don't you and Thurston try getting together and playing guitars?" she suggested. Barely a week later, Moore, Gordon, and Ranaldo met to rehearse at White Columns and began banging out the beginnings of what was later that year to become *Sonic Youth*, the band's debut EP.

"There was the bass line to 'Burning Spear,' which they were already trying to do something with in a reggae sort of version," says Lee. "Mostly we just made up things between the three of us, those first few nights of rehearsal." Sonic Youth did four or five gigs as a trio, sans drummer.

"She Is Not Alone," which appears on the first EP, was an early number, albeit in a different arrangement. In true noise-rock spirit, Ranaldo came up with the idea of running a power drill through a wah-wah guitar pedal. (The effect can be heard on the studio recording of "Burning Spear," the first track on *Sonic Youth*.) Performing drummerless, the band tried to compensate; those first performances featured little singing and "a lot of banging on guitars with metal pipes and sticks."

Sonic Youth played its first show with Lee at an opening at the Just Above Midtown/Downtown Gallery, on Franklin Street in Tribeca, a funky exhibit space that boasted comedian Martin Mull on its board of directors. Lee had practiced with them only once. Sonic Youth appeared again soon after, at a yuppie club called Stillwende that had opened where Tier 3 had been. A cluttered bill allowed the band only ten minutes, enough time for one song, "Burning Spear."

"I beat the shit out of this drum and played my guitar with a drumstick,' says Thurston. "And Kim was holding it down with this bass figure and Lee was going off on the drill, and I screamed out the lyrics and then it came to this crashing finale." At the end, Moore tossed the microphone stand into the audience.

"It was really hysterical," Lee says. "The audience was half kids that had come to see us, in the back, grooving—and half art snobs in the front with their fingers in their ears because it was so loud and abrasive."

"That was the first night where I felt like Sonic Youth was this really experimental thing," Thurston recalls, "but at the same time it was just sort of like 'get the fuck out of my way' art."

In Sonic Youth's first press release, Thurston described the band as follows: "Crashing mashing intensified dense rhythms juxtaposed with filmic mood pieces. Evoking an atmosphere that could only be described as expressive fucked-up modernism. And so forth."

Three months later, on September 18, 1981, Sonic Youth performed at Music for Millions, an East Village festival held in the spirit of Noisefest at the New Pilgrim Theater on East 3d Street. (A brand-new quartet from Athens, Georgia, named R.E.M., also made its New York debut at the festival.) Desperate not to miss such a promising appearance, Moore, Gordon, and Ranaldo pleaded with Edson to return. In rehearsal, Edson helped shape the band's first real set.

The day after the show, Glenn Branca called to say he had seen it; he was planning a record label called Neutral and he wanted Sonic Youth to be his first act.

Glenn Branca had stumbled upon a golden opportunity. Since *Lesson No. 1*, Ed Bahlman at 99 Records had taken to following Branca's recommendations as far as which happening New York acts he might sign to his independent label. Having scored with Liquid Liquid, a Branca pick whose three albums went on to sell around 50,000 copies, mostly out of the MacDougal Street store-front, Bahlman had begun to rely on Branca's intuition.

Sonic Youth was one of a number of local bands Branca had been pushing on Bahlman. Yet Bahlman balked when it came time to sign this particular act. "He actually knew Thurston, because Thurston was a very heavy record collector and Ed's store was the main record collector's store in town if you wanted English releases and all that shit," says Branca. Yet Bahlman went so far as to vow he would never sign Sonic Youth.

Thanks to Josh Baer, the owner of White Columns, Bahlman's vow proved spurious. Baer, a well-to-do scenester, had already begun exhibiting the works of cutting-edge visual artists at his SoHo gallery. So it was only natural for him when he asked Branca, "What would you like to do if you could do whatever you wanted?" Branca dreamed of starting a record label; Baer offered to grant Branca's wish. Branca subsequently suggested Sonic Youth as the label's first act.

Branca's offer—and Sonic Youth's acceptance of that offer—to produce a record for the newly dubbed Neutral Records, was the first of many fortunate turns for the band.

The notion of independent labels devoted to distributing the musings of the "underground" rock scene was a relatively new one in 1981. In fact, Neutral was one of a very tiny group of indie labels extant in New York at the time, a close circle which included 99 and Labor. Unlike the punk bands of the seventies scene, such as the Ramones, Television, and Blondie, the premier No Wave acts of the early eighties had no hope of getting signed to major labels. And the paucity of independent labels further ensured that few would ever make it to vinyl at all.

Kim took Thurston on his first trip to Los Angeles in 1981, to meet her parents. While Thurston had purchased issues of *Slash*, the premier Los Angeles fanzine, in New York, his first direct exposure to the burgeoning hardcore scene was a revelation. "Before then, all I knew about was X and the Germs," he says.

By 1981, SST—a small, southern-California independent label started by Greg Ginn and Chuck Dukowski, guitarist and bassist for the already legendary L.A. hardcore outfit Black Flag—had already released its seminal records, such as Black Flag's *Six Pack* and the Minutemen's *The Punch Line* which presaged the hardcore punk–independent label connection. While SST's earlier acts were more closely tied to a basic three-chord rock-and-roll energy than Sonic Youth, those acts' code of operation would deeply influence on their New York counterparts.

Early on, SST set the decade's standard for loud, literate music recorded on shoestring budgets by bands set off as much by their geographical origins and pugnacious personalities as by their loud, fast music. Many of the early SST album covers featured crude, comic book–like etchings with mystical erotic and violent themes, rendered in pen and ink by Ginn's older brother, Raymond Pettibon.

In July 1981 Henry Garfield—the twenty-year-old lead singer for a Washington, D.C., hardcore band named S.O.A. (State of Alert)—moved to Los Angeles to become Black Flag's new front man. Redubbed Henry Rollins, he soon became one of the most visible standard-bearers for a new, postpunk aesthetic—one that valued creative breadth over production values, and frightfully dynamic performances over handsome recording advances.

"New York had a hardcore scene, but it wasn't as good as D.C.'s," says Don Fleming, a Georgia-born punk aficionado/musician and later air force recruit who got transferred to the D.C. area just as hardcore began to flourish. "D.C. was sort of like L.A.—there was a real D.C. pride at the time: 'We've got the best hardcore scene.' " Although Fleming didn't conform to the D.C. hardcore dress code—jackboots and a crewcut or shaved head—he found the scene relatively amenable to outsiders. The Velvet Monkeys, a deliberately slapdash outfit he started in 1981, wasn't even a hardcore band.

Back in New York, Thurston bought a record by the Circle Jerks, an even faster, sloppier Black Flag offshoot. "At the same time, I guess, people who were a few years younger than me also bought that Circle Jerks record," Thurston says. "And they were *way* more into that than they were into DNA."

Hardcore changed everything at the grass-roots level of the underground, even in New York. "Black Flag and those bands just got in vans and cars, called each other up," says Thurston. "And if they couldn't find any club in a town that would allow kids in, they would play in a basement or a skate party." The first time Thurston saw an ad for a Black Flag show in a New York paper, it was a revelation. How, he wondered, had this virtually unknown band from California made it all the way to New York?

A couple weeks after the Music for Millions festival, Sonic Youth was offered a Friday night gig at CBGBs. Mark Coleman wrote a glowing half-page review—Sonic Youth's first—of the show for *New York Rocker*. Taken by surprise, the band had to run out and get a photo taken to accompany the piece.

"All we were playing were the five songs on that first record and maybe two other sketchy things," says Ranaldo. Coleman admitted to not having understood the lyrics, but praised "a stunning purity in the range of sounds the guitars encompass" and rhythms that "hit in the pit of the stomach, instead of the cerebellum." Edson is referred to in the review as "Richard Smith," an everyman-sounding *nom de guerre*.

In December 1981 Sonic Youth entered Radio City Studio, a gymnasium-size studio upstairs from Radio City Music Hall in midtown Manhattan. Under its former name, Plaza Sound, the twenty-four-track studio had played host to the debut efforts of the Ramones, Blondie, and the Voidoids only five years earlier. The band, only a month old since Ranaldo had joined, rehearsed seven nights in a row to prepare for the session. Branca and Baer arranged for time with a house engineer, Don Hünerberg. (In the same studio, Branca's ensemble recorded *Bad Smells*, music commissioned for a dance piece of the same name choreographed by Twyla Tharp; Thurston performed as the group's fifth guitarist.)

For $2,000, $1,000 each day for two days, Sonic Youth had itself a debut release. *Sonic Youth*'s five songs—"The Burning Spear," "I Dreamed I Dream," "She Is Not Alone," "I Don't Want to Push It," and "The Good and the Bad"—were recorded the first day and mixed the next.

Despite the fact that Branca had no input into the end product (he never even heard the material until the final tracks were mixed), *Sonic Youth* had "New York art rock" written all over it. Robert Palmer of the *New York Times* noted that "instrumentally Sonic Youth sometimes recalls [Glenn] Branca's carefully formal, numbingly loud overlays of massed electric guitars. The music's beat, and the even strokes the guitarists favor, are controlled and relentless, especially on the generally dark and desperate-sounding side one. The second side of *Sonic Youth* offers some brighter moments, but the concern with order and clarity is still evident." Palmer also observed that the lyrics seemed like "afterthoughts," although he cited "I Dreamed I Dream" as a standout track.

The album received other brief but praiseworthy reviews in the *Los Angeles Times*, *Heavy Metal* magazine, and the U.K. tabloid *Sounds*. The local *East Village Eye* offered considerably less praise: "Too much Killing Joke and not enough Buzzcocks," its critic sniffed in a capsule review.

Most critical assessments inferred that *Sonic Youth* was not what one expected. Written accounts of the No Wave aesthetic trumpeted its worship of heightened, unearthly clatter—yet *Sonic Youth* is not especially noisy or chaotic. Considering its status as the first release by Neutral Records, *Sonic Youth* does not contain many of the important elements that later came to embody the "indie label" sound: It is crisply recorded and carefully mixed to keep each instrument in full focus at all times.

"Everyone was amazed at how well the first record came out," says Kim. "We had been together two months. When we played live before that, the songs were less structured. Then when we went to record it, it was a little more arranged. Richard Edson had a lot to with that."

Evenly metered and carefully composed, Sonic Youth bears little resemblance to the work that eventually set the band to cross genre lines. On it, one can hear the influence of British postpunk acts like Public Image Ltd. and the Raincoats; one can also hear a little of the underground reggae sounds popular in downtown New York clubs at the time (the Jamaican reggae star Burning Spear was a particular favorite). But in comparison to the early work of the Velvet Underground, another New York band with downtown art-world credentials who went on to influence subsequent generations of rock experimentalists, Sonic Youth's debut work sounds deceptively tame.

Yet from the sharp cymbal bursts that introduce its first track, "The Burning Spear," the EP sows, in some form or another, all the seeds from which Sonic Youth would later reap its creative bounty. The rat-tat-tat of Edson's drumming lays out form and tempo in "The Burning Spear." Thurston got the song title from the reggae act Burning Spear, "but the lyrics don't have anything to do with Jah love—they were more about living on 13th Street," he says.

Thurston plays the song's first terse guitar strains with drum sticks, setting the standard for Sonic Youth song-beginnings-to-come: An oddly tuned guitar sounds its first notes, clearly out of tune but testing the waters, adapting to the tempo, making motions toward a new vocabulary. Gordon repeats a simple bass pattern, remarkable only in the way its resonates under her heavy hand. And then Ranaldo starts the power drill—surprisingly enough, this particularly grating effect hardly stands out in the slickly produced mix.

The guitars ring like chimes, the tempo is moderate; even the vulnerable first line Moore bleats—"I'm not afraid to say I'm scared"—more immediately connects the music to New York performance art circa 1978 than to the raw, unleashed power of the early SST acts.

"If you listen to the first album," says Edson, "it's kind of like we purposely tried to make every song different. I was being very experimental with the rhythms, I was playing a lot of polyrhythmic stuff, not real straight-ahead rock rhythms."

"I Dreamed I Dream" features two more basic elements that Sonic Youth would later develop further and make staples of its stylistic roster. Kim Gordon whisper-talks the lyrics—presumably the thoughts of a woman done in by her junkie boyfriend—over a simple, repetitive melody, sung by Ranaldo. The intertwined thoughts of man and woman swirl and intersect at key words— "dream," "drift," "money's gone." Next, Gordon intones the phrases "Fucking youth" and "Working youth" over and over, the first in a series of many instances where the band used its name as lyrical inspiration. Edson and Gordon wrote the song's lyrics in the studio, gathering phrases by cutting up newspapers and working out lines while listening to playbacks of the instrumental tracks. Kim didn't decide which lines to sing until she went to record her vocal. "It was very random," says Kim. "And I still think that sometimes that's the best way to write lyrics. Because we didn't know any better, we were doing whatever we wanted."

On "She Is Not Alone," Edson gets the opportunity to demonstrate his beholden Latin/jazz percussion techniques. With its title virtually the sole lyric, "Alone" comes off as the most leaden of the EP's five tracks. Clearly a jam session in search of a shape, it unfolds in a style that the band would rarely, if ever, touch upon again. Only Moore's singsongy repetitive melody bears any resemblance to the band's later work.

The guitar work on "I Don't Want to Push It" closest approximates what later became a Sonic Youth signature sound. Its distorted phrases imply speed while not actually being played particularly fast. Again, the lyrics are fragmented allusions to an alienated acquaintance. Forced to rerecord the vocals for "Push It" on the second day in the studio, Thurston had no choice but to sing through a cold. "So if you listen to the song, you'll hear the stuffed-up-nose take," he says.

An instrumental, "The Good and the Bad," finishes off the disc, alternating between a bass-heavy, Gang of Four–style funk (that's Thurston on bass guitar) and repetitive guitar jabs reminiscent the ghoulish scores Bernard Hermann wrote in the fifties and sixties for Alfred Hitchcock films.

While *Sonic Youth* possesses a distinct sensibility, it is by no means a full reproduction of what the band was reportedly capable of live at the time. Charged by the amped-up volume generated during live performance, Sonic Youth thrashed about in a kind of choreographed apoplexy. In addition, much of *Sonic Youth* utilizes standard guitar tunings. It was only later that the group began exploring the world of unorthodox tunings.

Bob Bert, a twenty-seven-year-old committed fan of the downtown scene, saw the Edson lineup perform a couple times, once at the Mudd Club. Then again, Bert saw everything. As a matter of fact, he had moved to New York, at seventeen, from Clifton, New Jersey, with the express purpose of following the punk scene.

Patti Smith, Television, Talking Heads, the Heartbreakers—by the time Bert had experienced Sonic Youth, from his perspective the scene just wasn't happening anymore. "People in other places might think No Wave was a heavy-duty scene," says Bert. "But you never had to worry about whether you were going to get into a Mars show. And every time Ut played, they emptied the room completely. It was just three people watching them, at the most."

But it was No Wave's extreme draft of the do-it-yourself credo that finally compelled Bert to take up the drums—a childhood obsession he had put aside to take classes at the School of Visual Arts and pursue a career as a silk-screen printer. Having only jammed sporadically with a few pickup groups in downtown dive bars, Bert decided to respond to a flier posted in the back corner of Rocks in Your Head—a tiny, ephemeral record store on Prince Street—which announced succinctly, "Sonic Youth needs drummer."

When Bert met with Thurston Moore, the guitarist immediately recognized him from the clubs; the two hit it off and Bert was in the band. "When I played the first gig with them at CBGBs," Bert recalls, "and I saw Arto Lindsay and Lydia Lunch in the club, to me at that time, I was just like, Wow, this is the greatest thing in the world.

"It's meaningless in the scope of things," Bert continues, "because there weren't that many people there, and Sonic Youth really didn't have their shit together at the time. It seemed like hour-long gaps between the songs, changing guitars and figuring out this and that. But I dug what they were doing right away."

After playing only a few gigs together, the new Sonic Youth hit the road in November 1982, on its first foray outside Manhattan. The band paired up with Swans—Michael Gira's Circus Mort off-shoot band that Sonic Youth shared a rehearsal space with—for two brief jaunts: One down the East Coast, through the Deep South; the other, up through the Midwest. Introduced to each other by Kim, Thurston and Gira had become tight friends; Sonic Youth and Swans had shared a few bills together at CBGBs and another downtown dive called 2+2. "We had similarities in attack," says Thurston. "And there was nothing else like us. 'Hardcore' at that time wasn't such a big word, it was confined to hardcore kids."

Dubbed the Savage Blunder Tour by Gira, the two-week series of makeshift dates established what underground fans outside New York perceived as the New York sound: Bone-jarring, coruscating, dissonant rock music that arrogantly, and perhaps erroneously, purported to be the living end of the genre. Although, in Swans' case, the description couldn't have been more accurate.

Swans' slow, sludgy, dirgelike music, while surely influential for the subsequent generation's dark-minded "goth" rockers, had little in the way of humor or musical variety to hook listeners into its deafening roar. Determined to explore the limits of what Gira characterized to one interviewer as all that is "blunt, clear, undeniable, stripped raw, unintellectual," Swans piqued curiosity among hardcore punk's burgeoning ranks, but frequently came off as too narrow to more worldly types. Later on, Swans acknowledged the limitations of their grating thump and began recording more conventional pop songs, with Gira's baritone bolstering a sound reminiscent of the British band Joy Division.

"Mike Gira really brought with him this great animosity," says Thurston. "He was kind of a freak that way and everybody knew it. So you just sort of dealt with it. A very extreme person, but at the same time a really good person—it was a real conflict."

"When we first started in New York, there were the more folkie, music-oriented bands, like Mofungo, and the art-world composers," Kim says. "We decided early on that we definitely didn't want to go those routes. We definitely wanted to break out. We were really kind of isolated until we met up again with Mike and Swans. But even Mike—I guess he saw himself as doing rock music, but he was very unrealistic as far as what the demands of it would be."

In early November, nine people piled into a rented van with a U-Haul attached, to carry the two bands' equipment, and drove South. The first leg incorporated about ten gigs, including stops at the Marble Bar in Baltimore; the 9:30 Club in Washington, D.C.; The Pier in Raleigh, North Carolina; Cat's Cradle in Chapel Hill, North Carolina; the 40 Watt Club in Athens, Georgia; and 688 in Atlanta. (At The Pier, Sonic Youth recorded a performance of the Stooges' "I Wanna Be Your Dog" that eventually appeared on *Confusion Is Sex*, the band's follow-up to *Sonic Youth*.)

The on-the-road experience wasn't a pleasant one. "It was insane," Bob Bert recalls. "Every single one of them smoked cigarettes, except me. So it was like riding in a total cloud the whole time." Ranaldo remembers getting into a bad fight with Gira, whom he describes as "the most difficult person on earth to deal with." Despite the fact that most nights the two acts played to audiences numbering in the tens and twenties, the first tour generated a flurry of interest and a few memorable incidents.

Many of the audiences that showed up at the Savage Blunder dates were expecting two brand-new hardcore acts from New York City, brandishing the kind of double-speed, metronomic rhythms pioneered by the Ramones. And local promoters billed the shows as such, not having any real idea what kind of music would transpire anyway.

"Right around the time when *Sonic Youth* came out, we started seeing hardcore kids," says Thurston. "The first thing I saw was a kid wearing a leather jacket on St. Marks Place, with spiky hair and big letters on the back of his jacket in white that read 'Reagan Youth.' My first response was, What's this 'youth' thing? I hope there's not another 'youth' band. Because there hadn't been anything."

Outside of New York, young kids came to see the two bands with skateboards in hand, assuming they were hardcore bands from New York, and *especially* because one of the bands had the word *youth* in its name.

Both Sonic Youth and Swans felt compelled to rise to the occasion. At the 40 Watt club in Athens, Michael Gira of Swans got into the spirit of hardcore in his own unique way. Perturbed by the audience's pogo-dancing antics, de rigueur in hardcore/new wave circles of the day, Gira jumped off the stage mid-set and started beating up one young audience member who had been smiling and jumping around with his girlfriend. Then Gira returned to the stage and announced, "I'm really sorry, but you were having too much fun."

Bob Bert remembers one gig, in a church: ". . . and there were two guys with cowboy hats that spent the whole show yelling out, 'Freebird!' " Sensing a redneck presence, Gira started spewing incendiary between-song patter—for example, "This next song is about two cops butt-fucking each other."

In Atlanta, most of the bands' potential audience was drawn away by a Plasmatics show down the road.

Sonic Youth responded more to hardcore's innovative organizational techniques. Hardcore was a close-knit scene that channeled activism into the creation of records. Suddenly teenagers around the world were releasing their own singles, writing their own fanzines, and creating their own intricate musical network. The members of Sonic Youth, unperturbed by being significantly older than the hardcore kids, found themselves relating better to hardcore's enterprise than to the willful obsfucation proffered by most of their New York art-rock colleagues.

"I can remember the first flier I saw for a NYC hardcore gig," Moore later told *Reflex*. "It had this great line on it: 'The Sex Pistols weren't enough.' I told Branca about it, and he just said, 'The Sex Pistols were *more* than enough.' That's when I realized I had to break away from the old men of the scene."

Sonic Youth developed its wild live show in part to win over the more fickle skate punks. Ranaldo and Moore began experimenting with the alternate tunings that both had been exposed to while playing with Branca; they also took to attacking their guitars with drumsticks and screwdrivers in concert.

"Onstage, Swans were just ferocious," says Thurston. "People would just go, 'Holy shit!' And we were just going all out, all those shows were at a time when we were just damaged." One of the few New York bands of the era to bother reaching out to audiences outside of Manhattan, Sonic Youth had stripped down its effete SoHo sound to suit the raucous tenor of its newfound environs.

The tour found its most receptive audiences in Chapel Hill and Raleigh, college towns both. "I noticed that that whole area had a sense of broadness developing," Thurston says, "an acceptance of things that were a little out of the ordinary."

A month later, Swans and Sonic Youth embarked on another journey, this time through the Midwest, all organized around a date at the Walker Arts Center in Minneapolis. In the same way Branca had used a high-paying Walker gig to justify a full tour, Lee arranged other dates along the way.

This adventure was even more trying, though; a mere case of one shoestring tour following too closely on the footsteps of another.

Thurston took to jeering Bert about his lack of drumming skills. "I really wanted to get ferocious," he recalls. "And Bob would just sit back there and he would play his thing. I wanted somebody who was more of a wildman. And he was not a wildman.''

The rest of the band asked Bert to leave as soon as they returned to New York.

6 | Harder Than Hardcore

' ' I remember when hardcore came,'' recalls Mike Watt, the burly bassist for fIREHOSE and, formerly, for the Minutemen—post-punk's most revered trio. ''In a way I was glad that it wasn't just old glitter people, you know, from the burned-out Hollywood scene. But in another way, I was bummed out that they all wanted to play one song and they didn't have time to realize that it could be lots of different kinds of sounds.''

The Minutemen—Watt, drummer George Hurley, and the late singer, songwriter, and guitarist D. Boon—came together in San Pedro, California, in 1980. Taking the raucous energy of punk, filtering it through blues, funk, and jazzlike riffs, and infusing it with a distinctly proletarian intellectualism, the Minutemen went on to make some of the most joyously provocative rock of the mid-1980s. And for D. Boon—who died in a 1985 car crash—and Watt, rock-and-roll aesthetics began and ended with Creedence Clearwater Revival.

''D. Boon—his daddy was totally into [country musician] Buck Owens,'' Watt says. ''The only rock D. Boon had ever really heard was a little bit of Beatles. So he was really unaware of the whole rock thing and Creedence was kind of a bridge for him." The two childhood friends were taken to their first rock concert by D. Boon's dad, a 1971 T. Rex show. Sometime after, Boon and Watt found salvation from their small-town rock-and-roll fantasies in the music of Creedence Clearwater Revival's John Fogerty.

Watt, like the members of Sonic Youth, saw in Fogerty a plain-spoken American humility that helped the sixties icon temper his anger at coming of age during the Vietnam era in succinct, melodic pop songs. "Another trip was, his songs were like, *econo*," Watt says of Fogerty. "And this is way in our youth, before we even understood economics—you know, music, moneywise, any-wise—conceptually. But the idea of getting all these sounds, making a whole body of music with just a couple sounds . . ." Clad in flannel shirts and jeans, the Minutemen skipped and tripped through their brief, existential pop songs by the dozens, allowing each to last only as long as the moment it took to absorb its precepts. The Minutemen's finest work, 1984's double-length *Double Nickles on the Dime*, features 44 tracks—none longer than three minutes, most less than two—concise tone-poems on topics ranging from Central American politics to proto-punk history, selling out to buying in.

Watt maintains that the main lesson he learned from the punk revolution was pragmatism—keeping recording budgets small and manageable, arranging your own tours, and making music people could witness up close.

For Sonic Youth, too, the hardcore rumblings from less preening American ports pointed toward a self-affirming pragmatism alien to the pre-hardcore art-rock bands. Ian MacKaye's D.C. band Minor Threat, San Francisco's Dead Kennedys, L.A.'s Black Flag, Saccharine Trust, and consequently SST Records—all impressed the members of Sonic Youth, especially Thurston.

"It wasn't just hardcore music and that stance," he says. "It was also how it was promoted—the whole DIY self-promotion of it was just so pure and so American. The whole network of it, from city to town to city to town, little dots all over the map. People were just doing Xerox sleeves in bags. And you'd put it on, and it'd just be this eight-track thrash. That didn't exist before."

Synchronously, bands such as Austin's Butthole Surfers, Berlin's Einstürzende Neubauten, and the Birthday Party (the Australian band which included Nick Cave and Rowland S. Howard), were exploring hardcore's unbridled intensity from different angles. The immediate goal became to take the music beyond what Thurston once referred to as "the fifteen-year-old, assassinate Reagan, thirty-second thrash song with an eight-second skank interlude."

Sonic Youth had an oft-cited affection for the music's high-energy freshness (tracks from albums as late as 1992's *Dirty* attest to that), although the band was more eager to tap into hardcore's sonic bombast than its single-note sentiments. The members of Sonic Youth were older than the hardcore kids and consequently had more of a perspective and musical history from which to draw.

"A lot of stuff about that scene inspired *Confusion Is Sex*," says Lee Ranaldo. "From the album graphics, which were very like the Xerox art that was going with those kind of records, to some of the more punky songs, like 'Confusion Is Next.' "

During the period in which the band's second record, also released by Neutral, was written, Sonic Youth caught a lot of the New York hardcore bands of the day—False Prophets, Misguided, Heart Attack—in concert. "New York was not considered cool on the hardcore scene across the country," says Thurston. "The big city was not cool—the smaller the city, the smaller the town, the cooler it was. New York had the whole sleazy, black-leather punk history—it just didn't fit into the straight-edge concept. 'Fuck New York'—that was the big thing." Straight-edge bands—most of which hailed from Washington, D.C., and the Midwest—were usually younger, less worldly, and more self-serious than their East Coast and West Coast hardcore counterparts. The straight-edge credo angrily preaches abstinence from alcohol and drugs.

"From D.C.'s perspective, we certainly saw Swans and Sonic Youth and Lydia Lunch as really hot things," says Don Fleming. "When they would come to town to play, there would be huge turnouts. Even then, they were perceived as the hot scene from New York.''

Even before recording *Confusion Is Sex*, though, Thurston set about sating his thirst for hardcore energy: In late 1982, he briefly played with Even Worse, a band formed by Tim Sommer and Jack Rabid, then DJs at New York hardcore shows.

Ranaldo, Gordon, and Moore, however, were eager to release new Sonic Youth material—specifically, a single. Seven-inch singles were the primary format for the hardcore bands. Phenomenally cheap to produce, most hardcore singles consisted of the 45, a photocopied sleeve, and a lyric sheet in a plastic sheath. The band's limited means, consequently, joined nicely with an aesthetic it just happened to admire. Sonic Youth hoped that the same kids that bought hardcore 45s would buy its similarly fashioned product.

But Neutral Records was in trouble. In the interim since *Sonic Youth* had been released, Neutral had continued releasing albums, most at a financial loss. Before long, the label ran out of funds.

After borrowing some money from two friends they'd met in New York but who lived in Rolle, Switzerland (Catherine Bachmann and Nicholas Ceresole), the band approached Wharton Tiers, the onetime drummer for Rhys Chatham.

Tiers had just installed an eight-track tape console in his Chelsea basement. ''Confusion Is Next,'' ''Shaking Hell,'' and ''Making the Nature Scene''—all new compositions—were the three songs considered for the single.

But when the band revealed it had enough material written to record more, it was encouraged to do so. ''It ended up going from a two-song single to a five-song EP to a full-fledged album,'' says Ranaldo. ''And it was a really chaotic process, where we worked forever at Wharton's. We worked for days and days and weeks and weeks on it. And it was really low budget to the max, and he had a good tape machine but he didn't have a lot of gear.'' *Confusion Is Sex* was also the first record Tiers had ever worked on.

A rough pencil sketch that Kim had done of Thurston, photocopied more than once for proper effect, became the cover of the album. "It wasn't meant to be used," Thurston says. "She just sort of drew it on a piece of paper. It was a fuck-up—my head was too big. [Kim says it wasn't even supposed to be a drawing of Thurston.] But I kind of liked it, so I made it into a flier for a show. And then we made it into the cover."

The creation of *Confusion* was plagued with disasters. It took three months in early 1983 for Sonic Youth to bang out the muddy, violent-sounding tracks that appear on the final product. The dark, hissy results were as much a result of the wildly uneven recording process as they were a document of a band that had become known for its jarring live shows.

"We ended up remixing a lot," Kim says, "because we did all kinds of weird things. First everything was too muddy. We remastered it, too."

Disorganization was the reigning aesthetic on *Confusion*. What the band members agree was the best take of "Shaking Hell" was accidentally erased from the master tape when they redid Kim's vocals. After recording more takes, the band decided to go with the original one; unfortunately, the only copy left existed on an ordinary cassette tape. The version that appears on the album was recorded from the low-fi cassette mix.

For "Freezer Burn," the album's only instrumental track, the band recorded inside a walk-in freezer of a deli down the street from the studio for improved low-end bass tone.

Work on another track was hobbled when the tape got crumpled up in the machine. Strapped for time and funds, the band had no choice but to smooth it out and repair it with strips of Scotch tape. And, in unintentional homage to a recording practice initiated by the Beatles while recording the White Album, a can of Coke was accidentally spilled on the master tapes and allowed to soak in.

It's not surprising that *Confusion Is Sex* is rarely cited as one of the seminal albums of the early 1980s. Although Greil Marcus hailed it as the only record of 1983 to affirm pop music's essential need to communicate "a burden of negation," he did so in the pages of *Artforum*, an esoteric if well-respected journal of the art world, read by relatively few people. While hardly bereft of wonderfully chilling moments, *Confusion* is a difficult listen. And even Marcus—who compared the album's revelatory power to that of the Sex Pistols' *Never Mind the Bollocks, Here's the Sex Pistols*—predicted that "the power of Sonic Youth's *no* will be negligible: few will hear this music."

To listeners not caught up in the machinations of the foundering avant-garde or the burgeoning hardcore scene, *Confusion Is Sex* was a tough sell. For rock fans initially unreceptive to nontraditional song structures, off-kilter harmonics, and garbled, impressionistic lyrics, even R.E.M.'s debut album, *Murmur*—recorded and released the same year—was a bitter pill to swallow. In retrospect, it's difficult to appreciate why *Murmur*, a subtle, carefully wrought round of melodic folk-rock ditties, was not an immediate success. Not so with *Confusion*.

Yet the album remains a landmark. Steve Albini—at the time a perspicacious fanzine publisher and leader of the impressively abrasive Chicago band Big Black—argues that *Confusion Is Sex* radically changed audience attitudes and perceptions. "Up until that point, there had been several schools of thought: There had been people who played rock music in many permutations and people that played sort of head-case music that did not really rock," Albini says. "Sonic Youth were one of a few bands that sort of staked out a territory within head-case music that would, in fact, rock.

"Thurston, who was sort of the aesthetic guru and propaganda-meister of the band—I think his enthusiasm for hardcore was largely window dressing," Albini continues. "It was sort of a comical take, because here is this guy who is significantly more experienced and older and more intellectual than these hardcore-punk kids, sort of displaying that kind of exuberance toward a music that was totally separate from hardcore music. Anybody that won't acknowledge the humor in that presentation is really missing the point."

In retrospect, then, all that *Confusion Is Sex* may lack is an overt dose of self-deprecating wit. No doubt, in the throes of its hardcore thrashing, Sonic Youth felt the need to keep faces straight. Not that they were wholly successful.

Already reviewers had begun mentioning Thurston Moore's gangly features. With a shock of blond hair covering his eyes and a penchant for wearing plain, baggy clothes and flailing about in a rather impressive way for someone of such height, comparisons to various cartoon characters, most frequently a too-tall Dennis the Menace, became common.

Furthermore, "Confusion Is Next"—the song from which the album culls its title and which is ostensibly the band's first contribution to the hardcore canon—has some especially amusing lyrics, courtesy of Thurston Moore. Drawn out, in a tempo closer to that of a Led Zeppelin–style strip-bar blues number than the double-time pogo-punk produced by the likes of the Dead Kennedys and the Circle Jerks, "Confusion Is Next" purports to be a recipe for anarchy. Yet its equation for the future, which Moore shouts out in a typically monotonal hardcore fashion—"Chaos is the future / And beyond it is freedom / Confusion is next and next after that is truth"—is diffused by the song's refrain: "Sonic tooth."

The band, whether consciously or subconsciously, reveals its art-friendly roots by sacrificing stern punk sentiments for assonant puns.

Similarly, "Shaking Hell," Kim Gordon's first thoroughly chilling performance, taps into the force and imagery of hardcore without subscribing to its tenets. "Shaking Hell" begins with a brisk introduction reminiscent of a spooky B-movie, which quickly segues into a section in which a woman describes an unrequited seduction scene. Escalated to horror's peak, Gordon's refrain, "I'll take off your dress," changes to "I'll shake off your flesh." Confusion is sex indeed. With a few brief lyrical turns and a simple song structure that consists of three distinct segments, each with different tonal colorations and a different tempo, "Shaking Hell" captures both the appeal and danger of a seducer's come-on in broad strokes that are easy to visualize.

"Making the Nature Scene," another Gordon vehicle, takes a mathematical approach to lyrics, similar to that used for "Confusion Is Next," but applies it to living in the city. In a clear, modulated song-speak that Gordon would soon abandon for a rougher-sounding vocal, she outlines her world, an urban landscape, as if it were a pine forest or a savanna. Brighter, more upbeat, and better-recorded than the rest of the album, "Nature Scene" is the shaky album's most memorable track.

While the album was being put to tape, confusion ruled the band members' lives as well as the recording process. Unable to survive off the $50 or $100 the average punk-rock dive paid at the time (and really, only playing about once a month around New York), each member juggled sundry day jobs. Ranaldo took an apprenticeship with a metal-welding sculptor named David Klass in Chelsea; Moore did a number of stints as a street vendor, selling ice-cream sandwiches and fruit; Gordon found work as a waitress at Elephant & Castle, a SoHo restaurant, and at Todd's Copy Shop, a photocopying establishment owned by A's cofounder Todd Jourgensen; and Bert worked for various silk-screening operations.

And although Bert had helped write all the material included on Confusion Is Sex, his services were terminated before the band recorded. He was quickly replaced with Jim Sclavunos, a veteran of of the No Wave scene. (He was a member of Red Transistor, Teenage Jesus and the Jerks, and Lydia Lunch's follow-up project, Eight-Eyed Spy.)

"Kim called me up and she was kind of cold about it," recalls Bert. "And then Thurston called me up later, and was like, 'Naw, we really like you, we just wanted to give Jim a try.' It was much more of a friend thing." ("The boys were too chicken to call Bob," Kim counters. "They made me do it. Then they were friendly. Typical—they made me out to be the bad guy.")

* * *

Meanwhile, Thurston had befriended Lydia Lunch. Lunch (née Koch), instantly recognizable with her punkish shock of red hair, was already a fixture on the downtown New York circuit by 1982. Her confrontational persona, which played with people's perceptions of whether she was performing or whether she was simply acting out, helped transform her into a New York punk paradigm. She was the New York music underground's Elizabeth Taylor, the uncontested "queen of the scene."

Lunch and Moore had lived a block away from each other—he on 13th Street between Avenues A and B, she on 12th Street—in the late 1970s, when Lunch was performing with Teenage Jesus and the Jerks. They would spot each other on the subway tracks; Thurston recognized her, but according to Lunch, was too intimidated to introduce himself. Through Richard Edson, an occasional Lunch cohort, the two formally met. Edson admired Moore's bass-playing and recommended him to Lunch.

Lunch characterizes her musical leanings of the time as "anti-rock and anti–punk rock." Speaking perhaps for a generation of downtown New York performers in describing punk rock simply as "Chuck Berry on speed," Lunch remembers the East Village scene of the late 1970s and early 1980s in New York as profoundly disinterested even in rock's most basic impulses. Punk was a fashion statement; what was going on in New York was grounded in personal rather than communal urges.

As testament to her vision, Lunch spent the years following the breakup of Teenage Jesus and the Jerks creating an oeuvre piecemeal, with whichever musical collaborators were available to come along for a ride—which at times included Australia's Birthday Party, Michael Gira, and Jim Thirwell (a.k.a. Clint Ruin, Jim Foetus). For In Limbo, an EP recorded in November 1982 at Surf Sound in New York, Lunch recruited Moore to play bass. Other musicians included Richard Edson on drums, Pat Place (formerly of the Contortions and the Bush Tetras) on guitar, Jim Sclavunos on saxophone, and Kristian Hoffman on piano. Intent on making "the slowest record ever recorded," Lunch on some level succeeded: In Limbo is a slow-as-molasses collection of songs, seemingly bent on exposing everything dirty and disappointing about life. Four out of the EP's six tracks were cowritten with Moore. "Thurston and I went into a rehearsal, I had the words," says Lunch, "and we just tried to get up a few basic bass riffs."

Lunch was immediately struck by the difference between Moore's personality and the music. Moore's upbeat countenance had little to do with the dire nature of the resultant tracks. But his understanding of music that could be "very beautiful, very melancholy, and very tortured," in Lunch's words, allowed the unlikely pair to work quite well together.

"I was getting into L.A. punk—and then full-on into D.C. and Midwestern hardcore," says Thurston. "When I played Lydia some Black Flag she was just like, No way! Too fast, too loud. She was more into this moody, gothic shit with a real scum-of-the-earth kind of attitude. Which was cool." The two finally found common musical ground in the Birthday Party, a dark, decadent Australian band—one of the few non-hardcore acts favored by hardcore fanatics.

Sclavunos, Moore, and Lunch played a few shows together in New York and Washington, D.C., but the aggregation soon dissolved. Once the tracks were finished, Lunch went on tour, performing over the prerecorded tracks.

It's not surprising that Sonic Youth thought of Jim Sclavunos when it went looking for a new drummer. After kicking out Bob Bert, the band tried out a few different drummers, including Lee's friend David Linton. But Sclavunos had credentials and, even Bert admits, was the more adept musician. "When I first hooked up with them, I was pretty amateur," Bert says. "I really didn't have my shit together. I had this chintzy little drum set that I had when I was a kid."

"We came to a 'we'll give it a try' kind of agreement, but without any guidelines for what kind of try it was going to be," says Sclavunos. "So we started rehearsing for the album." Sclavunos performed only two live shows with Sonic Youth, one with Swans at the Kitchen. He also ended up playing on virtually all of *Confusion Is Sex*.

"This was a really bad thing," says Ranaldo, "because then we ended up feeling like Bob wasn't good enough. We thought, Bob's not going to play this stuff good enough." On *Confusion Is Sex*, Bob plays drums only on "I Wanna Be Your Dog" (recorded at The Pier in Raleigh, North Carolina, during the Savage Blunder tour in November 1982) and "Making the Nature Scene," a song which he played a major role in creating.

But Jim Sclavunos ended up being a much more temporary member of Sonic Youth than the other members of the band had expected. He first walked away right in the middle of the *Confusion* sessions (Bob Bert was even tentatively invited back) convinced that the amateurish setup at Wharton's would result in an unplayable record. In time, Sclavunos made it clear he had no intention of sticking things out—he had previously made a commitment to play in a new band with his wife (coincidentally, Truss de Groot of Plus Instruments). "It wasn't like I was going to leave them without a drummer, because Bob was still floating around," says Jim. "I never quite understood their on-again, off-again relationship with Bob, but it seemed like whenever they needed him, he was there."

Confusion Is Sex also marked the debut of alternate tunings on a Sonic Youth recording. Both Moore and Ranaldo had been privy to the ways in which Glenn Branca used oddly tuned guitars to drastically alter the tonal palette. Branca had gone so far as rigging guitars with drastically different string gauges and assigning them chorus parts—i.e., soprano, alto, tenor, and bass. While radically different from the approach taken by virtually any conventional rock band, alternate tunings are a technique that Sonic Youth has understandably been reluctant to ascribe solely to Branca's work.

"Before the Flucts even left Binghamton, I was playing a guitar with drumsticks and stuff like that and experimenting with weird tunings," says Lee. "Because when I learned to play guitar in junior high school, I learned about tunings from a cousin of mine. When

I learned to play guitar, I was really into *After the Gold Rush* by Neil Young, the White Album by the Beatles, stuff like that. The Crosby, Stills and Nash and Joni Mitchell folkie thing. And I had an older cousin who showed me how to play some of that stuff, and basically those guys all used open tunings. All of a sudden I could play 'Suite: Judy Blue Eyes' with an open-tuned E-chord. I've experimented with that all the way along. Then when I was in college, I was really into Jorma Kaukonen—the first Hot Tuna album, that acoustic one. And again, a lot of his stuff was in open tunings."

Branca, however, had taken things one step further, restringing guitars to achieve the most alien effects possible.

Creating music under a restricted set of circumstances, by now a Sonic Youth signature, played as much a part in retuning guitars as anything. Early on, the band only had cheap guitars, many of which wouldn't hold normal tunings for long anyway. Rather than abandoning them and saving up for better ones, the band would figure out specific tasks for which the chosen instrument would perform, oftentimes a sound that didn't rely on intonation.

"Early on, I took frets on one guitar we had," says Ranaldo, "which we still actually use on 'Eric's Trip'—this guitar called the Drifter—and I took all the frets off it, just as an experiment, and put bass-guitar strings on it instead of guitar strings."

After a while, people began giving the band more guitars, noting the onstage tangle that would ensue when Moore and Ranaldo tried to elicit the proper sounds out of their inferior equipment. The band even began buying new and different guitars when they could—with each new guitar would come new tunings and new songs.

The sum of *Confusion Is Sex* is fueled by the two environments habituated by the band—the hardcore milieu and the foggy notions of the New York experimental performance scene. "Songs kids make up when they're banished to their rooms," Greil Marcus called tracks such as "(She's in a) Bad Mood" and "Protect Me You," presumably referring to their solipsistic nature.

"I heard in that record a kind of extremism, a kind of nihilism that I wasn't hearing anywhere else at that time," Marcus says today, "and that I don't think crops up in their music all that often afterward—or in anyone's music."

Work with Glenn Branca remained intermittent, allowing Thurston and Lee to continue performing with Branca on subsequent symphonies in between Sonic Youth dates. May 1983 brought an opportunity to tour Europe with Branca's expanded ensemble, for performances of his *Symphony No. 4*.

Few New York bands at the time had played Europe; in general, only performers with "composer" status, such as Branca, were given grant and festival opportunities overseas. So when Sonic Youth was offered a chance to play at a Vienna new-music festival, the band devised an inventive if precarious plan. Unable to justify the cost of flying the whole band over for one show, but bent on getting the most out of what they viewed as two free plane tickets, Moore and Ranaldo took a gamble.

At each venue in Europe at which they performed on Branca's two-week tour, Moore and Ranaldo secured a Sonic Youth gig for a month later. Kim flew over to catch the last few dates of the Branca tour.

Once it became clear that Jim Sclavunos had no intention of touring with the band, Kim asked Bob Bert back. "It was kind of funny," Bert says, "because they had this gig at the Speed Trials festival at White Columns [in May 1983]. And I rehearsed with them to do that show. Then they said, 'Do you want to come to Europe?' And I said, 'Well, only if I'm going to be a member.'"

Bob flew directly to Lausanne, Switzerland, for the first date on Sonic Youth's impromptu European tour.

According to Branca, doubling up in the name of a creative opportunity was something he always encouraged—he considered it a show of gratitude in lieu of decent pay. In general appreciative toward his players, including Moore and Ranaldo, for coming out on short notice for gigs that were neither profitable nor opportunities for individual expression, Branca lost it this time around.

"There wasn't any backlash until they went out on the last tour with *Symphony No. 4*," Branca recalls. "They were always very good about it. But when they knew that this was the last time they were going out with me, then they decided to be assholes."

"Glenn hated hardcore," says Thurston, "mainly because I embraced it, I think. He really wanted to prove me wrong on it—he used the word 'bland' all the time. He totally didn't get it—or if he did, he refused to get involved with it."

"I didn't mind the fact that they were wearing their leather jackets with 'Sonic Youth' written on the back—that didn't bother me, I didn't see why it would," says Branca. "I didn't even mind that they had 'Sonic Youth' written on their guitars. But when they were spray-painting 'Sonic Youth' on the stage, that definitely was a little too extreme."

Sonic Youth's first jaunt through Europe ended up a rousing success.

Bob Bert, having quickly forgiven his fellow bandmates' transgressions, flew from New York to Paris on his birthday and waited seven hours to catch an eight-hour train to Lausanne. He was picked up at the train station in a Volkswagen Bug and rushed him directly to the show. Onstage twenty-four sleepless hours later, Bert was behind a borrowed set of drums—a seventies-style travesty with numerous horn-shaped tom-toms—banging out the rhythms of Sonic Youth's first gig on foreign turf.

The band played every song it knew, which amounted to the whole of *Sonic Youth* and *Confusion Is Sex*. The encore was a twenty-minute-plus version of "I Wanna Be Your Dog." The rowdy, drunken crowd refused to let the band stop playing, and as Thurston and Lee bent back for yet another relentlessly repetitive round, a riot ensued. Bottles flew through the air. The same thing that Ranaldo had experienced touring with Branca early on had happened again. "People in Europe were astounded," says Ranaldo. "Nobody had any idea that anything like this was going on in

America. It was so easy and so much fun to totally freak audiences out with the kind of stuff we were doing back then."

Another particularly memorable show took place at a bar directly across the road from a cow pasture in a tiny German town. The band arrived at the venue to discover an particularly well-lubricated audience. After two and a half hours of playing virtually everything they knew, including an improvised rap number, the band left the stage. A largish German woman grabbed them, plied them with shots of tequila, and pushed them back onstage. They began playing "Satan Is Boring," a newer number (later to appear on *Bad Moon Rising*). Kim ran out into the audience and continued playing from behind the soundboard. Audience members jumped onstage, grabbed stray guitars and began playing along.

One particularly inebriated participant took Bert's place at the drum kit and began hammering away. Lee and Thurston had had enough, but the German drummer just kept pounding. So the band stopped playing, grabbed him, and wrapped him up in duct tape. "It turned out that the guy was some kind of epileptic or something," says Bert. "He was just freaking out and his eyes were bugging out of his head." Even as the audience member was unwrapped, the other self-appointed band members continued screwing around with the guitars.

In December 1983 Sonic Youth got its first chance to play London, at a club called The Venue. Through a connection at London's Rough Trade label, Sonic Youth was put on a bill with SPK, a British noise-group-turned-dance-act, and a forgotten chanteuse named Danielle Dax. Unsympathetic to the band's pleas—this was the band's first time to London; it had traveled far—Dax demanded that Sonic Youth perform first.

Sonic Youth played for fifteen minutes to a nearly empty house. It turned out to be the most disastrous gig the band had played to date. Thurston's guitar broke in his hands. The drum set fell apart. In the middle of one song, the stage curtain was lowered and the power shut off. "The curtain opened and there wasn't any people out there," says Thurston. "We immediately just did 'Confusion Is

Next,' 'Burning Spear,' and one or two other things. But it was a totally ferocious set. I remember two young kids up in front, they were really into it."

"Thurston just went nuts and started taking the monitors and sliding them across the stage and smashing shit," says Bob Bert. "At the end, one of the amps started glowing and exploding," Lee recalls. Hours later the band was sitting at the train station realizing it had blown its first big chance in England.

By the time Sonic Youth returned to New York, the British reviews had come out. A write-up in *Sounds* mysteriously praised the band's "hypnotic noise and quirky lyrics."

"Sonic Youth were mind-blowing, psychedelic without the amoeba slideshow," purred the *New Musical Express*. "The best thing on eight legs all night."

Somehow, either through the sheer incompetence of the night's headliner or just plain American panache, the show's opening act had received unanimous praise in print. The next time Sonic Youth played CBGBs, there was a line around the block.

7 | The Boosters and the Critics

''I HAVE NO DOUBT THAT THURSTON LEARNED FROM LIVE
SKULL, BUT I DON'T THINK LIVE SKULL IS A VERY
INTERESTING OR IMPORTANT BAND. NOBODY GIVES A FUCK ABOUT
LIVE SKULL ANYMORE.''
—ROBERT CHRISTGAU, MUSIC CRITIC FOR THE *VILLAGE VOICE*

The evolution of rock criticism often seems to trail that of the music itself by about a decade. By the time bona fide writers began covering the rock-music scene in any broad, coherent fashion, the notion of pop musicians as a shared obsession of the masses no longer existed.

In the late 1950s, few rock-music fans didn't have an opinion of Elvis Presley; in the late 1960s, the largess of acts such as the Beatles and Bob Dylan could not be ignored. By 1980, popular music had become much more diverse; no one performer or style of music could lay claim to the current listeners' collective psyche.

The consequence has been that only a handful of writers have ever been able to acquire long-lasting reputations for themselves based principally on their rock criticism. And even for the biggest names, recognition outside the music community remains hard-won, if not altogether elusive.

In the halcyon days of rock's primacy as a cultural force—the late 1960s—most musicians seemed unaware of, or at least oblivious to, what was being written about them. To this day, sixties rock icons are keen to give the impression that they don't read and never have read the reviews. In *Rolling Stone*'s twentieth-anniversary issue, Lou Reed was the only musician interviewed to bring up the magazine's initial critical appraisal of the Velvet Underground: "I remember [*Rolling Stone* cofounder] Ralph Gleason wrote this editorial telling how much he liked Lenny Bruce and how the trouble of being in favor of free speech was that you had to defend the likes of Lou Reed. I never forgot that."

But by the early eighties, the tables had turned. More and more frequently, the writers covering the culture were older and more established than the up-and-coming performers. When critic Jon Landau wrote in 1974, "I saw rock and roll's future and its name is Bruce Springsteen," it became so. While the critics still did not possess the ability to make or break the artists, their words were at least respected as a definitive opinion. For the progressive rockers of the late 1960s, FM radio stations had gotten the latest sounds across to the fans.

Print was an important medium, too, for the underground network being established by independent labels such as L.A.'s SST and D.C.'s Dischord (headed by Minor Threat's Ian MacKaye), and later, Touch and Go in Chicago and Homestead on Long Island. This time, though, things were different. FM radio had ossified; the soon-to-be-influential college-radio culture had yet to become structured.

Alternative newspapers and "fanzines"—a conflation of the celebrity-struck publications from Hollywood's golden era and the booster mentality of rock groupies—became the maps between points for this new counter-counterculture. Hardcore was especially reliant on fanzines to relay information. The mainstream media, after all, were run by adults; and hardcore didn't have time for adults.

In 1983, inspired by the swath of hardcore fanzines that had popped up around the country, Thurston began publishing his own, called *Killer*. *Killer* aped the look and tone of its genuine hardcore counterparts—record reviews and interviews were purposely plagued with misspellings, and stapled to the layouts. The hardcore scene was its purported scope, though Thurston decided to cover the New York "art-core" scene as well.

"I would send Killer to all the other hardcore fanzines," Thurston says. "And they would write back and go like, Wow, great." The first issue featured an exhaustive typewritten interview with Ian MacKaye, and a goofy, hand-scrawled recount of a chat Thurston had with Mike D of the Beastie Boys. Between 1983 and 1985, Thurston produced a total of seven issues. In 1984 he took the concept even further by selling homemade cassette copies of an album-length sound collage made from early Sonic Youth concerts. Sonic Death, as it was titled, was the first release on Ecstatic Peace, Thurston's very own indie label.

Killer was an inspired excuse for Thurston to introduce himself to musicians he admired in other cities; it also served as an ingenious way to promote the New York bands that were Sonic Youth's friends, like Ut, Swans, and Misguided. (It took until the second issue for Thurston to brave a mention of Sonic Youth—he even put a photo of Kim playing bass on the cover—though he stopped short of penning unsigned reviews of his own band's records.)

Rest assured, Thurston's scene-boosterism was of the most genuine sort. Mike D (né Mike Diamond), a Beastie Boys found-ing member, remembers Thurston offering to drive his band—then a hardcore act—to a gig. "We were like, fifteen, and he was the only one we knew who was old enough to rent a van," Mike D says. The young group had just released Polly Wog Stew, a 1982 EP that Thurston cites as one of his hardcore favorites. (The Beastie Boys, like Sonic Youth, later played the Speed Trials festi-val at White Columns in May 1983; by coincidence, it was the first at which the Beastie Boys attempted incorporating rap and turntables into their show.)

In this light, a letter written by Thurston to the editor of the Village Voice, published November 1, 1983, makes perfect sense. The Voice's popular-music coverage, edited since 1974 by one Robert Christgau—Dartmouth graduate, obsessive critic, and self-pro-claimed child of the sixties—had taken on a virtually monolithic role in New York by the time Sonic Youth had formed.

While other downtown Manhattan publications—*New York Rocker*, the *East Village Eye*, and the *SoHo Weekly News* (all now defunct)—were covering the club scene, the *Village Voice* was (and remains) the established press of the antiestablishment.

According to Christgau, he perceived the *Voice* music section as a critics' and not a boosters' section. "I knew that the tendency of highbrows, or people who define themselves as highbrows, or avant-gardists or alternative—that word wasn't used then—*counterculturists*, say, was always to underestimate what was going on in popular culture," Christgau explains. "And I believed that history proved, as well as my own aesthetic experience, that popular culture was as aesthetically valid, or perhaps more aesthetically valid, than anything else."

Christgau assigned writer John Piccarella to cover a Sonic Youth show at CBGBs in September 1983. The review was largely unfavorable. "Robbed of the intensity of their best recorded work, and forswearing their access to an engaging pulse," Piccarella wrote, "Sonic Youth is reduced to the merely numbing effect of their loudness." Praising the band for plumbing the "plodding monotony of Branca's own works" while making "abrasive intensity accessible," Piccarella felt the band had lost their way. *Confusion Is Sex* was reviled in comparison to its precursor.

According to Thurston, it had been an off night for Sonic Youth; Rat At Rat R, the other New York band on the bill, put on the better show. The maxim reads that all publicity is good publicity, and at the time, Sonic Youth needed the mention. But Thurston was upset. "Christgau was always the butt of everybody's jokes," he says. "He wasn't even reviewing records we were listening to. He ignored hardcore, he seemed kind of out of it—but he was the only rock critic that everybody read."

So Thurston wrote a fanzine-style letter to the *Voice*; much to his surprise, they printed it: "Before we get onstage to play a live gig we run down to Spring Street and collectively suck Glenn Branca's cock until it bleeds inspiration into our souls," Thurston's obnoxious screed began. He went on to brand Piccarella's review as "sleazy venereal journalism" and challenged Christgau as to why the *Voice* rock section had virtually ignored the "collective rock underground of New York City" and refused to publish weekly coverage of the local scene.

"My basic view of the avant-garde is that it's where interesting ideas get started but aren't necessarily brought to fruition," Christgau says in retrospect. "Bands think other bands are important because those people are working on little details of ideas that also concern them." And judging from the list of acts Thurston included as examples in his letter—Live Skull, Don King, Misguided, Ut, Toy Killers, Chris Marclay, Bag People, Sue Hanil, Susie Timmons, Heart Attack, and Carbon—Christgau's assessment in that respect proved correct. Few survived.

"There seemed to be a certain attitude developing in New York," says Steve Albini, a Chicagoan. "The progression went something like this: In the beginning of the punk-rock era, if a band was really outstanding, then they could get someplace. The next step was that if a band was really outstanding, people would put up with them being assholes. The third step was people didn't even have to be any good—as long as they were assholes."

"My conception of the *Voice* music section from the time I began editing it, in '74," Christgau adds, "was first of all, that it was critical. It was not a booster's section. It engaged in a kind of cultural criticism that was appropriate to New York. Not as a scene, but as a center of world communications."

Tim Sommer—hardcore DJ, musician, and rock writer—bugged Christgau early on to write about Sonic Youth. Christgau says he wouldn't assign the piece to Sommer since he was friend of the band. (A fair sentiment, but one that doesn't square with the fact that, mere months later, Christgau assigned a Branca review to Sommer.)

Thurston was incensed. Even before the letter, his ire had already fueled one of Sonic Youth's defining anthems, a song written during the rehearsals for *Bad Moon Rising* called "Kill Yr. Idols." While "I don't know why / You wanna impress Christgau / Ahh let that shit die / And find out the new goal" are not exactly lyrics that pop legends are made of, they did elucidate a predicament common today among "alternative" acts, though relatively rare in 1984. But the band emerged unscathed. Even as Sonic Youth continued along as a credible force in underground circles, it had begun garnering praise in the pages of the *New York Times* and other mainstream outlets.

Thurston later characterized the song as "advice to the lovelorn"—a claim that could not be extended to a subsequent live version of the cut, which appeared on the B-side of a "Making the Nature Scene" giveaway seven-inch enclosed with an issue of *Forced Exposure* magazine. This time the song was retitled "I Killed Christgau with My Big Fucking Dick" by Sonic Youth cohort and FE contributor Byron Coley. "It had credence at the time," Thurston says with a chuckle.

Zensor, a small German label that had plans to rerelease the first two Sonic Youth albums in Europe, also agreed to put out *Kill Yr. Idols*, an EP never released at the time, in the U.S. Side two of the EP—which includes "Kill Yr. Idols," "Brother James," and "Early American"—was recorded at Wharton Tiers's studio, live on a two-track tape machine. "Those songs depended on this white guitar I had that had a whammy bar on it that could go 360 degrees," Thurston says. "Early American" remains one of his favorite Sonic Youth compositions.

In order to transport *Kill Yr. Idols* overseas for production, the band squirreled away the master tapes in the back of their amplifiers before a European tour. When they arrived at a German studio to present their newest work, the band discovered all the highs and lows in the mix were missing. "We were really humiliated," Thurston says. It took a fair bit of effort on Sonic Youth's part to convince Zensor that the band had foolishly demagnetized the tapes with their speaker magnets. Fortunately, Tiers had a safety master back in New York and sent a replacement copy.

Because *Kill Yr. Idols* was released prior to Zensor's version of *Confusion Is Sex*, "Protect Me You" and an alternate take of "Shaking Hell"—two songs off the earlier record—were included as enticement to buy *Confusion*.

Although the scope and influence of the New York scene up through 1982 was minimal outside the city's environs, a quick read through the pages of a publication such as *New York Rocker* could quickly bring the enterprising fan up to date. Mark Coleman's half-page *New York Rocker* feature on Sonic Youth, for instance, prompted Gerard Cosloy—a bespectacled teenage hardcore fan from the Boston suburb of Wayland—to pick up a copy of *Sonic Youth* at Nuggets, a local used-record store.

Cosloy was by no means the typical rock fan. By his mid-teens, he had all but consumed the current offerings of the Boston music scene. A college-radio DJ before he was in college, a club booking agent before he was old enough to drink, a rock fanzine publisher before he graduated high school—Cosloy was as precocious as they come.

In December 1979 a fifteen-year-old Cosloy began publishing *Conflict*, his own rock fanzine, with the aid of a typewriter and photocopier. "I was living in Boston, writing about Boston-based bands, writing about hardcore and stuff," he says. "Other than the occasional trip to New York, to see music, I didn't really know what the hell was going on there."

Though Cosloy was already familiar with the sounds coming out of Hoboken, New Jersey, a relatively urbanized suburb right across the Hudson River from Manhattan—Hoboken's jangly guitar acts like the dB's had much in common with the standard Boston fare of the time—the downtown Manhattan scene still seemed a bit daunting.

It was on one Cosloy's infrequent trips to New York that he visited 99 Records on MacDougal Street. He was selling 99 owner Ed Bahlman copies of *Conflict*. Not surprisingly, Cosloy bumped into Thurston—by now a devoted record-bin denizen if ever there was one. "It was just kind of funny because I sort of knew who he was," Cosloy says. "And I think he had seen the fanzine before."

In the wake of recording *Confusion Is Sex*, Thurston was even more attuned to the hardcore doings of the day, so he and Cosloy had a lot to talk about. Soon Cosloy was sending Thurston copies of his fanzine, which Thurston would in turn bring around to stores like 99 and sell for him.

Cosloy was soon able to return the favor; he arranged for Sonic Youth's first Boston-area gig in August 1982, at a club called Storyville. The show, hardly untypical of this period for Sonic Youth, was a bomb. "It was the same night that David Bowie played some big stadium gig somewhere, and Sonic Youth ended up drawing like, three people to the show," says Cosloy. "But they were great. I mean, they were absolutely amazing. A really terrifying band to see live."

Before long, the members of Sonic Youth were Cosloy's New York contacts—i.e., the only people whom he knew in New York with a place for him to stay.

In a minor twist of fate that arguably affected the independent recording industry in ways that still resonate to some degree today, Cosloy, at eighteen, dropped out of the University of Massachusetts at Amherst. During the summer of 1984, he moved to New York, and that September got a job at Homestead Records, a brand-new independent label based on Long Island. Sonic Youth was one of his first signings.

Cosloy, having had no previous contact with the New York art crowd, saw in Sonic Youth what few early supporters had recognized in the band: commercial potential. In Cosloy's vision, Sonic Youth was a rock band, like his favorites, Black Flag and Boston's Mission of Burma, were rock bands. "They just had a different way of putting the words together and the sounds together," says Cosloy. "But there was something very elemental about it that I thought would appeal to anybody with a belief in good music."

* * *

I f Sonic Youth's signing with Homestead was the group's first genuine opportunity to be marketed like a rock band, then the Gila Monster Jamboree, a tripped-out music festival held at a remote desert location outside Los Angeles on January 5, 1985, was its first full-fledged opportunity to act like a rock band.

Upon meeting California promoter Stuart Swezey (who later went on to found Amok, the infamous California distributor of twisted and macabre books) through Michael Shepard—who had released a new Sonic Youth single, "Death Valley '69," on his own Iridescence label—the band was inducted into the Los Angeles underground scene.

Organized by Swezey's Desolation Center agency, the Gila Monster Jamboree was also Sonic Youth's first West Coast show. Previous Desolation Center events had included a boat cruise around San Pedro Harbor featuring the Minutemen, and a Mojave Desert show starring the coruscating German band Einstürzende Neubauten and high-gauge explosives. The Sunday-night bill pitted Sonic Youth against the Meat Puppets, an acid-punk trio from Phoenix, Arizona, signed to SST; Redd Kross, a seventies-inspired punk band led by teenage brothers; and Psi-Com, a unfortunate group headed by one Perry Farrell—later front man for the infinitely more successful Jane's Addiction.

A map to a halfway point, Victorville, was provided with each ticket; exact directions to the festival site were given verbally from there. Despite a rash of free LSD and a late-night slot that forced Sonic Youth into the chilly desert air, the show was an unqualified success. Regardless of the prevailing hippie aesthetic (which the members of the New York band found nothing if not anachronistic), Sonic Youth for the first time met their true contemporaries face-to-face: postpunk musicians who regarded rock and punk with equal doses of admiration and derision.

Meeting Redd Kross particularly made a lasting impression on Sonic Youth. The earliest Redd Kross shows, in the the late 1970s, featured a fifteen-year-old Jeff McDonald and his eleven-year-old brother Steve. The Partridge Family, the New York Dolls, Kiss, Buffy Saint-Marie, the Osmonds, and the Ramones all carried equal weight in Redd Kross's skewed vision of American pop culture. *Born Innocent*, the band's 1982 debut, featured a song titled "Linda Blair," after the star of *The Exorcist*, and a cover of "Cease to Exist," a Beach Boys song notoriously cowritten by serial killer Charles Manson.

Even by the mid-1980s, the idea of underground pop musicians lampooning their more mainstream counterparts remained relatively unexplored. The bulk of punk's heroes regarded stardom with awe, as a transforming force that remained both appealing and unattainable. Hardcore's stance was extremely anti-celebrity, stemming from the admirable if essentially naive belief that mass recognition connoted squandered creativity and self-delusion. In general, neither world felt comfortable acknowledging the effects that the essentially American notion of superstardom wrought upon virtually every native-born teen.

Redd Kross deserves credit for being the first band to revel in seventies junk culture by approaching it with only the most razor-thin slice of irony; Sonic Youth immediately detected the technique's endless potential. Bob Bert recalls being visited by Thurston only months earlier, and being given a hard time for the copy of Madonna's first album among the drummer's home collection. "He was just like, 'Man, what're you doing with this?' It's so funny because a year or two later he was wearing Madonna T-shirts and covering her songs."

Judging from a video of the band's powerful Gila Monster performance, Sonic Youth had yet to find a place for its pop-culture obsessions in its nonetheless affecting vision.

Around the same time, in England, a young music entrepreneur named Paul Smith began looking for a new creative outlet. Smith—a partner in Doublevision, a video and recording company devoted primarily to the output of Cabaret Voltaire, an experimental outfit inspired by British punk, yet deeply involved in U.K.

pop's synthesizer revolution—had become caught up in the quest for extremes that characterized the London scene of the day.

Having approached Lydia Lunch, then a London resident, in hopes of coordinating a video release of a Lydia Lunch–Nick Cave collaboration which quickly fell apart, Smith learned of Lunch's unfinished In Limbo project. Smith quickly signed Lunch to Doublevision, enabling her to finish up the mixing on In Limbo and return to New York.

In August 1984 Smith had received a tape from Thurston, one of a number of New York musicians whom Lunch had informed of this open-minded label in England. The six tracks on the tape were eventually to become Bad Moon Rising.

"It was one of those real moments of epiphany," says Smith. "I had this little terraced house in Nottingham, that used to have a little tree in front of the window. It was a day that I wasn't actually going to work; and it was really bright sunshine, the sun had come through the trees and it was reflecting on the wall. And I just put this cassette in and I played these six numbers and thought, My God, someone makes music like this. It was just an amazing thing, a really interesting blend of what at that point was partly industrial, but then with guitars, but then the guitars were all really weird and fucked-up, and there were sort of pop and rock bits in there, but it wasn't a pop or rock thing. It was just sort of like this hugely exciting noise. I certainly couldn't understand why other people weren't interested in that, why they weren't excited by it."

Smith took the tape to Stephen Mallinder and Richard Kirk, founders of Cabaret Voltaire and the other two-thirds of Doublevision, and recommended Sonic Youth for immediate release. For an act to be signed to Doublevision, all three invested parties—Smith, Mallinder, and Kirk—needed to agree on its merits. Yet Mallinder and Kirk hated the Sonic Youth tracks; thus, they were not to be released on Doublevision. But Smith felt betrayed and began shopping the tape around to every independent label in London—Cherry Red, 4AD, and Mute, to name a few. No one was interested.

A beleaguered Smith couldn't figure out why no one saw what

he saw in Sonic Youth. While England was in the throes of an all-synthesizer revolution—the Human League, Depeche Mode, New Order—Sonic Youth was by no means an old-fashioned rock band. Finally, Pete Warmsley, a friend of Smith's at the independent Rough Trade, made Smith an offer. Rough Trade, a pioneer in the boutique marketing of independent releases, had been having success selling just a few thousand copies of promising young bands. If Smith could get the rights to the recordings, Rough Trade would release the album under a label name of Smith's choosing. Smith called his label Blast First, after the debut issue of British antimodernist critic Wyndham Lewis's literary journal, Blast.

According to Smith, at first Sonic Youth asked for $10,000 for the rights to the Bad Moon Rising tracks—a claim at least one band member flatly denies. Sonic Youth ended up settling for around $500, paid by Smith directly out of his own bank account.

The final album tracks were recorded in September and October of 1984 at Martin Bisi's studio, Before Christ, in downtown Brooklyn.

Almost immediately Smith played witness to Sonic Youth's controlled, opinionated approach. All parties agreed upon Bad Moon Rising's striking cover photo, a flaming pumpkin-headed scarecrow, set against a Manhattan sunset, taken by artist-photographer James Welling; the back-cover collage submitted by the band met with consternation from Smith. "It basically had lots of pictures of them when they were young," says Smith. "Lee's got a full beard, hair down beyond his collar, and there's some photograph of him getting out of a Volkswagen van. There's pictures of Bob Bert with a row of people obviously smoking pot. When I saw that, I said, 'This is a mistake, because if people look at this record and they're interested in turning it over, they'll think that you're a bunch of fucking hippies.' " Many of the photographs in question later appeared inside a subsequent CD release of the album.

"I wanted to have pumpkin imagery on it because I really liked the American scary thing," says Thurston. "The only place you really saw pumpkins was on Misfits records. And the early John

Carpenter movies [Halloween, The Fog], which were just sort of like, Here's middle America—what's lurking there?''

In England, Bad Moon Rising was released to surprisingly favorable reviews, especially considering the anti-guitar climate that prevailed at the time. Edwin Pouncey reported in Sounds that the album "lifts off where Confusion Is Sex touched down, the same concentrated howl of anguish is artistically amplified and thrown out in a shadow show of different musical shapes and collage effects." "If Bad Moon Rising doesn't totally add up," the New Musical Express argued, "it can still be enjoyed as an exercise in the macabre." Melody Maker characterized it as "a record to commit suicide to" while admitting that "Sonic Youth represent some vague sort of outer sphere" that "groups like [British oddballs] Psychic TV fumble about looking for."

No one in the U.K. was doing anything innovative with electric guitars, except for the Jesus and Mary Chain, the British band notorious for their fifteen-minute sets and arch, feedback-heavy bubblegum pop. "I remember going to see them play and being wholly unimpressed with them because they were so British about it," says Smith. "Backs to the audience, hair in their eyes, they were just frail white boys making noise. But it wasn't a wholehearted noise: It was obviously something that they had developed from listening to a lot of Velvet Underground bootlegs."

Sonic Youth, having already learned how to tour a network of small clubs around Europe, nonetheless had not played England again since their ill-fated Venue gig in 1983. But positive Bad Moon reviews and Paul Smith's contacts made England a more likely touring prospect by late March 1985. So Smith secured a slot for the band at an independent music festival being held that month at London's Institute of Contemporary Art (ICA).

Smith met Sonic Youth for the first time at Heathrow International Airport; a proud, young label head ready to meet his first prospect. "I said to them, 'Well, guys, do you want to change some dollars into cash here so you've got some money?' " Smith recalls. After a few awkward minutes of silence and scrounging around, the four members produced $64 between them. They also informed their newly anointed would-be Svengali that they had only purchased one-way tickets from New York to London.

"The only thing I had to parallel that against was a band like Cabaret Voltaire, who wouldn't even think about leaving the country if the foreign promoter had not bought them return tickets, promised them a good hotel, and was generally looking after all their costs. It was like, Wow, these people are insane. They'll just come over here, and trust themselves to luck or fate that it would work out."

Sonic Youth remained in the enviable position of being able to shock British observers unaccustomed to seeing rock music delivered with such brute force. The Wednesday-night performance (the band appeared on a bill with Boyd Rice & Frank Tovey and Tools You Can Trust) was notable for its ferocity; the band repeatedly launched themselves at their equipment and at the mikes while playing a set comprised primarily of material from *Bad Moon* and *Confusion*. The band had covered the stage with jack-o'-lanterns, a distinctly American-gothic touch. During a chilling rendition of "Shaking Hell," Kim fell off the stage while she sang but kept singing nonetheless.

By the end of the show, nearly half the audience had left; the rest were pressed against the back of the room. Prominent British writers such as Jon Savage and Chris Bond were ineffably impressed, even as they remained pinned against the wall in horror.

"I must have been totally scared, but I kept it under wraps," says Thurston. Playing a London showcase was the biggest deal the band had yet to experience. "As a result, I got really sick on the way there. All of a sudden I got incredible cramps and wasn't able to function very well. . . . Before the show, I was in the back of the stage in this little room. I had four coats on, everything I brought with me I had on." The sound check had been discouraging; Boyd Rice (otherwise known as the California tape-loop experimentalist Non) put on a bone-jarring performance that Sonic Youth was convinced would obliterate its force.

"Michael Stipe came backstage and I was really sick. I didn't even look at him," Thurston recalls. "Then we went out, and as soon as we started playing, after the first song, 'Burning Spear,' I felt really good and the audience was really responsive."

As the set continued, Thurston removed his jackets and shirts and T-shirts, the final one being a Madonna T-shirt. (The band had bought Madonna, Bruce Springsteen, and Prince T-shirts to wear for British photo shoots, "just to fuck with people.")

"No one had ever seen people do that to a guitar," says Smith. "Glenn Branca had been over and played before, and that had sort of created an interest, but Branca's thing had more to do with high art and volume. This was more physical—there was no sort of 'Hey, aren't we cool, and we make this cool noise.' This was like someone having their hands around your throat and throttling you."

Not everyone was so taken with Sonic Youth's cacophonic delivery. "These art school dilettantes conceal their soft-centre behind an unsmiling intensity that's so revoltingly elitist, I'd like to slap them silly," a *Melody Maker* critic scowled. Other reviewers mocked what was perceived as the band's premeditated fascination with the macabre. Simon Frith, in the *Sunday Times*, characterized the band's hour-long set as "clever people playing stupid music."

Kim and Thurston married during the summer of 1984. It was a traditional Catholic wedding held near Thurston's childhood home in Connecticut. Lydia Lunch and Jim Thirwell were the most obtrusive scenesters present—upon arriving late, Thirwell's leather pants and sleeveless T-shirt and Lunch's wild red-and-black hair turned heads in the pews. Ranaldo and Bert each also married that year. (A year later, Lee's wife Amanda gave birth to their son, Cody.)

"I think at that time we were all in love and wanting to get married," says Bert, "but I almost think part of it was, If we can get some wedding money we can keep playing. We were all broke."

8 | California Dreaming

The late 1960s were impetuous times for the United States. So impetuous, in fact, that many Americans still blame that era's collective questioning of traditional values as the heresy that ignited our present-day woes, then fanned them into firestorms.

Unlike the ideological conservatives who helped elect Reagan into office, few of today's rock musicians can claim to be unmoved by the fertile counterculture of the sixties. While a popular motto of the time—Sex, Drugs, and Rock and Roll—rings resolutely naive and cliché in contemporary ears, its cant marks some elusive yet manageable utopia which popular music has pursued ever since.

Ronald Reagan began his second term as president in 1985 and thusly set into motion a fin de siècle party for the country's privileged which sought nothing less than to exorcise what conservatives knew as the "sixties myth." To right-wingers, the era's dramatic social upheavals—the civil rights movement, the Vietnam War, the sexual revolution, the impending drug culture—represented a wrong turn, a fundamental betrayal of modern civilization's precepts. In strangulating the welfare state and celebrating "trickle-down" economics, the Reagan administration sent a clear "Don't worry, be happy" message to anyone predisposed to not worrying and being happy.

That Sonic Youth's next album, Bad Moon Rising, drew inspiration from the year 1969 and the state of California couldn't have been more apropos. "In the image of Reagan, the whole of America has become Californian," the French philosopher Jean Baudrillard wrote in 1986 in America. "Ex-actor and ex-governor of California that he is, he has worked up his euphoric, cinematic, extraverted, advertising vision of the artificial paradises of the West to all-American dimensions." Again, Sonic Youth had hooked into a national rumbling, like hardcore, a nearly subconscious social force that had only just begun affecting the fringe of the mainstream.

"Every little group of friends gets into their Manson kick," in the words of Bob Bert, who remains amused by what at the time was perceived as Sonic Youth's death trip.

For Thurston, the album's dark overtones carried more emotional weight. "The whole meaning of America is death," he told NME in April 1985. "Reagan's talking about the final peace, but the image you get from his tone is a mushroom cloud. An image of the total annihilation of humanity. Our culture is like, death."

Recorded for under $7,000 in a little more than a week's time at Before Christ, a tiny Brooklyn studio made unique by a mixing board that sat inside the recording booth with the musicians, Bad Moon Rising became a defining album not only for Sonic Youth but also for what would blossom into the "indie" era.

Ironically enough, Before Christ began as a studio for rap artists and jazz avant-gardists. Started by a nineteen-year-old New Yorker named Martin Bisi in 1981, Before Christ played home to the crucial fusion experiments of bassist and producer Bill Laswell and his group Material, as well as early rock-rap collaborations, such as "World Destruction," which featured Afrika Bambaataa and John Lydon fusing hip-hop's beats with postpunk's fury.

Although other downtown New York oddball musicians like Arto Lindsay (DNA, Ambitious Lovers) and avant-garde composer

John Zorn had already trucked out to the barren Brooklyn warehouse district in which Before Christ sits to record, Bisi believes it was his hip-hop credentials that first brought Sonic Youth to his studio. That and the relatively affordable, albeit crude conditions.

"I remember describing Sonic Youth to some of my friends," says Bisi. "I actually said that it was sort of folkie, because I associated it with certain kinds of rock stuff, like Creedence Clearwater Revival." Although the members of Sonic Youth were New Yorkers by address, their approach to music was by no means solely defined by the band's birthplace.

"What was interesting to me was that Sonic Youth cherishes aspects of American pop culture, stuff that came before them," Bisi adds, "whereas people like John Zorn had no sentimentality about America whatsoever, or about any sort of American rock-music tradition. You know, they were throwing that out along with everything else."

Bad Moon Rising, a continuous cycle of seven songs, marked Sonic Youth's first overt break with the European-derived theory that in many ways had allowed the band to deconstruct, and thus re-create, American rock tradition. "It was kind of hippie-ish, but it wasn't hippie-ish," Moore says. "It related a lot to Black Flag growing their hair out."

Days before Sonic Youth played the Gila Monster Jamboree in January 1985, Kim and Thurston had tried to clarify the band's newfound tack in an interview with the Los Angeles Times. "We really have this feeling about ourselves as being an American band," Moore said. "People tend to think of our music as German-influenced, industrial. But there's this big American uprising of Byrds-like jangly guitar bands. We love Creedence Clearwater, the music of that [late sixties] time. We feel akin to all that, in the same manner of bands like Green on Red. Only we don't sound the same."

Of course, Thurston was right. Sonic Youth stood out in the New York circuit simply because it was so American. Sonic Youth's New York contemporaries—bands such as Swans, Live Skull, Don King, and Rat At Rat R—prided themselves on their relative inaccessability. Having created a malevolent-seeming scene based out of the S.I.N. Club—a dive club on drug-infested Avenue C in the East Village, which booked all the aforementioned bands at the time— New York rock's extremists seemed bent on keeping a cool, artist's distance from their dark songbooks.

"Everybody applauds Laurie Anderson because she made it out of the art-world ghetto, but she's not that interesting to me," Gordon said in the same interview. "I may not be into Michael Jackson, but as a multimedia experience, it's gotta be more exciting than what Laurie Anderson does. I'd much rather go see Ratt." By stating her preference for commercial heavy metal over art rock, Gordon made an easy but rarely evoked point about good rock music. Why assume that the mind and body are opposed—she seemed to say—when acknowledging both, even if in direct contradiction, makes for the most exciting results?

Iggy Pop and the Stooges, and Creedence Clearwater Revival served as musical touchpoints on *Bad Moon Rising*. The title of the album is also the title of a 1968 Creedence song by John Fogerty, written as a harsh commentary on the Vietnam War. A snippet of "Not Right"—written by Iggy Pop and Ron Asheton, recorded by the Stooges, and doctored by Lee Ranaldo—appears between "Society Is a Hole" and "I Love Her All the Time" on the first side of *Bad Moon*.

Having toured extensively by this time, the band had a much better handle on the inherent strengths of its sound. Although Sonic Youth's recording career had begun in studio situations which were relatively staid compared to the band's live performances, *Confusion Is Sex* and *Kill Yr. Idols* were reasonably accurate documents of a band that valued its chaos theory.

While touring, Thurston and Lee found that their ever-increasing number of alternate tunings made for long, energy-sapping pauses between songs. Although the band tried to compensate by adding a few pre-tuned cheap guitars to their arsenal, à la Glenn Branca, the dead time between numbers remained a frequent frustration. In Europe, the band had gotten used to lugging four or five guitars on and off trains. Oftentimes guitars would be passed through train windows to ensure the band met a connecting departure a couple minutes later three or four platforms over.

"Throughout all that touring, we were really into this thing of making all the songs go together, and segues became a big part," says Ranaldo. "Before we'd go out onstage every night, we'd talk through the segues of the set: 'What are we going to do when this song ends?' 'Well, you keep something going while I switch guitars, and then I'll pick it up and when I get it going, then you'll switch guitars and then we'll get into the next song.' "

Inspired in part by the West Coast imagery utilized by Black Flag and the Minutemen, Sonic Youth also became set on making its first distinctly American album. "Brave Men Run," the album's leadoff track, takes its central image from a painting by California artist Edward Ruscha, of a schooner riding a wave accompanied by block letters reading "BRAVE MEN RUN IN MY FAMILY." During the increasing number of trips taken to Los Angeles to visit Kim's parents, Thurston and Kim fueled a common interest in the dark underpinnings haunting the world's glamour capital.

"It was all very much lighthearted," says Thurston. "We didn't want to make a big deal out of it, but nobody else was writing stuff about that. It was sociological." For many musicians and listeners raised on punk, history began in 1977. Only from the perspective of the mid-eighties—a time that found many young people caught up in a hyper-capitalist feeding frenzy—did the underground start looking back for causes. For the members of Sonic Youth, the search ended with Charles Manson.

Manson, a California hippie drifter with a juvenile record, transfixed a generation by fostering a group of teenage followers with whom he enagaged in sex orgies, blood rituals, felony binges, and finally, in August 1969, the systematic slaying of seven people, including actress Sharon Tate, the twenty-six-year-old bride of director Roman Polanski.

That drugs and hippie accoutrements were favored by Manson and his followers, whom he called "the family" (Manson even claimed to have found apocalyptic messages in rock songs such as "Helter Skelter," off the Beatles' White Album) made it easy for establishment naysayers to label the burgeoning counterculture "evil." The made-to-order symbolism afforded by other "freaky" occurrences—such as Hell's Angels security guards murdering a fan during the Rolling Stones' set at an Altamont Speedway rock festival in November 1969—left a pall over the utopian notion of a mass bohemia.

As a teenager, Kim Gordon witnessed the repercussions of Manson and Altamont firsthand. "My brother had a girlfriend who was killed by the Manson family," she confessed in a 1985 Melody Maker interview. Yet Gordon's (and for that matter, Sonic Youth's) fascination with Manson was as much the calculated maneuver of a craftsperson as it was a means of genuine cultural catharsis.

An exceptional piece of criticism written by Gordon titled "American Prayers" appeared in the April 1985 issue of Artforum. Within its few pages lies a near blueprint for Sonic Youth's next few years.

In the article, one image Gordon chooses to focus on is the cover drawing of Raymond Pettibon's 1982 self-published book Other Christs. "I'm glad to see someone from our group making it," reads the caption over the heads of a drawing of four men with halos over their heads, who are watching the crucifixion of a "Christ-like Manson figure" on television. As Gordon notes, Pettibon's drawing manages to equate mainstream religion, cultism, and media worship in a single crudely rendered pen-and-ink image.

"If you've ever heard him talk," underground filmmaker Richard Kern says of Manson, "what he says makes a lot of sense. It's kind of that idiot-savant thing, the crazy person that speaks the truth—at least, it seemed that way to me at the time. The world of the future was going to be all fucked up; he was going to set up his commune in the desert and they were going to be these revolutionary types. Also, the fact that Manson's in jail and he never did anything—he simply told people to do stuff. He never did any of the crimes he was put in jail for. The obsession was about the secret longing for chaos and genocide that a lot of people carry around with them. Of course, this all makes a lot more sense if you're on drugs.''

The sixties obsessions of other disenfranchised artists—CalArts whiz kid and Gordon friend Mike Kelley's long-standing Iggy Pop obsession; and New York video artist Tony Oursler's 1985 output titled Evol, a reference to the sixties love backlash (and subsequently the title of Sonic Youth's next album)—similarly inspired Sonic Youth's mid-eighties output. Pettibon, Kelley, and Oursler were all using crude, appropriated images as a way to simultaneously emerge from and detach themselves from popular culture in order to discuss its newfound establishment status. Soon enough, Sonic Youth would be approximating this effect in their music.

''The most unpretentious pretentious band in the world'' is how Village Voice writer Tom Carson described Sonic Youth in 1988. In 1985, the pretense had yet to meld fully with the abandon.

Tattered copies of The Family, by Ed Sanders, and Helter Skelter, by Vincent Bugliosi with Curt Gentry, were passed among the band members. Sonic Youth attempted to glean meaning from reading of Manson's exploits, much in the way sociologists study deviance as a method for finding behavioral patterns. Comprehended by many observers as a childish gothic obsession, Sonic Youth's Manson kick nonetheless served its purpose within the band's artistic vision. ''I think it annoyed people, us using that kind of imagery,'' Thurston gleefully recalls.

From the open-tuned, declarative guitar phrases of ''Intro,'' Bad Moon Rising's opening track, Sonic Youth set off in a whole new direction. Hardcore's double-time tempos and blood-curdling vocals—no longer filled with the expressive power they possessed a few years earlier—were replaced with a slower, churning sound that made the most of the band's increasingly complex harmonics. While Bad Moon retained the band's penchant for volume, the chimelike guitar fragments that gather about tracks such as ''Brave

Men Run" and "Society Is a Hole" seem to cascade like a warm wind across a Midwestern wheat field. Sonic Youth had become more at home with its own ragged glory: new alternate tunings began to shape songs; "mistakes" were mined for aesthetic gold.

The lyrics for "Society Is a Hole," for example, were written by Moore after hearing "Rise Above" by Black Flag. "I always thought Henry Rollins was singing one thing, when in reality he was singing something else," he later explained. "Rise Above" contains the line "Society's arms of control"—which Moore mistook for "Society is a fucking hole." "I was thinking, What great imagery, what an amazing line—then I found out I had completely misheard what Henry was saying." Moore's singsongy vocals add a dreamlike quality to "Society" which renders its nihilistic sentiments almost inert. This sensation of political urgency demurring to aesthetic pleasure was soon to become one of Sonic Youth's strongest suits. The song is followed by a garbled snippet of the Stooges' "Not Right" (a diffuse political anthem if ever there was one)—a device that made its debut at a Maxwell's show where Ranaldo cranked a cassette tape of the song through his amp at full volume.

"Death Valley '69," the album's centerpiece and ironic "tribute" to Charles Manson and the Family, evolved out of a riff the band had tossed about in rehearsals but had originally dismissed as too much of a goofy seventies-rock throwback (they thought it sounded like Steppenwolf). Then Thurston and Lydia Lunch came up with lyrics; she wrote the verses and he wrote the chorus. "Thurston and I wrote it on a bus going up to Spanish Harlem," says Lunch.

"Death Valley '69" became the band's first "crossover" single, as it were—a straightforward rock song that incorporated all of the distinctly Sonic Youth musical devices to date: Bert's primitive but forceful drumming; Gordon's simple, thumping bass line; and Ranaldo and Moore trading guitar parts so fiercely strummed that they sounded like dueling air-raid sirens. Lunch ended up singing on the finished version, harmonizing with Moore in an off-kilter manner reminiscent of Exene Cervenka and John Doe's evocative performances on X's earlier albums.

"Lee didn't show up for rehearsal, and Thurston goes, 'Oh yeah, I want to do this song about Manson with Lydia, I have this riff,'" Bert recalls. "I came up with that drum part immediately. It was written in like five minutes or something. We rehearsed it a million times after that, but it came together in a few minutes."

The album version of "Death Valley '69" (it also exists as a rare Iridescence single, a cruder version recorded at Wharton Tiers's studio) is a wonderfully vertiginous romp—the guitars buzz and whirl as lyric fragments like "Sadie I love it," "Hit it," "I got sand in my mouth," and "I didn't wanna" spray out like the genuine yelps of mesmerized Manson-ites.

A choppy video clip of the song, codirected by Richard Kern, captures the song's art-skewed blood lust in gory color. (The band made this first video—which features the band members, including both Bob Bert and Steve Shelley, covered in buckets of fake blood—well aware that it would have no chance of being aired on MTV. It eventually did air on "120 Minutes," MTV's late-night new-music showcase, in a drastically truncated form.)

Bad Moon Rising was Sonic Youth's official departure from the New York scene. While many critics and writers not stationed in New York took its dark edges as evidence of the band's pretentious "scum rock" aspirations, the content pointed in many new directions, an aspect laboriously reemphasized by the band in its increasing number of encounters with the press.

"When that record came out," Ranaldo says, "journalists fixated on it, thinking it was about the glorification of Charles Manson. That was so far from the truth: Our interest in it was more just observation of a cultural epoch. It was very different from Genesis P. Orridge [of the splatter-gore group Psychic TV] in England, sporting Charles Manson T-shirts like, 'I'm down with Charlie.'"

"I Love Her All the Time" was (as the band was quick to point out) Sonic Youth's first true love song, a swirly, seductive testament to loving someone's mind and body simultaneously. "Brave

Men Run" presented Kim at her most confident. Her husky voice lends a perfect blend of sex appeal and detachment to the song's clever lyrical hook. "Brave men run"—she pauses—"in my family," and then, "Brave men run"—"into the setting sun."

The album's three remaining tracks are its most musically daring and subsequently its least accessible. "Ghost Bitch" is a Kim Gordon–penned ode to the bastard nature of the United States' origins. Its harshly distorted accompaniment, which revolves around a Ranaldo-devised acoustic guitar pattern, only makes Gordon's monotonal vocals harder to follow. "I'm Insane" harks back to Sonic Youth's rudimentary structures, built up from a two-note bass pattern, yet its lyrics are Thurston's first real attempt at free-associating and punning away in a specific mind-set. "Justice Is Might" seems unusually rote, incorporating what by now had become virtual Sonic Youth catchphrases—"Lee is free," "Sonik life"—into a brief equation of power, perhaps another reference to Ronald Reagan's justice-hungry, might-gorged America.

Despite the album's overt sampling of American imagery, Bad Moon Rising's reception in the U.S. was middling. As late as early 1985, Sonic Youth had trouble pulling in an audience of over twenty-five people at Maxwell's in Hoboken, New Jersey—on a Friday night. The band's latter-day status as college-radio darlings was as yet unearned—the College Music Journal, the most influential college-radio trade publication, didn't even review Bad Moon. Rolling Stone totally ignored the album—as it did virtually every major independent American act of the mid-eighties until they began to sign to majors. Only after delayed stateside reaction—a feature in Spin, a favorable review in the New York Times—did Sonic Youth's American fan base begin to grow. Warner Brothers Records even requested a copy of the album from Homestead; after listening, someone called up wondering whether Cosloy had sent the right album.

In England, Sonic Youth created a minor sensation. In the first six months Bad Moon Rising was available in the U.K., it sold 5,000 copies, an altogether reasonable amount for an independent release at the time.

The nature of the record industry in the United Kingdom allowed Sonic Youth to blossom organically. In Britain, record labels, even some major ones, often resemble glorified art projects rather than high-stakes profit machines. And because the total population is reasonably small and concentrated, distribution costs amount to less than in the U.S. In the U.S., the burgeoning world of independent labels was acting in direct opposition to a restrictive corporate monolith, a big-money recording industry which conveyed the message—by refusing to sign different-sounding young bands with devoted cult followings—that "alternative" (at the time, still called "underground") music was creatively invalid.

The United Kingdom also had the fortune of being able to support three national music weeklies—the *New Musical Express*, *Melody Maker*, and the now-defunct *Sounds*. Sonic Youth had graced the cover of all three publications by the mid-1980s. To this day, Sonic Youth has never appeared on the cover of a major American magazine, music-oriented or otherwise. British music fans—despite their deserved reputation for being overly fickle and trendy—were better informed and more receptive to the newest sounds. Even when those sounds came courtesy of a bunch of seemingly sullen New Yorkers brandishing electric guitars instead of synthesizers.

Paul Smith then proceeded to release *Death Valley '69*, a twelve-inch EP meant to capitalize on Lydia Lunch's name-brand popularity in U.K. hipster circles. Smith issued the EP with a pink cover and graphics by underground illustrator Savage Pencil (a.k.a. British music journalist Edwin Pouncey). The A-side featured "Death Valley '69"; the B-side consisted of one track off each of the first three Sonic Youth releases, plus the muddy and malevolent "Satan Is Boring," inspired by the highly publicized 1984 case of Ricky Kasso, Jr.

Kasso was a Long Island teenager who, while loaded on angel dust (PCP), coerced his friends into helping him gouge out seventeen-year-old Gary Lauwers's eyes—after having tortured the youth for three hours and stabbing him seventeen times. A day later, Kasso committed suicide in a jail cell. His father told the national press that all his addled son ever talked about was "drugs and rock music." "Satan Is Boring" had been recorded during the *Bad Moon Rising* sessions and offered reasonable closure to the band's fascination with death cults.

Sonic Youth toured Europe through the first half of 1985, starting off and finishing in England. Long and grueling, the European stint nevertheless provided the band with more time on the road than they'd ever experienced before. Smith also had begun urging the band to think ahead. "Where do you want to be in six months?" was a question Sonic Youth had rarely put to itself before. After the last date in England, Smith again asked the band about its future plans. "And Bob said, 'Well, I'm not going to be in the band anymore,' " Ranaldo remembers. "Big shock to us all."

"I get the impression from people today, 'Wow, how could you leave Sonic Youth?' But back then, people were leaving bands every second," says Bert. "The last tour of Europe, I was just kind of getting tired of it. I knew the Homestead Records scene was pretty bogus. And Paul Smith, who in the long run turned out to be really great—I was really skeptical of that guy at first. He kept saying, 'I'm going to make you guys as big as the Birthday Party.' He was planning out the next six years. The whole time I was in Sonic Youth, too, I was holding down full-time jobs. I was working for Warhol's company, doing his silk-screen prints. I was doing the same thing for other places and different artists. That's how I was trying to survive."

Bert later became drummer for Pussy Galore, a raucous Washington, D.C., guitar band formed by Brown University dropouts Jon Spencer and Julie Cafritz. Pussy Galore relocated to New York in 1986 and for a brief period out-attituded Sonic Youth in downtown New York's paramusical noise circles. Bert also formed Bewitched, a band that became best known for occasionally opening Sonic Youth gigs. Today Bert, thirty-eight, looks about the same as he did then, though his large frame carries substantially more weight these days. In the fall of 1993, a chance to become the drummer in the Muffs—featuring two former members of L.A.'s legendary all-women garage-rock group, The Pandoras—fell through.

"Sonic Youth was always touring, and we'd mainly break even or make a little bit of money. But that's not really why I left," he says. "At the time, I wanted a change, and I knew it was the right time to do it."

9 | Love Spelled Backward

Homestead was a tiny, inefficient label that, despite the best efforts of Gerard Cosloy, couldn't give *Bad Moon Rising* the attention it required. Cosloy's friendship with Sonic Youth only made matters more difficult.

To outsiders, Cosloy was the "Homestead college rep"; in actuality, he was the label's A&R department, promotional department, and "custodial services" (his words) all wrapped into one. Compared to SST—by 1985 home to what amounted to the American independent scene's brain trust (Black Flag, the Minutemen, Meat Puppets, Hüsker Dü)—Homestead was a mere speck. Technically, it wasn't even an independent; it was distributed by Dutch East India Trading, a disinterested corporate parent.

SST had become a brand name—a boutique, if you will—for well-crafted, fury-filled postpunk product. Greg Ginn's older brother, the gifted illustrator known by the name Raymond Pettibon, rendered distinctive album covers for many of the releases. MTV had begun its late-night college-rock show, "120 Minutes," allowing SST to produce videos for under $4,000 that were assured six weeks of airplay. With the addition of Global Booking, an in-house booking agency run by Chuck Dukowski, the kind of distribution and exposure SST afforded an act could simply not be matched.

While Homestead's roster featured a prominent number of soon-to-be alternative darlings—Green River (an early incarnation of Seattle's Mudhoney), Naked Raygun, and Big Black—college rock had already begun to pull in its reins. The success of R.E.M.—a reasonably independent-minded band who by 1985 had already parlayed its distinctive jangly sound into a Top 40 hit with "So. Central Rain (I'm Sorry)"—was leading many American indie labels toward more sixties-influenced guitar acts. Muzzy pop bands like the Long Ryders, Green on Red, and the dB's were easier to peddle to radio programmers, college and commercial, and to retailers than more free-form, aggressive fare like Sonic Youth.

Personal passion, rather than commercial demand, fueled Gerard Cosloy's organization of Sonic Youth's first full-fledged U.S. tour in late 1985. Fortunately, Cosloy came equipped with an impressive list of independent contacts, booty from his years as a local promoter in Boston and as the publisher of *Conflict*.

Cosloy contacted Ray Farrell in San Francisco and asked if he might arrange some California dates. Farrell, a New Jersey native living in San Francisco, had been a part of the independent distribution world since its beginnings in the late seventies. Having worked for Rough Trade (a transplanted British indie), Subterranean (Flipper), and CD Presents (Billy Bragg), and as an erstwhile radio host and concert promoter, Farrell was well versed in the art of making the most of a shoestring budget. An early West Coast fan and a friend of Iridescence's Mike Shepard, Farrell was happy to oblige. He booked Sonic Youth at the hip Mondays-only I-Beam club in San Francisco for January 14 (nine days after the Gila Monster Jamboree), and another at a Santa Cruz reggae hardcore club.

In Santa Cruz, skinheads showed up, expecting one more in a line of local hardcore bands with names like Radical Youth, Impatient Youth, Rational Youth, and Wasted Youth. The small audience seemed disappointed that the band didn't have mohawks. Furthermore, the Rastafarian promoter had paid the band in advance—he had $19—expecting a paltry turnout. Sonic Youth agreed to play seven songs, at $2 apiece.

By 1985 SST was on a roll. No longer known solely as Black Flag's label, and having gained broader public acceptance and a better cash flow via the success of the Minutemen's *Double Nickles on the Dime* and Hüsker Dü's *Zen Arcade*—both double albums and both masterworks from their respective creators—SST expanded its ranks in order to go where no independent punk label had gone before.

In April, Ray Farrell accepted a job offer from his friend Joe Carducci, one of SST's four principals. Farrell became the label's first employee (other than the partners)—"the last guy to sleep on the floor," as he puts it. Upon arriving, he almost immediately began talking up Sonic Youth. As with Doublevision, all four SST owners—Greg Ginn, Chuck Dukowski, "Mugger," and Joe Carducci—approved new signees. Initially, Sonic Youth was vetoed by Carducci, who felt that SST needed to reinforce its local character, rather than branching out. "Record collectors shouldn't be in bands," was another criticism allegedly leveled against the band from within. Soon after, Carducci left the partnership; in 1986, Greg Ginn called Sonic Youth.

The members of Black Flag weren't initially familiar with the New York band's music, though the name rang a bell. All along Black Flag's most recent tour, the band had found messages spraypainted on club walls that read, "Hello to Black Flag, From Sonic Youth." Sonic Youth becoming SST's first East Coast band wasn't so much a matter of fate as it was one of coerced inevitability.

Midland, Michigan, isn't much different from most American suburbs—except that it isn't really a suburb. Detroit, the closest big city, is two and half hours away.

Home to Dow Chemicals, Midland is a company town, the same way its more infamous neighbor Flint, Michigan (Flint's an hour and a half away) is a company town. But unlike most Midland heads of households in the early 1980s, Steve Shelley's father worked for the City of Midland instead of Dow. In Midland, that counts as exciting.

However, "boring" is the adjective that comes up within the first few sentences every time Steve mentions his hometown. Of course, this automatically puts Steve Shelley, born June 23, 1963, in better stead with the whole American indie rock scene than anything the members of Sonic Youth collectively or individually could devise. The "Think globally, act locally" of the hardcore circuit was predicated by young teens—kids—who were, simply put, bored out of their skulls. Growing up in the part of middle America where cultural enlightenment equals a trip to the mall, smart kids learn to enlighten themselves. Rough-hewn, raucous, homemade culture sprang forth from the blandest of bland environs. For all the above reasons, New York was not cool in hardcore circles—after all, New York was the capital of established culture.

From an early age, Steve—a skinny, geeky-looking bespectacled youth—banged drums in the high-school marching band, and for as many Top Forty basement bands as he could find. "You pretty much had to start doing everything yourself," he says. "Set up a concert at the library or play a lawn party, make fliers—trying to keep people excited about doing something was pretty difficult."

The Beatles, the Who, the Rolling Stones, the Steve Miller Band, Bob Seger—all staples of mid-seventies FM radio—filled the playlists of Steve's earliest combos. The advent of "new wave," middle America's idea of rock esoterica, gradually allowed songs by the Police, Elvis Costello, and Talking Heads to replace the older fare.

After graduating high school in 1980, it took two semesters at a local community college for Steve to realize that he wanted a different kind of education. Occasional road trips to Detroit and East Lansing, home to Michigan State, exposed Steve to a better variety of music, lots of live shows, and a more happening crowd.

When Steve and his friend Scott Begerston, a bassist, grew weary of playing with one in a line of pickup outfits, a new-wave trio, they decided to form a new one with a twisted old punk character named Doc Dart. Doc's sixteen-year-old cousin, Joe Dart, played guitar.

Hardcore's Jerry Lewis, Doc Dart dubbed the band the Crucifucks, an ambitiously offensive name that perfectly characterized the band's mix of vaudevillian charm and brazen puerility. Provocative but jokey leftist songs such as "Hinkley Had a Vision" and "Cops for Fertilizer" won the Crucifucks a small following on the fringes of the liberal-minded scene in nearby Madison, Wisconsin (Die Kreuzen, the Tar Babies). Slower and more varied than most hardcore outfits, the Crucifucks were able to quickly carve a niche for themselves on the hardcore circuit.

Steve first became aware of Sonic Youth after listening to a friend's copy of *Confusion Is Sex*. "She's in a Bad Mood" and "Making the Nature Scene" immediately caught his ear. "The other stuff I don't think I got right away," he says.

Intermittent bookings and Dart's mercurial personality kept the Crucifucks in constant flux—the band broke up and re-formed on a regular basis. Occasional career opportunities—such as an attractive offer to play a string of West Coast dates with San Francisco's Dead Kennedys, and a Rock Against Reagan tour—prompted such reconvenings.

The pairing with the Dead Kennedys, a similarly unflinching antiauthoritarian outfit, was most apt. In 1985 the Crucifucks recorded a debut album for Alternative Tentacles, the label run by Dead Kennedys lead singer/raconteur Jello Biafra.

The Rock Against Reagan tour brought the band to CBGBs for a hardcore matinee, the band's first New York appearance. Audience members Thurston Moore and Lee Ranaldo, impressed with the band's unusual instrumentations, introduced themselves to the band after the show. ("Steve was the most interesting thing in the band," Moore says.) When Steve got back to Midland, he called up Ranaldo and asked if he was interested in producing a follow-up Crucifucks album. Although Steve left the band before Ranaldo could accept the offer, Ranaldo soon delivered a more lasting favor.

As the Crucifucks' youngest members (Joe Dart left after the first year), Steve and Scott frequently felt weighed down by the adult commitments of their older bandmates, most of whom were in their thirties, with real jobs and wives or girlfriends. Steve subsisted on a string of short-order-cook and dishwasher jobs and satisfied his thirst for limitless drumming opportunities by playing with other bands during the free time between Crucifucks commitments.

Spastic Rhythm Tarts, based in Kalamazoo, Michigan, was one such band. Spastic Rhythm Tarts (later known as Strange Fruit; and without Steve, Strange Fruit Abiku; then simply Abiku)—which included Steve's Midland buddy Tim Foljahn, and Michael Love and Shari Feight, two students at Western Michigan University— came the closest to what the young drummer hoped to be doing. "It wasn't an outright political band or a band that was saying, 'Cops suck,' " says Steve. "It was a more artistic band with more poetic lyrics, if you will. More abstract."

The group played songs based on unorthodox verse structures and one-chord raves—songs inspired by the influential British postpunkers of the early eighties, particularly Joy Division, New Order, Pop Group, and the Slits (the band had a female lead singer).

The state of Michigan is shaped like a mitten, with Lake Michigan forming the western border (the pinkie finger) and Lakes Huron and Erie forming the eastern border (the thumb and forefingers). Midland, near the crease between thumb and forefinger that is Saginaw Bay, forms a triangle with Kalamazoo to the southwest and East Lansing, Ann Arbor, and Detroit to the southeast. Each side of the triangle is a three-hour drive. "On weekends, Tim and I would go to Kalamazoo and rehearse, and then we'd go to Ann Arbor and see the Gang of Four, and then we'd go to East Lansing to hang out," Steve says. "We would drive just all the time. We were just totally into it." On occasion, the two friends would drive six hours to Chicago in order to see bands play.

After a few years of interminable driving and gigging, Crucifucks bassist Mark Hauser and Steve decided the time had arrived to leave Michigan. San Francisco—home to the Crucifucks' label, Alternative Tentacles, and a reasonably fertile independent music scene—looked to be the most appealing destination. San Francisco, or New York.

Early in 1985, Steve called Lee Ranaldo asking about apartments in Manhattan. Ranaldo suggested that Steve contact Kim and Thurston, who sublet their Eldridge Street digs whenever they went on tour. A chat with Thurston assured Steve that New York was the place to be. "Everybody's *always* looking for drummers," Moore assured him. So Sonic Youth fled to Europe; Steve and Mark agreed to mind the Moore-Gordon household.

While house-sitting, Steve explored the many moods of Bad Moon Rising, the newest album from his newest friends. "I can remember sitting in Kim and Thurston's apartment, listening to Bad Moon and staring at the cover," Steve says. Sold on its merits, he also became sold on New York. Going so far as finding menial work to tide himself over when Sonic Youth's U.K. stint was extended, Steve began to audition around town, hoping to stumble upon a satisfactory band situation. A Bauhaus soundalike band in New Jersey, a bunch of Smiths copycats in the East Village—Steve initially had poor luck finding a suitable group of New York–area cohorts. Fortunately, Steve's timing proved more prodigious than he ever could have imagined. On returning from England, Sonic Youth found itself, once again, drummerless.

"One day I came home from work and there Kim and Thurston were in their apartment—it was the first I'd actually met Kim," Steve recalls. "And then they asked if I wanted to be in the band." Without so much as an audition or a practice—without, in fact, ever having seen the band perform—Steve Shelley became Sonic Youth's fourth full-time drummer.

"I knew I wanted to do something like Sonic Youth—but, of course, I didn't want to copy Sonic Youth," he says. Soon after Steve accepted the band's offer, Sonic Youth played its last show without him—a twenty-minute performance at the Pyramid, a dilapidated East Village haunt on Avenue A best characterized by the transvestite go-go dancers that gyrate atop its front-room bar.

The Pyramid gig was a grand Sonic Youth homecoming; the joint was, in the best proverbial sense, jumping. Outgoing drummer Bob Bert watched his replacement, Steve Shelley, who was watching his predecessor drum his final beats with the band Steve had just joined, as a packed house reveled in the sounds of its new favorite hometown act. "It was a very up night," Steve says.

Mere weeks later, Steve began rehearsing with Gordon and Moore. Early tasks included teaching a new drummer old tricks (the band was scheduled to return to Europe for subsequent *Bad Moon* tour dates) and working up a few new songs. Steve helped create "Expressway to Yr. Skull" and "Green Light"—the first tracks written for *EVOL*, Sonic Youth's first SST release—from the bottom up.

One of the first shows Steve played with the band took place at New York's Folk City on Bleecker Street. One in a series of concerts titled Music for Dozens and arranged by writer-turned-musician Ira Kaplan and Michael Hill, the night was unique, even by Sonic Youth's standards. Thurston, Kim, and Lee stood on the stage, which was in the center of the room; Bob Bert and Steve Shelley each sat at full drum kits in separate corners of the room. King Coffey and Theresa from the Butthole Surfers filled the other two corners of the room with kettle drums. As the band played, all four drummers hammered away—in the dark. Amplifiers in the rest rooms blared distorted tape loops. Disturbing, gory slides by Richard Kern (a man with a spear through his throat, for example) flickered on a screen. A mesmerized audience basked in the massive, tremorous quadrophonic scape.

"To me, the most important aspect of their music at that time was just that they had these incredible buildups that were so beatifically escalating," says Lydia Lunch. "The whole sonic holocaust that they presented—every song was so long and so unrelenting and yet so beautiful at the same time. They were really some of the originators of making something so terrifying so beautiful.''

Another show set Sonic Youth and Das Damen—a local quartet whose 1986 debut EP was one of the first releases on Thurston Moore's own Ecstatic Peace label—in an outer-borough New York subway station, where the bands were forced to play under strobe lights. Steve's first out-of-town Sonic Youth gig was at Stash's in Columbus, Ohio.

By June, Steve's place in the band was secure. Appropriately enough, one of the first tasks required of Sonic Youth's new drummer was to attend a photo shoot for a *Village Voice* review. The notice, written by Rosemary Passatino, praised *Bad Moon Rising* as "heavy stuff" and characterized the band as having its "heart in the right place." The critical tide had begun to turn: "All this is pretty astounding," Passsatino added, "considering that Sonic Youth's previous output was sometimes transcendental and intelligent ('chaos is the future and beyond it is freedom') but frequently irritating, mean-spirited, or stupid ('sonic tooth?')."

No doubt Sonic Youth had improved with age, yet the New York music press, too, had changed. The independent world had turned inside out; the extremes of what had come before, mainly punk and hardcore, suddenly seemed less outré. And Sonic Youth had everything an ascendant American independent act required—a remarkably new sound, a wild stage show, and scene credibility. Everything, that is, except the one thing that could provide instant status within the mainstream recording industry—hits.

Sonic Youth's new lineup spent the following months touring the U.S. Local critics were quick to remark how Steve's skills far exceeded those of the average hardcore drummer. Steve, of course, avoided playing the adversarial role previous drummers had held in Sonic Youth. "There were all those old songs," Steve says. "I found it very easy to pick those up and put what little of myself in them that I did." The first track Steve recorded with the band was a cover of Alice Cooper's "Hallowed Be Thy Name" for the sound-track of *Lovedolls Superstar*, directed by a young filmmaker Sonic Youth had met in California named Dave Markey.

"I've always felt that we became more conventional when Steve joined the band," says Kim, "because his drumming is more agile. He was also more straight-ahead, so it became harder to sort of jam and write songs that way."

Back in Europe, Paul Smith scored the band a healthy number of publicity-generating gigs near the end of the year—one was a November concert performed on the sand at Brighton Beach, England. Another, at the Pandora's Box festival in Rotterdam, the Netherlands, placed Sonic Youth among an impressive roster of its heroes and contemporaries—Einstürzende Neubauten, Nick Cave and the Bad Seeds, Alex Chilton, Echo and the Bunnymen, and Crime and the City Solution.

In the meanwhile, the band planned a new twelve-inch single for release. "Flower" caused a minor sensation with Rough Trade, Blast First's distributor. Based on a poem Thurston wrote about a Puerto Rican calendar he found in a New York grocery, from which Kim extrapolated lyrics, the song "Flower" furthered Gordon's obsession with matters not fully addressed by establishment feminists. Its provocative lyrics—"Support the power of women / Use the power of men / Support the flower of women / Use the word fuck / The word is love"—caused less of a huff than the single's sleeve, a photocopy of the topless woman who appeared next to the words in the calendar. "It's not that the naked form is sexist in itself," Rough Trade's Geoff Travis told the NME, explaining why he chose not to release the single, which included "Halloween" as the B-side. "It just *looks* like another sexist piece of shit. . . . We don't want to be a party to their muddleheadedness."

Lee, Kim, and Thurston—miffed that Rough Trade had taken their seriously considered cover image for a gag—simply found a new European distributor, The Cartel, for the single and went ahead with their version.

*   *   *

''**They** never went out of their way to alienate me or cut me out of the picture," admits Gerard Cosloy. "To their credit, they were very honest about it. . . . It was never meant as some kind of statement on their part about me or even about Homestead, which turned out to get worse later on." But Cosloy couldn't help taking the news of Sonic Youth's departure from Homestead personally. He had never worked so hard or believed in a band so much.

Not only had Cosloy arranged the Sonic Youth's first real U.S. tour, sold them more albums and garnered them more publicity than ever before—he had made possible an event the band had long believed impossible. His efforts allowed the members of Sonic Youth to quit their day jobs.

But SST's appeal proved undeniable. "It was the fucking legacy of the early eighties," explains Ranaldo. "Every good record you had in your collection was on SST—the Minutemen, the Meat Puppets, Saccharine Trust. All those bands were our heroes and they were all on that label."

Cosloy soon had one more reason to resent Sonic Youth's departure from Homestead: Sonic Youth quickly convinced Dinosaur (later Dinosaur Jr.)—a Boston-area band fronted by Cosloy's friend J Mascis, and one of Cosloy's first Homestead acts—to jump ship and follow to SST. (Sonic Youth played Pied Piper once again when it subsequently pointed the Butthole Surfers, Big Black, and Dinosaur toward Paul Smith's Blast First for European distribution.)

Sonic Youth had been attracted to SST for all the right reasons. But SST's distinctive operation also came with distinctive ways of running things. Sonic Youth's ways clashed with SST's ways almost immediately upon signing, when Paul Smith released the double-disc live "bootleg" album *Walls Have Ears* on Not Records—an offshoot of Blast First created by Smith to release semiofficial live recordings of Blast First artists—without Sonic Youth's approval. *Walls Have Ears*, later hailed by critics as a triumphant document, consisted of live *Bad Moon* tapes (Bob Bert plays on one disc, Steve Shelley on the other) that the band had listened to and decided against releasing. That there had been such a gross misunderstanding between Sonic Youth and its British business representative proved an unfathomable prospect to the total-control stalwarts at SST. Fortunately, Sonic Youth's emergence as independent rock darlings coincided with the rise of a new and improved SST.

As popular as SST had become among college-age Americans, by as late as 1985 SST still had little contact with college radio, ostensibly the most reliable channel by which to expose new independent music. Early-eighties college radio in the United States usually chose to focus on British bands over American ones. Consequently, Black Flag had little faith in the tastes of college programmers and therefore rarely catered to them.

In the early eighties, West Coast record distributors such as Green World and Systematic were set up by young people to distribute independent releases, which at first were primarily imported independent releases. Later on, specialized American independents joined the fold—including folk labels (Rounder), reggae labels (Shanachie), and blues labels (Alligator). What made punk labels like SST, Alternative Tentacles, and Dischord different is that owners, musicians, and fans were all around the same age—that is, young.

By 1984, enough independent record stores that stocked independent rock-related releases existed across the country to support a network of small labels. What had begun merely as a means of existence had magically transformed itself into a grand triumph of youthful expression.

Within the underground (made underground primarily by a mainstream that chose to marginalize it), SST came closest to creating a reduced-scale star system. Each top-shelf SST act came equipped not only with an impressive set of material and a powerful live show, but also with a full-blown mythos. Artfully rendered album covers implied whole undiscovered worlds, worlds that came with their very own values, vocabularies, and icons.

The cover of Black Flag's 1985 album *In My Head* consists of a series of Raymond Pettibon drawings floating around a silhouette of a man's head. Like individual frames from lost comic books, the drawings hint at characters and stories. "An 'A' in the school of life," reads the caption to a drawing of a seedy-looking man in academic garb who appears to be removing a young woman's brassiere. A sketch of two hands cleaning a handgun is accompanied by the words "I've been good too long." On the back, a more mystifying one shows a man dressed only in briefs resting against a wall as a clothed arm shuts the door to the room: "I don't know any language," the caption states. Listeners coming to the album or group afresh were unsure whether the words were lyric fragments and the pictures moments from the lives of characters expounded upon within.

The sleeves of Meat Puppets albums such as 1983's *Meat Puppets II* and 1985's *Up on the Sun* featured colorful, primitive landscapes painted by lead singer and guitarist Curt Kirkwood. The fiery oil paintings gave good indication of what lurked within—country- and blues-inspired rock twisted by bouts with punk fury and hallucinogenic drugs.

Hüsker Dü's *Zen Arcade* (1983) and *New Day Rising* (1985) came complete with stark, steely-colored covers that hinted at the Minneapolis trio's grayish, impressionistic take on power pop's high-volume extremes.

By 1985's *3-Way Tie (For Last)*, even the Minutemen had found distinctive cover graphics (lead singer D. Boon painted the comical images of the band members as taxidermy victims on the front cover) to distinguish their work visually from their Lawndale, California, SST brethren. The photo of bassist Mike Watt suited up as a ghoulish Fidel Castro on the back says worlds about the brash but bright artistic perspective from which the band was hailing at that time.

Similarly, Sonic Youth's *EVOL* gave a glimpse into a world largely unfamiliar to the average young rock fan. The album's title, the word *love* spelled backward, was taken from the title of a video by New York visual artist Tony Oursler. In her 1985 "American Prayers" *Artforum* piece, Kim Gordon hailed one Oursler work, *Spin*

Out—an animated video in which a puppet is saved from disaster—for "poking fun at America's religion of optimism." EVOL, like Bad Moon Rising, referred back to the late 1960s as a crucial juncture in American history.

Oursler was concerning himself with imitating the ways in which America's mass media crafts its own ahistorical, hermetic versions of the past, present, and future. With EVOL, Sonic Youth made an analogous attempt at placing its encroaching quasi-celebrity within the mainstream notion of celebrity in 1986, à la Madonna, Michael Jackson, and Prince.

Considering EVOL's important role in Sonic Youth's transformation from a New York art-rock oddity to an independent-world supergroup, it's a frustratingly haphazard album. Nevertheless, its appealing mix of profane underground aesthetics and dreamy Hollywood references—as well as its assured navigation of decidedly experimental musical terrain—makes it a satisfying artifact of the schizophrenic mid-eighties.

"Expressway to Yr. Skull" (identified on the album cover as "Madonna, Sean and Me," and on the lyric sheet as "The Crucifixion of Sean Penn") is the album's centerpiece. "The Madonna thing was like, 'Into the Groove' was the big hit that year and it was just really infectious," says Moore. "I think one of the things was, 'There's something fun and exciting going on here.'

"Plus the fact that Madonna sort of came out of the New York downtown thing. We used to see her around. We made fun of her because we knew who she was. A friend of mine in New York went out with her a couple of times. I met her at Danceteria when she was sitting on his lap. She was really, really foxy. She was really glamorous. But when she would go on at Danceteria, we would leave. It was like, 'Let's get out of here.' Because she had put out a disco twelve-inch called 'Everybody.' And we just thought that was really stupid."

Within a year, Madonna Louise Ciccone became pop music's first female megastar, a worldwide cultural (and economic) force to be reckoned with. At the same time, independent rock blossomed. Black Flag, the Meat Puppets, the Replacements, Hüsker Dü, Soul Asylum, the Minutemen, Sonic Youth—while these groups couldn't match mainstream acts in sales, they more than superseded them in terms of recharging pop music, infusing it with more collective energy and content than it had experienced in over a decade. These bands and others like them were touring the country back and forth, bringing news of America's reclamation of its raucous rock roots. They, too, appeared unstoppable.

Then, in December 1985, the Minutemen's D. Boon met his end in a tragic van crash. "You know, with D. Boon I could hate the whole world, man," says Mike Watt, "because as long as I had him, it didn't matter." The Minutemen's lead singer, main songwriter, and guitarist, D. Boon represented the epitome of indie's alternative ways. The Minutemen had created their own musical and lyrical vocabularies, which they boisterously delivered in the shadows of a mainstream pop world they gladly and willfully ignored. "Mersh," as in commercial, was the word the group devised for pop music that pandered; and a life spent mostly on the road and in the small clubs made it easy to avoid the chart-toppers.

D. Boon's death provided a symbolic excuse for many independent acts to begin questioning their world's insular approach. For Mike Watt, of course, the passing of his closest childhood friend debilitated him. Taking solace in his romantic relationship with Kira Roessler, Black Flag's female bassist, Watt, too, began to look outward—and discovered Madonna. "I didn't really know about her until Kira turned me on to her," he says. "The last Black Flag tour she did [in 1985], Henry [Rollins] and those guys bought her all these fancy clothes to dress her up like Madonna." The Minutemen toured with Black Flag the first couple weeks of that tour, and when Roessler asked Watt what he thought of her getup, he had never even heard of Ms. Ciccone and her burgeoning career. After hearing some of Madonna's tapes, Watt became a convert.

In March 1986 Watt and Roessler headed East. (She left Black

Flag to study at Yale.) After dropping off Kira, Watt stayed a week with Gordon and Moore in New York, recuperating from what had proved to be the shock of his life. His New York friends invited them into Martin Bisi's studio, where they were laying down the basic tracks for EVOL. "We kind of took care of him," says Thurston. "He was still a little freaked out. D. Boon dying was a heavy thing." Watt ended up playing for the first time since D. Boon's passing.

"I always thought that [Madonna] was some kind of mersh version of punk," Watt says. "More than the Knack or Billy Idol—or the Clash. Those were really bad versions of punk. I think punk when it's mersh is more like Madonna used to be. And that's why I always kind of looked up to her in a weird way."

''**Expressway** to Yr. Skull'' remains as close to a signature song as Sonic Youth has ever mustered. Its first line—"We're gonna kill the California girls"—and its drawn-out, seemingly out-of-tune instrumentation perfectly captured the multi-hued moods of mid-1980s America's disenfranchised.

Yuppies, Reaganism, leveraged buyouts, unbridled acquisitiveness, willful ignorance—so much of what came to stand for the decade's excess bubbled over in 1986. As sung lackadaisically by Thurston, the song's next couplet ("We're gonna fire the exploding load / In the milkmaid maidenhead") seemed a mordant comment on the era's nearly pornographic penchant for sex, greed, and violence. The album's final track, "Expressway," evolves into a distorted vortex that culminates (on the original LP) in a locked groove, forcing the listener to remove the needle manually, perhaps another arch comment on how one ultimately determines one own's course.

If "Expressway" is EVOL's symphony, then "Starpower" is its étude. Kim Gordon sings the simple repetitive chorus as a worried schoolgirl who closes her eyes and hopes that thoughts of her celebrity idols will rescue her from ordinary existence. Kim later claimed the song was inspired by Joan Jett.

"Shadow of a Doubt," another whispery Gordon performance, takes its title from the 1943 Hitchcock film, but its lyrics clearly derive from another Hitchcock thriller, 1951's *Strangers on a Train*. Some are actual lines from the movie, which tells the tale of a man who tries to exchange murder motives with a man he meets on a train. The way its koto-like guitar phrases ease into a swirling maelstrom of rapidly strummed arpeggios perfectly complements the album's theme of rapture in the face of violence.

A cacophonous guitar pastiche that was constructed in the studio, "In the Kingdom #19," showcases Lee Ranaldo's narrative of a gruesome car crash. Mike Watt's cameo on bass contributes an added eerie dimension to what emerged as an oblique eulogy for D. Boon. While Lee recorded his voice-over for "Kingdom," Thurston skittered into the recording booth, tossed a lighted brick of firecrackers, and escaped. "All of a sudden you couldn't see Lee anymore 'cause it's all white smoke in there," Martin Bisi says. "And Lee comes out and I mean that was actually the first time I'd seen them in a horrible fight. We're sitting there for twenty minutes as Lee is completely fuming and Thurston didn't even say anything. Then we listened back to the tape—and I had a compressor on the mike, so it sort of recorded." One can hear the firecrackers explode and Lee scream midway through. The band decided to preserve Lee's genuine horror as part of the finished track.

"Green Light" couches a simple love-song lyric in an extended instrumental, the first glimpse at Shelley-propelled arrangements to come.

EVOL marked Sonic Youth's musical transformation—Steve Shelley's precise and complex drumming only served to clarify the groups's more streamlined pop structures and fanned guitar patterns—but more importantly, it signaled a seismic shift in pop music's firmament. For Sonic Youth, the appeal of hardcore—by 1985 a widespread and codified movement—had subsided. Suddenly what was going on in the mainstream seemed more provocative.

MTV had grabbed an important spot in the music culture. "It

allowed for all these previously detestable mainstream characters to be interesting all of a sudden," says Lee Ranaldo. "We found ourselves listening to and interested in people like Prince and Janet Jackson and Madonna and Bruce Springsteen." Rather than feeling threatened by this new, even more diluted presentation of pop culture, Sonic Youth had simply chosen to embrace it.

Not that Sonic Youth's music was in any danger of veering toward the pop charts. Back at Martin Bisi's, the band pursued a deliberately low-tech approach. Even though the occasional song, such as "Shadow of a Doubt"—for which Gordon spent a full day recording the multiple tracks of screams on the chorus—required overdubs, most of finished cuts are first takes. The band's instruments alone prevented the music from taking on anything remotely resembling a pop sheen.

"They literally had like thirty-five or forty guitars upstairs in my living room," Bisi says, "covering every wall and all the couches and chairs. And each guitar had like, a string missing, or two strings missing, or maybe only had one string and was covered with stickers or was banged up or torn apart and everything."

Soaking up Top 40 radio instead of the latest cutting-edge noise rock in fact added to EVOL's bristly texture. The lyrics to "Tom Violence," the album's opening track, describe some vaguely proscribed S&M nightmare, yet Thurston's forward-moving melody— slightly off-kilter but traditional in structure—implies a pop song's detachment. "Marilyn Moore" achieves a similar result from the opposite direction: Its lyrics, cowritten by the band with Lydia Lunch, allude to a Marilyn Monroe–type figure while its music mirrors her mental state. ("It's always a headache the size of a tow truck.")

But what of Lung Leg, the irascible young woman pictured on EVOL's front cover? The quintessential "death rock" moll, she was the star of a number of Super-8 film shorts, including Submit to Me, by filmmaker Richard Kern.

As a young art major fresh out of University of North Carolina at Chapel Hill, Kern made his way to New York in 1980, because "we were taught that everything that happens that is art is in New York." As a student, Kern produced a number of different fanzines on and off since 1975—alternately sordid and sardonic affairs with titles such as *The Heroin Addict*, *The Valium Addict*, *Dumb Fucker*, *Car and Truck*, and *A Key for the Streets of Fear*. A couple started off as music fanzines but they all later progressed into repositories for fiction, drawings, and photos. For *Streets of Fear*, Kern placed poetry made out of headlines from the *New York Post* alongside his own photos.

With encouragement from Scott and Beth B, the doyens of New York's late-seventies Super-8 movement, Kern began making his own Super-8 reels in 1983. Super-8, recognizable as the home-movie camera popular before the advent of the Camcorder, produces a grainy, jerky, crude-quality footage later duplicated ad nauseam by MTV video directors. In 1983 Kern had little competition.

Aiming to shock and culling his aesthetic from poorly filmed footage of the Sex Pistols performing live, Kern began to fashion a series of disturbing Super-8 shorts, starring his downtown New York friends. *Stray Dogs* is a humorous if unnerving account of a twitching straggler, played by the late artist David Wojnarowicz, who follows an artist home and suddenly starts spurting blood and losing limbs in the artist's studio. When a transvestite slits his/her wrists in the bathtub in the archly titled *Thrust in Me*, a character played by underground film star Nick Zedd, upon discovering her, pulls down his pants and ejaculates into his/her mouth. Kern's malevolent "you had to be there" sense of humor made him an instant draw on the downtown New York circuit.

Lydia Lunch soon caught wind of Kern's doings. "I hooked up with Richard when I moved back to New York from London and was looking for someone to do blood-and-guts performances with me," Lunch says. "I would do spoken-word nights at the Pyramid with four or five other people and Kern would jump in with his blood-and-guts explosions—he was doing a lot of fake bloodletting at that point." *The Right Side of My Brain*, an early Lunch-Kern film collaboration, stars Lunch as narrator and as a woman who gets serviced by a number of male and female friends (Clint Ruin, Henry Rollins, and Sally Ven Yu Berg) in an effort to satisfy existential urges. Saved from being purely pornographic solely by its art-conscious perspective and its antisex writhings, *Brain* draws a rather clear line between Sonic Youth's cool fascination with Kern's world and the experiences of those who inhabit it full-time.

Through Lunch, Kern met Sonic Youth. Sonic Youth asked Kern to provide gore effects for its "Death Valley '69" video, which Judith Barry was slated to direct. Kern agreed to participate if he could codirect. Two cuts of the video exist—Kern's is choppier, gorier, and includes snippets, from *Submit to Me*, of Lung Leg slashing at the camera with a switchblade.

"We never got involved so much with Kern that we became part of his dementoid coterie," says Thurston. "But Kern wasn't really like that. He did get hung up into a weird world, I know that. But he was very scientific about it."

Kern met the pseudonymous Lung Leg through Cassandra Stark, a friend of Nick Zedd's. He immediately took to the young actress's distinct look, topped off by a luring but demonic leer—she could have been mistaken for a young female member of Manson's Family. Lung Leg's death-rock demeanor inspired a number of Kern shorts, including *You Killed Me First*, an addled teen's parable of revenge, and *Submit to Me*, an S&M fantasia.

"We thought Richard was really talented," says Kim. "But we were not into the drugs and the whole East Village scum-rock scene. Probably a lot of people got that impression. But Richard himself had a real sense of humor. To him, his movies were hilarious. A lot of people didn't get that. I guess they thought it was our goth period."

"I was kind of into creating this mysterious myth, in the way that SST did with Pettibon," Thurston says. "It really did create this kind of weird in-house dialect. Pettibon's drawings were just unlike anything—they were just so loaded with ideas. We knew Kern was, too—some of the stuff he was doing was very controversial. And we were really into throwing that part of the New York underworld up into the record racks.''

10 | The World According to Sonic Youth

''IN THE FIRST YEARS WITH SST, PEOPLE IN EUROPE SAW US AS A BUNCH OF HEROIN ADDICTS—THEY'D LISTEN TO THE MUSIC AND LOOK AT PICTURES OF US AND THINK THAT WE MUST BE INTO HARD NARCOTICS. WE ALWAYS THOUGHT THAT WAS REALLY FUNNY, WHEN PEOPLE WOULD MEET US AND FIND OUT THAT WE DIDN'T HAVE TRACK MARKS ON OUR ARMS.''

—LEE RANALDO

By most indicators, 1986 was the year that Sonic Youth could have begun resting on its laurels. A contract with SST, a varied, innovative musical style, rave reviews, distribution and touring networks in place to conquer the world—the band had succeeded in turning its multiple interests and obsessions into a livelihood. Yet Sonic Youth chose to do the very opposite.

From the very time when the public's perception of Sonic Youth first galvanized, the band's members set about dashing it to bits.

Remaining true to their individual and collective sensibilities, the band, in theory, never had any qualms about messing around with its image. The problem, however, remained that few people outside of the band's inner circle were aware of the band's behind-the-scenes chicanery. Despite Sonic Youth's lyrics, which oftentimes consisted of strings of free-associated in-jokes and self-referential puns, the band was largely perceived as a ''serious'' band. In the world of American independent rock music, New York represented high art, ambition, detachedness, pretentiousness, jaded dispositions—all the things the scene railed against. All the things implied by the sour countenances worn by the members of Sonic Youth in most published photos at the time.

Never mind that Thurston's onstage banter increasingly consisted of jokey, anti-rock-posturing asides. ("This is not a rehearsal." "We shoot up on mayonnaise before we come on.") Never mind that the band had confessed its aesthetically incorrect allegiances to Madonna and Bruce Springsteen to the British music weeklies. Never mind that the nude pinup on the cover of the "Halloween" twelve-inch was meant as a laugh in the face of the self-serious avant-garde. Forget the fact that only one member of the band (Steve Shelley) could remotely still qualify as the "youth" in the band's name. In the minds of many in the larger audience the band had begun courting, Sonic Youth was a rough-and-tumble bunch of New York snobs.

The two videos the band had made didn't help any, either. The "Death Valley '69" Kern clip was too gratuitously bloody to be played in full on MTV; a crude video of EVOL's "Shadow of a Doubt," made by young director Kevin Kerslake paired artful but static footage of Kim riding atop the image of a moving train. Like most bands outside of the mainstream in 1986, Sonic Youth relied primarily on its live performances to communicate its vision.

Lee and Thurston still regularly attacked their guitars with drumsticks and screwdrivers, although their machinations rarely deteriorated into sheer chaos anymore. Lee's graceful guitar moves more frequently offset Thurston's studied awkwardness, their guitar necks tracing the air like two parrying fencing foils. At center stage, Kim had become a more willing sex symbol—she no longer wore glasses, and had dyed her hair blonde and grown it longer so that it wrapped around her gaunt face as she jumped up and down while hammering at her bass with her fist. Steve's square-toed appearance provided a clever contrast to his relentless drumming style. Onstage the band existed as four distinct personalities finely discernible to the naked eye in both appearance and performance style.

"They were tremendously funny," recalls Paul Smith. "It wasn't till probably EVOL that we got any pictures of them where they were actually smiling or having a good time. Anytime they got in front of a camera, they'd all do this very stern face. They obviously had that whole New York thing—these were people who would wear sunglasses when, in England, it was really quite overclouded. But it was part of that cool that they had at that point.

"There was a lot of laughing involved, but that was never apparent in the press. All the press was very, 'This is serious art. Look at these stern-looking people.' Which I always thought was a shame."

At the tail end of March 1986 EVOL sessions, the band took the first real step toward loosening its public image. Since Kim and Thurston had hit it off so well with their erstwhile house guest Mike Watt, his presence in the studio during the recording process was welcomed. According to Watt, Sonic Youth's recording process made the Minutemen's seem downright reactionary. "They didn't really have songs together," he says. "You know, they had like, parts. It wasn't flippant—it wasn't just to do it. It was another technique."

On whim, the band decided to record a cover of "Bubblegum"—an arcane seventies novelty tune cowritten by Kim Fowley, the infamous southern California songwriter, scenemaker, and producer (he also played Svengali to the Runaways, Joan Jett's first band). Instead of laboring over a brand-new arrangement, Thurston slipped a pair of headphones over Watt's head and had him play bass along with the original record. After the band added the other parts using the same technique (Kim sings lead), the original was erased.

Spurred by talking over the Madonna obsession they shared with Watt, the band recorded its own version of a Madonna hit—"Into the Groove," from the soundtrack to the 1985 movie *Desperately Seeking Susan*.

Thus was born Ciccone Youth, a post-postmodern tribute to Madonna Louise Ciccone, known to her minion fans simply as

Madonna. Again, the band played along with the original record-ing—this time, though, they kept part of the original's instrumen-tal track playing in the final mix, redubbed "Into the Groovey."

Rather than trashing the song—the obvious ploy for an under-ground act—Sonic Youth remained faithful to the original version. Moore sings over the percolating dance track, sounding somewhat bored but by no means hateful. Bits of Madonna's vocal seep in on occasion, the band plays crunchy metal guitar chords that accentu-ate the song's melody—everyone involved felt the end result to be quite entertaining.

"We did another mix that was much more of a dance mix, where we left in a lot more of Madonna's track," says Martin Bisi. "There was lot more consistent rhythm and it didn't fuck up as much—it was almost something you could have played in a club."

"Into the Groovey" was released as a twelve-inch through Blast First in England and as a seven-inch on New Alliance, Mike Watt's SST-distributed label. Back in California, Mike Watt recorded his own rocked-up version of "Burnin' Up," another Madonna single, at home on a four-track. These two tracks, along with "Tuff Titty Rap," Thurston's lame but good-natured attempt at a hip-hop track, comprised Ciccone Youth's first release.

"Our version is the exact same tempo as hers. It just sounds slower," Thurston told NME later that year. "We sort of feel like we're doing things alongside Madonna, but on a different level, maybe. It's like our arms are around her. And she knows what's goin' on."

The band was surprised as anybody when the single climbed the U.K. singles chart later in the year. "Into the Groovey" immedi-ately appealed to Britain's fickle pop audience. NME declared "Into the Groovey" its single of the year and gave Sonic Youth (or rather, Madonna) a cover—"Madonna on a Time Bomb?" the cover line read—in December 1986.

The recording of EVOL was followed up by a full-fledged American tour—this time done the SST way. Global Network, SST's in-house booking agency, managed to keep Sonic Youth on the road for virtually the rest of 1986.

The new songs were debuted live at the Continental Club on April 12 in Austin, Texas. Sonic Youth's EVOL summer tour began at CBGBs on June 13 and ended in Boston at the end of July. From Washington, D.C., the band headed down South, playing many of the clubs it had hit on the ill-attended Savage Blunder tour in 1982. This time, however, the band arrived to packed houses in Raleigh and Atlanta; the turnout in Athens, Georgia, was less impressive.

Carlos Van Hijfte—a Dutch agent who had previously arranged European bookings for the band—was flown over to act as Sonic Youth's de facto tour manager.

In Tucson, Arizona, Sonic Youth hooked up with its SST heroes and now labelmates Saccharine Trust. As others had done previously, the Backdoor club in Tucson advertised the show as an all-ages hardcore lineup. This time, though, no one showed— 1986 hardcore kids were unlikely to mistake Sonic Youth for their own. One of the club's owners allegedly pulled a gun on Carlos and refused to pay either band. Even SST, a small label at the peak of its powers, could not always prevent its bands from getting fleeced.

Upon arriving in California, the band met up with the folks at SST. For the first time, Sonic Youth felt part of a community. Of course, the band still stood out.

For one, the group hadn't been part of SST since its beginnings like the rest of the label's top-shelf acts. In addition, being SST's first East Coast band, Sonic Youth was perceived largely as a freaky art band by its West Coast compatriots. Conversely, the members of Sonic Youth found the post-hippie aesthetic of SST acts like the Meat Puppets somewhat alien. Sonic Youth simply couldn't conceal the fact that it hadn't begun as a bunch of kids banging out three-chord romps in their parents' garages.

At the Roxy in Hollywood, the band was joined onstage by Mike Watt for "Starpower"; Watt had formed fIREHOSE, a new trio featuring Minutemen drummer George Hurley and guitarist Ed Crawford (a.k.a. Ed fROMOHIO)—a Minutemen fan from Ohio who tracked down the band's remaining members after he heard D. Boon died and convinced them to form a new group.

In Seattle, Sonic Youth played with Green River—a long-haired punk band on Homestead, whose Iggy-inspired lead vocalist Mark Arm and guitarist Steve Turner later formed the archetypal grunge outfit Mudhoney. Traveling by van, the band spent the rest of July wending its way back East.

A mid-July gig in Minneapolis found members of Soul Asylum in the audience. Sonic Youth was regaled with stories of Hüsker Dü's signing to Warner Bros., one of the first independent-to-major singings of note: complete creative control; an office for Bob Mould at the label.

In Milwaukee, Dinosaur joined the tour. Chicago, Detroit, Indianapolis, Columbus, Cleveland—Sonic Youth performed to small, sweaty clubs packed with young fans, many of them newcomers to Sonic Youth. In Buffalo, New York, Lee joined Dinosaur onstage to sing Neil Young's "Cortez the Killer."

Steve Albini, who once had arranged a few shows for Sonic Youth in the Chicago area for Gerard Cosloy, and traveled in the same circles as Sonic Youth during that time as a member of Big Black, remembers 1986 as a remarkably exciting time: "It seemed like every week or so a totally different and totally mind-blowing album was coming out. There were records coming from all quarters on independent labels and from bands that nobody ever heard of that were blowing people's minds—and none of which sounded like each other."

The independent world's improvised structures were slowly becoming permanent ones; somewhere deep in mid-eighties Reagan America, rock music suddenly seemed as establishment as Hollywood or television. Even mavericks of style, like Sonic Youth, appeared to be at an aesthetic impasse.

Sonic Youth's popularity had grown enough by the middle of 1986 that the band received an offer to compose a movie soundtrack—and was just hungry enough for change to accept it. After the EVOL summer tour, the band agreed to be flown out to Los Angeles to spend two expenses-paid months recording an original soundtrack for Made in USA, ostensibly a road-trip movie with a cause, starring Christopher Penn (Sean's brother) and Lori Singer.

"We were given the money to work in a studio with a videotape of the movie—I guess we felt really cool about that at the time," Lee Ranaldo says. "Just the fact that we were asked to do it was a bit of credibility."

Made in USA was directed by Ken Friedman, a screenwriter (Heart Like a Wheel) being given his first chance at the helm. Friedman had heard the band's music and decided to give them a chance. A tale of two misfits from Centralia, Pennsylvania—the real-life site of toxic underground coal fires resulting from strip-mining—who drive cross-country, meet a wild young woman, and find industrial waste wherever they go, Made in USA is a disappointing piece of work. The studio cut deleted most of the film's social conscience and leaned toward its teen-titillation side. "The movie's terrible," admits Steve Shelley.

"Secret Girls," from EVOL, plays over the opening credits. Only little bits of the atmospheric improvisations the band created for the film remain in the final cut. The movie never made it to theaters, although it remains available on video.

K i m Gordon's old friend Mike Kelley provided Sonic Youth with yet another shot at engineering a soundtrack. In December 1986 Kelley invited the band to provide sound effects and incidental music for a three performances of his piece Plato's Cave, Rothko's Chapel, Lincoln's Profile at Artists Space in New York. Kelley recited an hour-and-a-half poem he had written and dramatized with the help of actress Molly Cleator while the band droned on.

Plato's Cave had begun "as a project about the possessive," Kelley said in one interview, "about how ascribing a quality of possession to something would equalize everything. Like, if I said that this was an exhibition of everything from Lincoln's house, it links all this random stuff together that has no link except as a possible way to psychoanalyze Lincoln. Everybody asked me why I picked those three people. I made a whole list of possessives that were in common usage and I just picked the three that sounded best together. . . . Then I wove a set of associations between them.''

The band got together with Kelley a couple days before the performance. Kelley went through the script and told the band what he wanted at certain cues—a chunky rock sound, a bang, a spooky noise.

"I wanted to play with rock staging," Kelley says. "For a lot of the performance, they were behind a curtain, so you didn't even see them. I was trying to play against this rock-star thing, where there's a shift of focus to somebody who in normal kind of rock-theatric terms would be the singer." Kelley's actions made him the center of focus—the singer, as it were—even though Sonic Youth's accompaniment accentuated his actions and words with kabuki-like synergy, rather than in the traditional way in which a rock band interacts with a vocalist.

As an art student at University of Michigan at Ann Arbor, Kelley had formed a proto-punk band with fellow student and future artist Jim Shaw, called Destroy All Monsters. He and Shaw moved to Los Angeles to attend graduate school at the California Institute of Arts (CalArts) in time to witness the scene's sea change from glam rock to punk. "In southern California—unlike on the East Coast, where there was more of an integration of art activity and music activity—punk was a teenage phenomenon," Kelley says. "It was really anti-intellectual. They didn't want to hear anything besides triple-time hardcore."

Not that the first wave of L.A. punk didn't have its share of avant-garde practitioners. In fact, the late-seventies Los Angeles scene cut a wide swath—from the conceptual (the Screamers, Nervous Gender, Boyd Rice, and Monitor) to the more straightforward (the Deadbeats, the Weirdos, and the Germs).

Kelley attempted to form another band, the Poetics, with fellow artists John Miller and Tony Oursler in 1978; their one club performance was summarily rejected by the Long Beach punkers in attendance. Discouraged, the group disbanded almost immediately. (By coincidence, though, John Miller later joined a formative version of the Coachmen in New York. And for a brief time, the Coachmen even rehearsed and performed Poetics material. Thurston didn't know Kim or Mike Kelley then—a testament, perhaps, to the tight-knit nature of the Los Angeles–New York underground-art nexus of the day.) "There was very little crossover between the art and the punk, except on a certain kind of club-performance level," he says. Short of a few profoundly underground outfits (the Doo Doo 'Ettes, Airway) that played non-punk venues such as L.A.'s rough-trade gay clubs, the two worlds rarely intermingled.

If only for the Los Angeles punk scene's relentless focus on fashion, the two worlds eventually collided. "People were trying to think of bands as sign systems," says Kelley. "The way they looked had just as much to do with it as anything else. The whole thing was a package, and people were really aware of that."

Kelley soon grew frustrated with the limitations inherent in keeping a musical group together; he began concentrating on individual performance pieces. "I wasn't interested in pleasing teenagers anymore," he says. "Even when I was making noise music, it was really about pissing them off—then it got to the point where you couldn't piss 'em off anymore." He met Kim Gordon heading in the opposite direction. Kelley's working-class Detroit roots had sufficiently inoculated him against overtly populist notions; Gordon saw a contemporary art world fraught with irrelevant class distinctions that were of little concern to pop-music fans.

Kelley had seen Sonic Youth perform during the *Bad Moon Rising* tour. "What I liked about them was how controlled they were," he says. "They had these huge, long walls of sound, but it was very complex. It wasn't like you took it as one sound: You had to listen in to it. They were really engrossing in that way. It wasn't like seeing a Throbbing Gristle show, where it was a big, huge wall of noise, but you didn't go into it—it sort knocks you on your butt and that itself was a physical experience. With Sonic Youth, it was this big veil of sound that you could kind of penetrate. With the two guitars, this big kind of swirling thing—it was actually very seductive."

Fall 1986 brought another cross-country jaunt, the Flaming Telepaths tour, that paired Sonic Youth with fIREHOSE. Saint Louis; Ann Arbor; Columbia, and Kansas City, Missouri; Norman, Oklahoma; Austin, Texas; Baton Rouge; Tampa—SST had provided Sonic Youth with the most rigorous touring schedule the band had ever mustered.

Middle America's club audiences treated the enthusiastic but weary band well. Yet long, close-quartered stretches in a van on the open road had a dramatic equalizing effect—clocking miles made Sonic Youth, for the first time, feel like virtually every other rock band on the road. In Lee Ranaldo's diary of the tour, later published in *Forced Exposure*, he describes the band being invited to stay at a college student's house en route to Kansas City: "I was reminded of the way kids live in college again—it was wet and damp, dirty and unheated, the electricity was mostly not working, one bulb swinging from a socket, and generally it was the last thing needed after an exhausting and sweaty night onstage."

Nevertheless, the tour elicited increasingly impressive Sonic Youth performances.

11 | Here Come the Cyberpunks

''THERE WAS A BEAUTY IN THE TRASH OF THE ALLEYS I HAD NEVER NOTICED BEFORE; MY VISION NOW SEEMED SHARPENED RATHER THAN IMPAIRED. AS I WALKED ALONG IT SEEMED TO ME THAT THE FLATTENED BEER CANS AND PAPERS AND WEEDS AND JUNK MAIL HAD BEEN ARRANGED INTO PATTERNS; THESE PATTERNS, WHEN I SCRUTINIZED THEM, LAY DISTRIBUTED SO AS TO COMPROMISE A VISUAL LANGUAGE.''
—FROM *RADIO FREE ALBEMUTH*, BY PHILIP K. DICK

''THE SYMBOLS OF THE DIVINE SHOW UP IN OUR WORLD INITIALLY AT THE TRASH STRATUM.''
—FROM *VALIS*, BY PHILIP K. DICK

Much has been made in the press of the image of William Gibson sitting at a battered 1927 Hermes 2000 portable typewriter, clacking out the pages to the definitive work of cyberpunk literature, 1984's Neuromancer. Some futurist, critics scoffed.

Yet few of the snickerers have allowed for how apt a metaphor the image has become for all that has arrived in the wake of its publication. The rough textures conjured up by notions of raw contact between body and computer parts are responsible for most of what's wonderful in the ensuing culture. It's no wonder sci-fi writer Philip K. Dick—dead by 1982, long before the term "cyberpunk" was even coined—is enjoying a renaissance. It's the eternally unlikely prospect of merging mind with metal that fuels cyberpunk's most engrossing and entertaining literature.

Ever notice how last year's "cutting-edge" science-fiction movies (check out 1987's Robocop) look twenty years old today? By deciding to record the archly futuristic Sister, Sonic Youth's second and final album for SST, at Manhattan's Sear Studio, a virtual temple to the finest in low-fi recording technology, the band insured itself against such a fate.

Sister sounds like tomorrow's music recorded yesterday. A time capsule filled to the brim with the detritus of fifties pulp science fiction, sixties acid rock, seventies punk obscura, and topped off with a warm dollop of sheer pop innovation that even today seems ahead of its time, Sister effortlessly flits back and forth between the archaic and revolutionary. It also divides old Sonic Youth from new Sonic Youth.

By 1987 Sonic Youth had become precociously aware of its place. Having survived the synth-pop revolution and hip-hop's lock-grip on the future, rock and roll's last greatest hope seemingly set out to prove the impossible—that electric guitars somehow figured into pop music's tomorrow. "Sometimes it's amazing that anything happens," Kim Gordon told Spin. "Like when you're in a plane and you realize that there's like three hundred people with you, and there's all this baggage. It doesn't seem very aerodynamic. It feels like you're on a boat, and it's flying. It's just amazing, and at the same time it seems so old-fashioned. It doesn't parallel the level of communication most of us operate on, like with fax machines. It seems almost archaic."

Philip Kindred Dick, born in 1928, grew up in the calm eye of Berkeley's burgeoning bohemia. His fraternal twin, Jane Charlotte, died soon after birth.

A quick study but a troubled student, the young Dick got hooked on the pulp science-fiction magazines popular among teenage boys during the late forties and early fifties and, in turn, fostered his own outsider literary persona. Throughout a tumultuous surburban life which spanned five marriages, scores of speed-fueled binges, and a history of depression and hallucinations, Dick managed to churn out over fifty novels and hundreds of short stories of varying quality.

He is best known to the general public through Hollywood screen adaptations of his works—the 1982 movie *Blade Runner* approximates his novel *Do Androids Dream of Electric Sheep?*; 1990's *Total Recall*, starring Arnold Schwarzenegger, is an unlikely reworking of the 1966 short story "We Can Remember It for You Wholesale." Dick developed a unique sphere of reference which combined wisdoms of the Western literary canon with shards of Eastern mysticism, contemporary situations, and the standard tropes of sci-fi trash.

Clunky, elegant, visionary, opaque—all are fitting descriptions of Dick's prose at one time or another. Dick classics such as *A Scanner Darkly*, *The Man in the High Castle*, *Radio Free Albemuth*, and *Valis* raise hackdom to an art. Tripped up with vaguely outdated hipster lingo and deliciously paranoid government-conspiracy theories, these novels buzz and crackle with half-received, half-probable communiqués. Long ignored by high-minded readers (due in part to turgid syntax and occasionally illogical narrative runs, but also for working in a lowbrow genre form), Dick has recently enjoyed a literary upgrade thanks to Vintage reprints of his major novels, long unavailable.

In a 1989 biography of Dick, author Lawrence Sutin lamented that the loopy maverick's books "continue to be shelved in the whorehouse." But judging from a recent *New Republic* cover story and a handful of hasty reappraisals from younger critics, Dick's vision of the future as an imperfect technological utopia—fraught with the same kinds of niggling annoyances that plague any era—has struck a communal chord. A whirl on the Internet, for example, today's version of the electronic bulletin board, is a maddening tangle of fiber-optic phenomena and disarmingly human disorder.

Ever the pop-culture junkies, the members of Sonic Youth mined Dick's work, both for reflection and flavor, way back in 1987, the year *Sister* was released.

"I didn't grow up as a science-fiction reader at all," says Thurston. But when Moore read *Radio Free Albemuth*, a newly discovered Dick manuscript posthumously published in 1986, he got hooked. "It was really great reading a book that was written as pop science fiction and yet had characters and incidents that were routine. And then getting caught up in these philosophical experiences." (Ranaldo *did* grow up reading science fiction; his tastes ran more toward Gibson's *Neuromancer*.) The new voices of science fiction—Lewis Shiner, Lucius Shepard, Rudy Rucker—many of whom were Sonic Youth's contemporaries, became popular reading among the band's members.

In the meanwhile, incessant touring and interviews (primarily with the enraptured British press) had acculturated the band's sense of self. *Sister* reflected a band that had devised a brand-new musical system and learned to work within its constraints. No longer did songs emerge out of pure chaos—Moore and Ranaldo had developed a regular cycle of tunings from which bona fide melodies regularly emerged.

Yet songwriting itself continued to be an arduous process. "With *Sister*, there were a bunch of songs that went through so many permutations that if you listen to rehearsal tapes you'd be amazed," says Lee. "We were really getting into this structural thing with *Sister*, and even more so with *Daydream Nation*, where if you talk about sections of songs in terms of the A and the B section, there'd be songs that would be like A, B, C, B, D, E, A, F. We'd actually have charts written down in front of us with just big letters—it would be a huge, long chart. It would get to the point where it would be so out of hand. We'd say, 'Listen we just have to take some letters out.' "

Thurston was attracted to Dick's works for their literate but plainspoken nuance. The wildly imaginative writer's notion of schizophrenia was more than a space-age freak-out—it was a homemade version of the "mind's reality versus the world's reality" quandary.

Moore, too, was inspired by Dick's everyman approach to philosophy and religion. "You didn't really have to read Kant or Hegel or the Bible or other things—you could read Philip K. Dick and get a lot of ideas through one writer," he says. Yet Sonic Youth's main lyricist, having read interviews in which Dick explained that his later works had been based on real-life experiences and put to page in trancelike states, also found himself freed by accounts of Dick's writing technique. "I always liked the idea that writing lyrics was more of a subconscious attitude, in a way. It really came to fruition while reading Philip K. Dick for a couple of years, and also while writing *Sister*."

Sister's ringing opening chords are almost immediately flattened to a dull thrum, their undeniable pop potential quashed by the limits of warm but frayed analog equipment. Steve Shelley's drums snap sharply on one beat, on the next they sound shrouded in thick flannel blankets. The album's opener, "Schizophrenia," takes its lyrical cues from the real-life details of Philip K. Dick's life, as filtered through *Radio Free Albemuth* and *Valis*, his penultimate works. (The album title itself refers to Dick's lost twin sibling.)

In March 1974 the real-life Dick answered his door to receive a Darvon prescription for a toothache. What he saw was "a girl with black, black hair and large eyes." Around her neck was a gold necklace in shape of an ancient Christian fish sign. Dick claimed the fish sign triggered memories of his celestial origins, mainly, a dual consciousness. Consequently, Dick's later novels explored the experiences of two personages somehow intertwined. In the cases of *Radio Free Albemuth*, written in 1976, and 1982's *Valis*, he wrote himself and his alter ego, as characters, into the books. Dick spent the rest of his real and fictional lives searching for truth and meaning in the fragmentary clues. The death of his sister, Jane, he decided, had triggered primordial mental impulses.

While most critics observed that *Sister* was Sonic Youth's most cohesive work—an album more easily comparable to the "concept" albums churned out by sixties rock legends—in fact, the album was every bit as open-ended as the band's previous work. Only two songs, "Schizophrenia" and "Stereo Sanctity," are in fact inspired by Philip K. Dick's writing. (A couple lines, such as "I can't get laid cuz everyone is dead," from "Stereo Sanctity," are straight out of *Albemuth* and *Valis*.) Yet the theme played out in those two songs—exploring dual realities as a way of finding yourself— permeates the whole album.

In "Schizophrenia," Kim and Thurston sing the parts of two entwined personalities (Thurston's part borrows the Christian-fish incident from Dick), each equally inquisitive and convinced of its own independence.

"At the time, it was a really heavy thing to claim that you had a dead twin," Thurston says. "If you hung out with Lydia Lunch, that was her claim; Nick Cave also claimed this." Elvis Presley also had a twin brother who died at birth.

"Stereo Sanctity" borrows Dick's pseudoscientific vocabulary to imagine a world where electronic currents run through everything; one's mind and the sky alternately light up as rickety connections fizzle and pop. "Sanctity" is also one of Sonic Youth's first perfectly crafted pop songs, written within the set of musical techniques created by the band. The way it speeds ahead, lurches to a stop, only to take off again—all the while dropping fragments of rattling, hissy guitar distortion—implies an implausible yet spooky *War of the Worlds* notion of a supernatural invasion. Sonic Youth had finally succeeded in funneling its avant-garde ideas about rock music through a conventional song structure. Yes, *Sister* engendered visions of spaceships, computer brains, and speed-induced hallucinations; but these spaceships were clunky, hand-built affairs; these computer brains were held together by Scotch tape; and these hallucinations were not warm dreams but carnivorous pests, closer to the imaginary bugs that plague the drug-frazzled Jerry Fabin in *A Scanner Darkly*.

For all its nods to cyberpunk "theory," *Sister* also possesses the first seasoned examples of Kim, Lee, and Thurston writing and singing as distinct and developed creative characters.

"(I Got a) Catholic Block" and "White Cross" are Thurston's nods to his own upbringing. The product of a Catholic mother and a father who counted the study of religion among his scholarly pursuits, Thurston admits both songs, especially "Catholic Block," were essentially a gag. "I always liked the use of Catholic-boy imagery—the starched white shirt and a plaid tie—rather than goth imagery as a punk device."

"Tuff Gnarl" again found Sonic Youth using a conventional song structure to suit the band's distinctively off-kilter guitar parts. Moore sings the song's lyrics, a nonsense narrative composed of phrases culled from music reviews he himself had once written in his Killer fanzine, as if they're the rhapsodic tones of a jilted lover.

"Beauty Lies in the Eye" is the rare case of a musical hook devised by Lee that was later taken over by Kim. Her combustion-themes lyrics ("Do you want to see the explosions in my eye?") complement the diffuse instrumentation, making for a love song that manages to find grandeur in violent affection. "Pacific Coast Highway" is a bumpy ride, an S&M trip fueled by Gordon's glee-fully coercive come-ons. (Its story, the tale of a hitchhiker on the highway being picked up by a serial killer, seems vaguely reminiscent of a Richard Kern short.) Slowly but surely, Kim was asserting her fine-tuned aesthetic sense.

"Pipeline/Kill Time" features Lee Ranaldo's first vocal turn since "I Dreamed I Dream." Lee, as it turns out, possessed the only naturally melodic voice (a true tenor). And "Pipeline" helped define him as the band's time traveler. Rather than adhering to a standard verse-chorus-verse pop structure, "Pipeline" accelerates as if being chased. Lines such as "Run ten thousand miles and then think of me" seem to allude to the cyberspace of Gibson's Neuromancer. The track also marks the first—and one of the few—instances the band has used a synthesizer; Thurston plays an old Moog original, courtesy of Walter Sear, in the fadeout.

Kim and Thurston paired up on "Cotton Crown" to perform their first duet. With its oblique Christ-like imagery and haunting melody, it makes for an apt coda to Sonic Youth's first successful front-to-back foray into the realm of pop songs.

*   *   *

A l l four members of the band contributed to *Sister*'s cover. "We couldn't come up with one single idea from one of us that was liked," says Lee. "So we ended up using a collage of all different things. Somehow that really fit that album a lot. It's really one of my favorite covers because it shows the multiplicity that Sonic Youth is all about." The original cover included, among other images, a photo of a young woman taken by Richard Avedon, and one of Disney World's Magic Kingdom with a hypnosis vortex scrawled over it with a felt-tip pen. Both were blacked out on subsequent reissues. (Avedon threatened to sue; perhaps someone at SST feared Disney would do the same.)

T o prepare for *Sister*, Sonic Youth holed itself up in, among other places, an extremely small rehearsal space in the East Village owned by Bradley Field, once drummer for Teenage Jesus and the Jerks. Close quarters helped give the songs written there a diamondlike clarity. Sear Sound—then a historic studio run by Walter Sear, a coconspirator in the invention of the original Moog synthesizer— was located on the mezzanine level of Manhattan's Paramount Hotel. Soon after *Sister* was recorded, the studio moved to its 45th Street location; the chicly renovated Paramount now plays host to many of the city's alternative-rock-industry visitors.

As always the music came first—only after song structures were established did the results get divvied up for lyrics. "Thurston said, 'I'll sing that one,' and Kim said, 'I'll sing that one,' back and forth till they were all gone," Lee says.

Chosen for its ancient (read: all-vacuum-tube) recording setup, Sear Sound provided *Sister* with its tonal "warmth." The band had been attracted to Sear after having heard *Don Gavanti*, a No Wave interpretation of *Don Giovanni* recorded there in 1981 by Mars leader Sumner Crane, DNA drummer Ikue Mori, and others. The band, particularly Lee and Thurston, had developed a protracted interest in vintage equipment, partly in reaction to the impending trend toward all-digital consoles. (When recording the band's latest album, the band insisted on returning to Sear Sound to run some of the digital mixes through an older board to add some analog character.) The term "grunge" might as well have been invented to describe the music on *Sister*.

Walter Sear—a squat, sixtiesh man with wire-rim glasses, a carefully trimmed moustache, and a penchant for 100s-length cigarettes—provided the requisite fifties sci-fi vibe. Awesomely knowledgeable about the history of recorded sound, and brimming with arcane anecdotes about the twentieth century's great music inventors and academics, Sear even helped program a Moog synthesizer for brief passages on the album.

Bill Titus, whose one "impressive credential" was as second assistant on a Billy Joel album, ended up as engineer on the album by dint of being in the studio's employ. Sonic Youth quickly came to resent Titus's condescending attitude toward the band's work. The band had decided against working with Martin Bisi again primarily because of differences over the way tracks sounded in the final mixes. Titus was difficult ("The tubes worked really well for guitars, but I was never really happy with how the drums sounded on that record," says Steve Shelley.), but the band was ultimately allowed to do what it wanted.

At the end of the *Sister* sessions, Sonic Youth decided to let loose once again, creating "Master-Dik." An in-studio construction that Ranaldo likens to *EVOL*'s "In the Kingdom #19," "Master-Dik" in fact was closer to the first Ciccone Youth session. Lee sat in the control booth and Steve at the drums. Ranaldo played sundry tape loops made from Kiss albums such as *Strutter* and *Kiss Alive* through Steve's headphones. ("She's looking good," "I know a thing or two about her," are two discernable Kiss lyrics.) Lee would turn one up and Steve would play along; then he would switch to the other. The rest of the band later added guitar overdubs.

The end result became the A-side of the *Master Dik* EP, another fragment of the unfinished portrait called Sonic Youth. Paul Smith assured the band that its release would be a professional gaffe. The EP was released anyway. The cuts on side B provide a kind of piecemeal tour diary—a Swiss radio performance, a jam done in rehearsal dubbed onto a cassette tape. Ultimately the record is a rousing disappointment—the wily work of band none too keen for your undue worship at its collective feet. But within its cryptic tracks, *Master Dik* had a flattering, celebratory message to its fans: "You *are* worthy," the band seemed to be saying.

In early 1988, *Sister* made number twelve in the *Village Voice*'s influential Pazz & Jop Poll. But although both *EVOL* and *Sister* had become college-radio favorites, SST failed to break Sonic Youth—not so, the Meat Puppets, fIREHOSE, and Hüsker Dü—on commercial alternative-radio stations. All told, the album sold around 60,000 copies—wildly impressive for a dissonant independent-label release.

By 1988 SST was being run primarily by Greg Ginn and Chuck Dukowski (Joe Carducci and Mugger had jumped ship). Around that time, allegations began to circulate that the members of Black Flag weren't interested in any SST band becoming more popular than they were, that every day at the office included a four o'clock "weed break" . . . Regardless of whether these rumors were true, more than a couple SST acts were finding it increasingly difficult to get paid.

Sonic Youth's allegiance to SST was a strong one, yet the label's prime East Coast contingent was one among the acts on the roster who felt they were getting short-changed. "We kept on selling more and more records with each release," says Steve. "And I guess it got to a certain point where they couldn't keep up on a quarterly basis with what they were contracted to pay the artist. They were trying to build their catalog—but in hindsight, they were alienating the bands that sold records for them."

Simultaneously, Paul Smith had set about consolidating his little American empire. In displaying Sonic Youth, his flagship act, Smith had attracted the likes of the Butthole Surfers, Big Black, and Dinosaur to Blast First in England. His dream, of course, involved expanding to the United States while retaining sovereignty over his largely American brood.

In 1987 Smith decided to head for New York in hopes of opening a United States office for Blast First, and soon succeeded in striking a deal with Enigma Records, an offshoot of Capitol.

12 | Rock and Roll for President

Anyone lucky enough to be tuned in to NBC's *Night Music* late one evening in 1989 witnessed a brief but nonetheless legendary moment in American pop history: an ultra-fierce Sonic Youth flickering across the screen, like some half-received cultural update faxed from the future.

"Night Music," a network anomaly, broadcast for only two seasons—in most markets, at around two A.M. Sunday morning—and featured the deceptively deferential saxophonist David Sanborn as host of the most daring new-music showcase ever to blitz the airwaves. The eclectic producer Hal Willner was its artistic director. Begun as a showcase for lounge-lizardy jazz acts, it quickly broadened its scope. Bootsy Collins, Leonard Cohen, Sun Ra, Diamanda Galàs—many legendary and underexposed musicians performed on "Night Music." In these halcyon days of independent rock—despite its primacy—"Night Music" was one of the few mainstream television shows available to a band of Sonic Youth's ilk.

"Now here's Sonic Youth with their manager Don Fleming on keyboards," the big-haired, soberly dressed Sanborn intoned. "The song is 'Silver Rocket.' " Then the camera quickly panned stage right as the band leapt into its first-ever nationally broadcast television appearance.

Dressed in a lime green neoprene biker's jacket zipped to the neck, his blond moptop carefully combed over his eyes, Thurston Moore ripped into the simple song's opening guitar arpeggios. Standing next to him, center stage, Kim Gordon shifted her balance from foot to foot, looking as if she might at any minute fall to the stage. In a purple print top, silver lamé hot pants, stockings looped with "Jetsons"-issue space rings, and straight, shoulder-length blonde hair that all but concealed her face, Kim was the attention-grabber—her big, unwieldy Fender bass seemingly powering the proceedings. To her right, Lee Ranaldo stood splay-legged in a black shirt and blue jeans, eagerly aping the guitar-hero archetype. Steve Shelley looked demure and businesslike, his sleeves rolled up, his glasses on straight, not allowing a big-deal TV appearance to detract from his duties. Don Fleming, leader of D.C.'s Velvet Monkeys, and the band's actual manager for about a minute, stood beside Ranaldo in a full-length black leather jacket and a large brown floppy hat, running his knuckles back and forth over a small keyboard.

Who the hell do these people think they are? the uninitiated must have thought. Here was a band virtually unknown to mainstream audiences—in fact, they'd rarely even appeared on MTV—hammering its instruments into the stage. Thurston spat out the song's lyrics from between clenched teeth (changing the second verse by adding lines like "Got a date with a girl named Cher"). Kim pogoed around the stage with her head bent over. It took Steve Shelley's machine-gun-tempo drum rolls to revive the band from the song's chaotic noise break. Then Thurston whipped out a drumstick and began slapping his guitar. When Lee crossed the stage to play alongside Thurston, the lanky guitarist pushed him to the stage as both continued playing. Minutes later, the song was over. Thurston fell to the floor, Lee dropped his guitar, Kim went limp, and Steve got right up and walked offstage. At the end of the show, Sanborn joined the band on sax for Kim's hoary rendition of "I Wanna Be Your Dog."

Sure, they acted a bit like a punk band, revved up and taut with energy. Yet to "Night Music" viewers, "Silver Rocket" must have sounded slightly off, its percussive chordings a little too dissonant, its shouted lyrics lost in the shrill siren sounds lurching forth from Lee Ranaldo's guitar, its elegant avante-garde flintiness rendering the band almost impossibly aloof. Like an important news brief lost in the newspaper's B-section, Sonic Youth's performance was a whispered warning to the unsuspecting: We're tomorrow's rock stars, it seemed to say. Louder, faster, more twisted, and buzzing in your head.

The power and promise inherent in American punk music— which during the eighties had been transmuted first through hardcore and later through indie rock—seemed curiously deteriorated. The stock market had crashed, Ronald Reagan had left office. What better setting for Sonic Youth—the band that had first embraced traditional rock instruments at the very time when the rest of the world had taken them for irrelevant—to make its grand statement.

Of course, these arbiters of punk taste were well aware that double albums were for seventies dinosaur bands. But that was all the more reason to release one—Sonic Youth's giant burst of rock bombast shot forth on the eve of the nation's post-greed hangover. The band even assigned pictograms to each member of the band— an infinity symbol for Lee, the Greek letter Omega for Thurston, a female symbol for Kim, and a winged cherub for Steve—for the labels affixed to each side of vinyl, in mock homage to Led Zeppelin's "Runes" album.

When *Daydream Nation* was released in the fall of 1988, it hovered over an impoverished and weary populace like a moldering hunk-of-cheese moon. "Never has music been so draped in irony as it is on *Daydream Nation*," Peter Watrous observed in the *New York Times*. "Though it sounds spontaneous and emotional, every literate move seems to have quotation marks around it."

* * *

By 1988 indie rock's "cause" was all but lost. As it turned out, hip-hop—not guitar rock—was the sound of the future. The new cutting-edge performers had names like Public Enemy, L.L. Cool J, and N.W.A. The anarchistic musical voices of the future were, for the most part, African-American. Hardcore hip-hop could be every bit as radical-sounding as punk; but unlike indie rock, hip-hop was astoundingly popular too. Furthermore, the phenomenal success of 1986's *Licensed to Ill*, the Beastie Boys' multimillion-selling Def Jam debut, was proof positive that even white, Jewish musicians could successfully test the limits of this relatively fresh African-American form.

"It was never like we said, 'Electric guitars are not it,' " says Mike D of the Beastie Boys' first hip-hop efforts. "It was just that we became overwhelmed and completely obsessed, even *more* consumed with hip-hop."

As if to acknowledge its own obsolescence with one grand gesture, Sonic Youth decided to ameliorate rather than ignore the changing of the guard. Having parted ways with SST and allied itself (indirectly) with a major label, Enigma, the band itself was experiencing something of an identity crisis.

For Thurston, Dinosaur's J Mascis—today the patron saint of slackers everywhere—represented a freshly cast rock archetype. A bright hippie stoner from Amherst, Massachusetts, who claimed making music was the only thing that kept him from spending all his waking hours in front of the television, Mascis offered the clarity of a rock-and-roll vision at a time when the future seemed unclear. "It seemed like the first time where you'd see kids who didn't draw any boundaries," Thurston recalls, "who were really young and were coming out of hardcore but at the same time buying into more sophisticated music."

Dinosaur's early albums, *Dinosaur* and *You're Living All Over Me*, startled Thurston. Mascis and fellow bandmate Lou Barlow seemed to effortlessly incorporate noisy guitar ideas into classic songwriting structures. "I remember thinking, hearing Dinosaur, Wow, there's this whole influx of kids who are going to come up and actually perfect some of the ideas that we were sort of leaning toward," he says. "For Mascis to write songs that were very Neil Young–like but with a very hardcore, American-youth edge to them was very new. Actually, discovering anything that was pre–Sex Pistols was kind of *dangerous*. But all of a sudden, it became the healthy thing to do."

Seattle was one of the first cities that Sonic Youth visited to display this new recombinant aesthetic in full force. In 1988, young kids with long hair who listened to Black Sabbath and Mötley Crüe as well as to the Sex Pistols and the Damned were an unholy crossbreed. "I remember playing with [Mudhoney fore-bears] Green River in Seattle," Thurston says. "They seemed genu-inely influenced by hard rock from '75 on, but they were punker kids." Local Seattle bands were incorporating elements of heavy metal into a punk-inspired format, a practice that only a year or two earlier had appeared distasteful to most listeners in the latter cate-gory. In the context of an impinging postpunk parochialism, how-ever, the mix came off as radical. As much a reaction to straight-edge hardcore's moralizing as it was to the avant-garde's social seriousness, the new punk-metal hybrid conspired to make the music fun again.

New developments on the rock scene, many of them in some way traceable back to Sonic Youth, allowed the band to settle in more while recording *Daydream Nation* at Greene Street Studios. The album's songs were consistently longer than those on previous efforts, a conscious move inspired by the work of the band's contemporaries—specifically, Black Flag's nine-minute "psycho-trauma" jams. "I remember Henry [Rollins] saying, I really like when you guys really improvise and stretch out," Thurston says.

"We never really *tried* to break out of conventional songwriting. Because it never really existed. I mean, we knew what conventional songwriting was—and we could utilize it—but we never really wanted to break free from it, because we were *already* free from it."

More than any other Sonic Youth album, *Daydream Nation* represents the band operating without constraints. Yet while no song on the album is under five minutes long, the record doesn't really succeed as an extended jam session. What it did achieve, though, remains a lot more impressive: It's a testament to the unexpurgated inventiveness of a revolutionary rock band at the peak of its compositional powers.

"We were all talking about dreams and, Where does a person get their ideas? Where does a person get their experiences?" Lee says. "Some things happen to you in the course of a day and some things happen to you in the course of an evening, when you're dreaming. And at a certain point, later, when you look back at your experiences, those things are just as much your actuality or your perceptions as what happens to you in the course of a day.

"It was also a period when the debate on sampling and appropriation was really raging, and our feeling was, If you go to a movie, you absorb those images into you, just as if you had had an experience on the beach that day. And they become part of your own mental library to draw on. Or if you read a book, or whatever it is. You clip something out of a newspaper. All of a sudden it's just as much yours—you have just as much right to owning it as anybody else. We were really interested—I still am—in that place where dreams are and waking hours and all the different ways in which you absorb someone else's film. Or from actually an encounter that happens to you in 3D out on the street."

Moore had intended the corrosive but catchy guitar riff that opens "Teenage Riot," *Daydream Nation*'s first track, to be a tribute to Zuma-era Neil Young and J Mascis. The song itself was Thurston's paean to alternative America—the lean, steely-eyed union that had flourished while the mainstream bloated up to bursting. Originally titled "Rock and Roll for President," it imagines J Mascis of Dinosaur (by now Dinosaur Jr., due to litigous threats from a California band called the Dinosaurs) as President of the United States.

Thurston likes to think of "Silver Rocket" as a compendium of everything the band was capable of: A simple but strange two-chord change-up, a noise break, and lyrics chock-full of knowingly invoked rock clichés souped up with a touch of technobabble ("You got to fake out the robot" / "And pulse up the zoom").

Despite the thematic continuity afforded by "Candle" (the cover of *Daydream Nation* features two photorealist paintings of lighted candles by the German artist Gerhard Richter, titled *Kerze*), the song was written and recorded long before Kim ever brought Richter's dark, beautiful works into the studio. The original title of the song was "I'm the Cocker," according to Thurston, the first line of the chorus. "That was kind of sci-fi ridiculousness—'I'm the cocker on the rock,'" he says. "I mean, what the hell's a *cocker?*"

But if there's any track on the album that approximates the limpid, umber hues of Richter's paintings, it's "Providence," a sound collage vaguely reminiscent of the Beatles' "Revolution No. 9." Built around an answering-machine message Mike Watt left for Kim and Thurston from Providence, Rhode Island, where fIREHOSE was playing a show at the Living Room club, "Providence" demonstrated how Sonic Youth's refined sense of taste could translate to even the most pared-down format.

"The night before, we'd played New York," recalls Watt. "And Thurston meets us and he had bought all these cassettes and cables and had them all in his arms. He'd smoked some 'mota' [marijuana]. And I have some trash—we're sitting in the van—and I say, 'Thurston, could you throw this trash away?' So when he goes out of the van, he dumps all the trash—I think he dumped everything in his hands in the trash can. Then we play the gig. Later that night, he said, 'What happened all those dollars' worth of stuff that I bought at the store, man?' We couldn't remember, see? The next day it dawns on me after I wake up and I call him and I tell him. That's why at the end, I said, 'Your fucking memory just goes out the window.'"

Combined with a melancholic piano part that Thurston recorded at his mother's house on a Walkman and a warm hum accidentally elicited from a Peavey tube amplifier that began heaving when its exhaust fan was blocked, "Providence" is an eerie yet oddly soothing piece. The band was especially pleased with the happenstance spiritualism implied by the word *providence*.

The album finishes with "Trilogy," a title which in virtually any other rock context would be construed as pretense. But as the cap to *Daydream*, it's just another gonzo pun—a backhanded homage to seventies-rock dinosaurs like Emerson, Lake and Palmer. Composed of "The Wonder," "Hyperstation," and "Eliminator Jr.," the set also works well as a thematic cap.

" 'Trilogy' came about because those songs were all kind of in the same tuning and they kind of could bleed into each other," Thurston explains. "That's how we rehearsed them and we decided to record them as such."

The original title of "The Wonder" was "The Town and the City," a reference to a lesser-known work by fifties Beat writer Jack Kerouac. But the settled-on title was culled from the work of hard-boiled mystery writer James Ellroy, who used "the wonder" to describe the awful beauty that is his native Los Angeles.

"Eliminator Jr." lays bare certain elements of Sonic Youth's self-styled method of songwriting. Frequently, when the band first establishes the basic guitar riff or chord change that grounds a song, a genre label will serve as the song's title. The music is put together by all four members; lyrics always come last. Kim is particularly reluctant to come up with anything beyond a working title early on. So the band members frequently come up with rock referents to remind them of a particular song's feel. "Eliminator Jr." derived from the fact that the song sounded to the band like something between Dinosaur Jr. and the ZZ Top album *Eliminator*. ("Skink," on *Experimental Jet Set, Trash, and No Star*, was originally called "Pete Townshend" because Steve thought Thurston's guitar part sounded particularly Townshend-like at one point.) Later, the title conveniently applied to Kim's lyrics—an impressionistic account of "preppy murderer" Robert Chambers, who strangulated his girlfriend Jennifer Levin in 1988 in New York's Central Park.

Lee Ranaldo sang lead vocals on an unprecedented three tracks for *Daydream Nation*. The band's most traditionally accomplished musician, Lee is also the member most fascinated with the farthest reaches of tonal experimentation. In 1987 he released a solo album on SST called *From Here → Infinity*, consisting of twelve tracks of Eno-like atmospheric noise which ebbs and flows like filibrating sine waves given voice. The original LP has a locked groove at the end of each track that repeats until the needle is removed from the vinyl. ("The only compact disc with surface noise," boasts the sleeve of the CD reissue.) Pieces with names like "Ouroboron" and "Slo Drone" expertly duplicate the amplified sound of Ping-Pong balls in a Cuisinart. Others use pleasantly distorted guitar patterns and unique tape loops to test the limits of the human attention span. *From Here → Infinity* is simultaneously remarkable and repellent.

As a songwriter for Sonic Youth, though, Ranaldo is relatively straightforward. Quick to cast himself as the group's reformed folkie, Lee is also the first member of the band to draw connections between *Daydream* and early Grateful Dead live double albums like *Live Dead* and *Europe '72*. Accordingly, his contributions to *Daydream* hit an unlikely middle ground—somewhere between Crosby, Stills and Nash and Joy Division—which is resolutely melodic, dreamy, lyrical. Whereas most Sonic Youth tracks crescendo and tense up, only to release right at the point of explosion, Ranaldo's songs are more likely to continue on, verse-chorus-verse, building to the very end. His lyrics for the most part eschew the detached cool personas constructed by Kim and Thurston—even when they're not specifically about himself they tend toward the first-person.

For "Eric's Trip" he used dialogue culled from Andy Warhol's lurid 1966 docudrama, *Chelsea Girls*. "It's based on this character from Warhol's group of people called Eric Emerson," he says. "In the film, there's this big sequence with Eric in it, and he's really tripped-out and he's talking in this really acid-babble kind of way. And he says all this stuff that I basically just wrote down verbatim and used as the first verse and the basic structural key of it."

"Hey Joni" was inspired in part by William Gibson's *Neuromancer*.

The play on Jimi Hendrix's "Hey Joe" and Joni Mitchell's name is somewhat intentional. "Rain King" is more introspective; its stream-of-consciousness punning seems more connected to Bob Dylan's "Subterranean Homesick Blues" than to anything written after 1970.

Thurston's originally proposed title for *Daydream Nation* was *Tonight's the Day*, a line from "Candle." But it was a lyric from "Hyperstation," part B of "Trilogy," that provided the final choice ("Daydreaming days in a daydream nation"). "We just said let's take the title out of a lyric," says Lee. "We had fifteen cool lyrical snatches from all the different songs and that was the one we all agreed upon."

Daydream Nation was planned for release on SST. But SST's impending financial difficulties encouraged the band to seek other options. In a pinch, the band asked Paul Smith, the album's prime financier, to release the new album in the United States. "I had six weeks from scratch to put a label together and the distribution deal and to get that record out," says Paul Smith. Smith came to New York and opened a Blast First New York office. He also worked out a distribution deal with Enigma, an arm of Capitol Records.

Smith's previous dealings with independent labels in the U.S. had proved fruitless. Unlike British independents, which habitually pay mechanical royalties (up-front fees based on the number of albums pressed) to artists, American independents were much more free-form.

Sonic Youth accepted Smith's offer. In March 1988 the band completed a full album as Ciccone Youth—*The Whitey Album*; *Daydream Nation* came to fruition in July and August.

Daydream was recorded in approximately six weeks, at a cost of around $30,000—a long and leisurely stint by Sonic Youth standards. Still bent on producing itself, the band was introduced to Nicholas Sansano—a young engineer and Berklee School of Music graduate who had worked his way up at Greene Street by assisting on hip-hop projects by top acts such as Run-D.M.C. and Public

Enemy. When the members came down to Greene Street to meet with Sansano, the engineer was immediately impressed by their resolve.

"They were somewhat conservative and worried—they were not as wild as I thought they would be," he says. Despite its close quarters, Greene Street was the most professionally set-up studio the band had been in since their first album; one of the first things they asked Sansano was whether they could record everything live, as opposed to doing lots of overdubs.

Sansano was also surprised by the number of technical concerns the band members had. Steve wanted to record with headphones; Kim didn't. Everyone wanted to know what kind of tape would be used. What types of microphones would be used. How long the recording process would take. Sonic Youth was not the slapdash thrash act Sansano originally mistook them for. Admittedly, Sansano himself hadn't really done much work with independently styled rock bands. But the band willingly took a chance.

"If Nick had been a better producer, it might not have been as good a record," Lee says. "It's a big record, it sounds better than the records did before, but it still has a really gritty, crunchy sound that ties it to what we had done before."

Again, the console was old-fashioned by the standards of the day; recording levels had to be set manually for each take. ("Everybody would have their hands on it," Sansano recalls.)

The relaxed atmosphere encouraged the band and Sansano to keep the tape rolling and let accidents happen. Kim's whispered nothings during the intro to "Teenage Riot" ("Spirit desire," "Say it, don't spray it") overlap because both tracks just happened to be playing on top of one another one day; the band decided it worked.

Lee became the project's most passionate tinkerer. He and Sansano would stay late into the evening recording additional lead-guitar overdubs and trying out all kinds of effects boxes. In many ways, the recording of Daydream Nation was the band's final opportunity to stretch out artistically without submitting to the corporate speculum.

Taking a break from the recording process, the band appeared in a segment of a BBC documentary, "Put the Blood in the Music," a television special meant to describe the downtown New York "noise" scene for foreign viewers. (It later aired on PBS in the U.S.) The hour-long show, directed by Charles Atlas, features segments on sax squawker John Zorn, Hugo Largo, Ambitious Lovers (Arto Lindsay's post-DNA project), and Sonic Youth. In the absence of a piece on Living Colour that was excised for space, Sonic Youth's twenty-minute segment represented the show's most straightforwardly rock-and-roll contingent. (Hugo Largo, while technically a rock band, played what was essentially pastoral New Age music.) The show also placed Sonic Youth perfectly—smack-dab in the middle of downtown New York's warring factions.

"It's our political record," Kim and Thurston soberly explained to any journalist that would listen. And by the time *Daydream Nation* was released, that amounted to a rather large number. Of course, many were taken aback by the band's straight-faced posture—were independent rock's master ironists ready to relinquish their cool demeanor in the name of political correctness? Well, not exactly. Sonic Youth's politics weren't of the soapbox variety.

Whether on purpose or by coincidence, the tracks on which Kim Gordon sings are *Daydream*'s most overtly radical. " 'Cross the Breeze" features the album's most awe-inspiring musical passages. Its expansive instrumental sections is comprised of sleek, slithery guitar parts that play cat-and-mouse with the beat. Gordon's lyrics offer a vague sense of sexual tension ("I took a look into the hate / It made me feel very up-to-date") without specifying the infraction. "The Sprawl"—whose title refers to the world described by William Gibson in *Neuromancer* (Kim says she got the title off the dust jacket of one of Gibson's later works, *Mona Lisa Overdrive*)—takes a narrative cue from the seedy scenarios of noir novels by the late Jim Thompson and James Ellroy, writers who romanticize the dark side of fifties Los Angeles.

But of all the Gordon tracks on *Daydream*, "Kissability" offers the clearest glimpse of Kim's developing persona at the time. Its lyrics describe a feverish sexual come-on—but not the wildly passionate kind rejoiced in most rock music. In an appealing but noncommittal singsong, Kim plays the part of a sleazy Hollywood producer. "You've got kisssability / You sigh hard, don't you wanna? / You've got twistability / You could be a star, it ain't hard." The words make it clear that the cheapest kind of desire is involved here, but the propulsive music and Kim's ambiguous vocal timbre send a different message.

"Kissability" sung by a male singer would lose its edge—one expects these words from the mouth of a man. Delivered by a woman, they communicate ambivalence. Female sexuality, traditionally evoked by men as the weakness that prevents women from being exceptionally creative, in this case serves as aesthetic strength. Gordon creates a confrontational rock posture—without acting like a man.

Daydream's initial pressing sold around 100,000 copies, an impressive number by 1989 independent-label measures. "Its influence outweighed its actual sales," says Lee. "And I think at this point I've just resigned myself to that being the fate of Sonic Youth—we're just that kind of band. We've always been a band that's attracted a lot of critical acclaim just because we're smart and we have ideas and it's interesting for journalists to talk to us."

By the time Sonic Youth finished *Daydream Nation*, the band had successfully accomplished every goal it had ever set before itself. For many, *Daydream* represented the pinnacle of all that was wonderful and revelatory about independent rock.

A few months later, Ciccone Youth dropped *The Whitey Album* into the arms of an unsuspecting public. *The Whitey Album* was not the note-for-note cover of the Beatles' White Album that the band had joked about releasing in previous years; rather it was Sonic Youth's haphazard homage to the genre that had sucked the wind from indie rock's sails—hip-hop. Recorded prior to *Daydream Nation*, at Wharton Tiers's studio, *The Whitey Album* was held back to prevent it from detracting attention from its more serious cousin.

"That was a record where we literally went in and made up stuff," Kim says. "That was the whole idea." Where *Daydream Nation* was austere, *The Whitey Album* was absurd. Where *Daydream* was ordered, balanced, *The Whitey Album* was haphazard. Using the two sides of Ciccone Youth's 1986 single "Into the Groovey" and Mike Watt's rendition of "Burnin' Up" as a jump-off point, *Whitey* poked holes in anybody's notion of what constituted meaningful pop product.

A grotesque black-and-white close-up of Madonna's face filled the album's cover. "We're not interested in Madonna's career because we think we're going to follow in her footsteps, or anyone's footsteps," Steve admitted at the time. "We're just doing our thing, and whatever happens with it, whichever way it goes."

Kim imagined the album as pop deconstructionism. "We're like the big garbage truck that goes along, scooping up the pop poop. Recycling it, kind of," she said. "We're interested in songs. We like songs." To prove her point, Gordon "covered" Robert Palmer's sexist pop hit, "Addicted to Love," for *The Whitey Album* in the most economical manner possible—she recorded her awesomely insouciant vocal track in a karaoke booth (where a prerecorded instrumental track plays, you sing the words off a lyric sheet, and get a finished cassette tape mixed from both tracks). An accompanying video took advantage of a similar kind of video service, available at Macy's department store in Manhattan: For twenty dollars, one could play an audio tape and perform in front of video images. Kim chose to strut her stuff in front of combat footage.

After *Daydream Nation* was released, Sonic Youth got to tour the U.S.S.R. and Japan for the first time, a testament to the quality of the band's impressive international contacts.

In the former Soviet Union, few people knew who Sonic Youth was, other than an American rock band. Whether in Leningrad, Kiev, or Vilnius, most audiences were pretty sure this clamant band from New York was doing it all wrong. "For the most part, there would be some kids who wanted AC/DC, or just artist onlookers," says Thurston. "And no sound systems. You'd be in a big hall with no sound system. You couldn't even hear yourself. It was that weird and that bad." While the trip was rewarding from the tourist's point of view—the main reason the band had agreed to go—as a musical voyage it was a disaster.

Sonic Youth's trip to Japan proved more fruitful. Upon the invitation of a young record-store owner in Tokyo, the band set off for what turned out to be both an exotic and a creatively energizing experience. "Our first gig in Tokyo was at this little club, and the Boredoms opened for us," says Thurston. The Boredoms, Japan's combined answer to both the Butthole Surfers and the Beastie Boys, quickly struck up a friendship with their New York counterparts. "They were a little different then," Thurston says. "They didn't make such a big sound. It was more sort of total weird noise improv. And every night was totally different."

"Previously, if you heard of a band coming from Japan, you would think 'very kitsch,'" says Steve.

Sonic Youth had no difficulty adjusting to a culture committed equally to record-collecting and generosity. When the band did an interview with a Japanese music magazine, each member was given a watch as thanks. "Japan's such a weird environment," Thurston says with fondness. "It has such a weird politic, and a social behavior that's unique to the Eastern tradition—the way they'll incorporate the West into their world but at the same time keep it at a distance."

In typical Sonic Youth style, the band has gone on to act on occasion as U.S. emissary for the Boredoms and Shonen Knife, an all-woman trio from Osaka that counts the Ramones as its prime influence. "Musically it's fascinating," Thurston says. "All this Japanese noise that's come out over the last couple of years is really amazing because it's based on American ideas of Zorn improvisation and Sonic Youth noise. It's not the noise that you heard coming out of Europe and England from Einstürzende Neubauten or Throbbing Gristle or SPK."

13 | This Guitar Kills Conformists

Jaguar, Drifter, Viper, Marauder—they could be the names of exotic sports cars. In truth, they're the imprimaturs of the various vintage guitars Sonic Youth has employed over the years.

But before Lee joined Sonic Youth, nonstandard guitar tunings were never even considered. "I remember we had to do some gig," says Thurston, "and there was one song Ann [DeMarinis] and I both played guitar on. So we had to borrow one from Glenn Branca—he was the only one we knew who had more than one guitar. He had a bunch of guitars, and they were all cheap, hundred-dollar guitars that he would get at pawn shops."

It wasn't till Thurston took the guitar home that he realized that all its strings were the same gauge—and that they were all tuned to A. Thurston had yet to play with Branca; and though he had seen Glenn perform, he had no reason to believe the composer's guitarists were doing anything different besides strumming furiously. "The idea that there are many alternate tunings isn't that surprising," he says. "But Glenn was definitely one of the first people I met that knew you could do music in other tunings."

The instruments-only "The Good and the Bad" on Sonic Youth was the band's first attempt to play guitars rhythmically without regard for the notes being hit. (Kim and Lee play the guitars on the Sonic Youth track; Thurston switched to bass.) To achieve the chiming effect heard on "Burning Spear," Thurston wedged a drumstick under the strings at the twelfth fret of his guitar and hit it with another drumstick—another technique inspired by Branca. (One unrecorded song written soon after the band's first sessions, called "Destroyer," required Lee and Thurston to detune all their guitar strings—i.e., to loosen the strings until they hung limp and emitted bass notes so low that they were hardly distinguishable from each other.)

"Some of it stemmed from Glenn," says Lee, "and some of it stemmed from this notion that we just wanted to keep trying different things out. People would give us guitars, because they saw that we were into guitars, and so we slowly started amassing them. We'd spend what little money we had and buy some new ones. And every new guitar brought new songs and new tunings, through those first years; now it's a little bit more of an established thing. It's not quite the same."

Thurston immediately cottoned to the idea of open tunings— guitar-tuning configurations that allow one to strum a full major-key chord unfretted, or simply by wrapping one finger across all six strings—for practical reasons. "I wasn't very good at chords so much," says Thurston. "My fingering was still kind of under-developed, so I was excited by the idea that I could play open strings with no complex chord thing, and use the left hand to tune it so that the open chord all of a sudden becomes this really amazing chord or something that sounds really good. And then you could start flattening it and creating other chords."

The songs on Confusion Is Sex were the first written in nonstandard tunings (the standard tuning for a six-string guitar is, from bottom to top strings, E, B, G, D, A, E); although Confusion relied less on established notations than on finding tunings that responded well to sharp, percussive attacks. " '(She's in a) Bad Mood' is basically just this Drifter guitar with a smashed black cowbell behind the twelfth fret," Thurston says.

In preparing *Bad Moon Rising*, Lee and Thurston began locking in tunings around which whole songs were written. The first such reworking, which inspired both "Death Valley '69" and "Brave Men Run," required the lowest four strings of both Lee's and Thurston's guitars to be tuned to F-sharp, the lowest two strings an octave lower than the next two. The second string is lowered to the E below F-sharp and the first string to B. (This tuning has prevailed throughout the band's history—it's used on "Kool Thing" and "Mary Christ" from *Goo*, and on "Self-Obsessed" from *Experimental Jet Set, Trash, and No Star*.)

For "I Love Her All the Time," Lee tuned his strings to D-sharp, D-sharp, C-sharp, C-sharp, G, G, and lodged a screwdriver behind the guitar's ninth fret and played on both sides of it; if played on the "wrong" side (the side closer to the tuning pegs), the strings tinkle like wind chimes. For the same song, Thurston put a drumstick under the twelfth fret of his guitar and rubbed it with a second drumstick until the strings began humming. Intent on experimenting even further, Lee and Thurston each began devising their own individual tunings for the same song; in most cases, Lee would listen to what Thurston had come up with and then simply detune his guitar until he heard something that pleased his own ears.

Early on, the band bought used, junked-up electric guitars and ripped out their insides, except for the pickups (the electromagnetic bars that amplify the sound of the resonating strings) and the two wires that lead to the output jack. As a result, each guitar retained a distinct, albeit extremely limited sonic palette. Sonic Youth's motley guitar collection has over the years included a Duo-Sonic, a Univox Plexiglas Dan Armstrong, an Ovation Viper, a Gibson Marauder, a Fender Telecaster Deluxe, and a twelve-string Kapa Minstrel, as well as dozens of Japanese-made copies.

As soon as they could afford to choose, Lee and Thurston began favoring Jaguars and Jazzmasters, two vintage electric-guitar styles issued by Fender in the late fifties and early sixties respectively.

Both guitars, unlike the more classically styled Telecaster and Stratocaster, feature a substantial length of string behind the bridge, which can be plucked to produce superhigh, tinny sounds.

"I had a very good Fender guitar from the days of the Flucts and Plus Instruments that I still use today," Lee says. "It's one of the few guitars that's been in the band its entire lifespan, that and the Drifter. But we've got a whole host of crappy guitars that have come and gone."

The band soon learned to capitalize on the otherworldly happy accidents afforded by inferior equipment. "Brother James," the song from Kill Yr. Idols with which Sonic Youth introduced a G, G, D, D, E-flat, E-flat tuning, was one of the band's first songs to take advantage of beat tones—the pulsing sounds that occur when two guitar strings are just about tuned to the same note. The beating effect is responsible for much of the out-of-tune feel that makes Sonic Youth's sound stand out. Which means that even on a Sonic Youth song that employs just a few basic chords, such as "Silver Rocket" on Daydream Nation, the notes ring in strange, unforeseen ways. (On "Silver Rocket," Thurston's guitar is tuned to A, C, C, G, G-sharp, C; Lee's is tuned A, A, E, E, A, A.)

For all the influence Sonic Youth has had on the sounds of younger, innovation-oriented guitar bands, few of their progeny have dared to explore the world of alternative tunings as extensively as Sonic Youth.

"I played a five-string open-B tuning for years with Velvet Monkeys on about half the songs," says Don Fleming, "but Sonic Youth's approach is unlike anyone else's who uses retuned guitars."

There are some not-so-surprising reasons why: Early on, when each member of Sonic Youth only owned one guitar, the band frequently lost momentum during live performances. "A lot of our early gigs were marred by too much time being taken tuning your one guitar to another tuning," says Thurston. Second, most young rock musicians have enough trouble mastering basic guitar chord theory, much less broaching the myriad difficulties introduced by a theoretically infinite number of tuning systems.

However, Sonic Youth quickly turned its handicap into a creative flash point: The garbled samples from the Stooges' "Not Right" and Lou Reed's *Metal Machine Music* that bridge tracks together on *Bad Moon Rising* were first used in concert; Thurston would plug his Sony Walkman Pro into an amplifier and let a tape blare while he and Lee returned. Even after Sonic Youth could well afford multiple guitars, each specially strung and tuned for particular songs (the specifications for each guitar are written on tape and attached to the back of its headstock), they continued using the tapes for continuity. Ratt's "Round and Round," Black Sabbath's "War Pigs," Gerardo's "Rico Suave," and *Artikulation*, a 1958 composition by György Ligeti, are some of the sounds that have emanated from Sonic Youth's speaker cabinets over the years. Today, Sonic Youth's racks of guitars onstage are a trademark.

Sonic Youth's guitar pyrotechnics frequently draw attention away from Kim's bass-playing. By her own estimate, Kim came to Sonic Youth with the least musical background of all. Perhaps it's because she almost always keeps her bass in standard tuning that her musicianship rarely gets its due. But Mike Watt, surely one of postpunk's most inventive bass players, avers that over the years Kim has more than compensated for her initial lack of experience.

"She's one of my heroes," he says. "She doesn't come from the polluted background of the guitarist that goes over to the bass. She's not as hedged in riffs. She goes more for parts." And no matter how unusual Lee's and Thurston's tunings are, Kim's bass remains in standard tuning.

As the band's center of attention onstage, Kim has also inspired a whole generation of women to pick up the bass guitar and join bands. "She once told me Thurston used to write some of the bass parts," Watt says. "In fact, Thurston plays bass and Kim plays guitar on some of the records—and you can totally tell. It's not as dreamy. When she plays bass, it's more like when [the late jazz innovator Charles] Chuck Mingus plays with a bow. It's more sound. It's in the low register, but it's not all these blues riffs that some of us are stuck in. More sounds."

Kim first set out in earnest to explore aesthetic pastures beyond the ones farmed by Sonic Youth with a side band called Harry Crews.

Kim and Lydia Lunch had long talked about putting together a band, as a onetime project. "With Lydia, she has the tour before the band," Kim says. Both women finally found themselves between projects in mid-1988. "We didn't really have that much time, so I thought it would be good if we had something in common that we could write the songs about."

Kim had over the years become a devotee of American noir fiction, an alternative canon of eminently readable novels that focused on the underbelly of America. Jim Thompson, James Ellroy, Carl Hiaasen—ever since the fifties, a small cadre of American writers have spun tales of hard-boiled pessimism culled from the same contemporary setting that others have pointed to as progress. Harry Crews, a gruff Hemingwayesque writer who doubles as a writing teacher at the University of Florida in Gainesville, is one of noir's best. In his darkly comic narrative world, there exist boxers who punch themselves out (*The Knockout Artist*) and evocative titles like *Blood and Grits* that conjure up visions of an unrepentant Deep South.

"There wasn't really a vast amount of female so-called rock bands at the time," Lydia says. "We wanted to do our own thing and decided to base it on the books of Harry Crews. Just the name itself, Harry Crews, seemed perfect for a three-piece female rock band."

Rather than plundering Crews's novels for material, Kim and Lydia decided to use the titles alone as inspiration. In September 1988 Harry Crews toured Europe (a friend of Lydia's, identified only as "Sadie," played drums). *Naked in Garden Hills*, an album made from live tracks recorded in London and Vienna, reveals a sloppy but distinct set peppered with Lydia's verbal assaults on the audience.

Though a number of songs, like the bluesy "Gospel Singer" and a version of Sonic Youth's "(She's in a) Bad Mood" sung by Lydia, show promise, Kim is clearly overshadowed by Lunch's antics. "Even though she said she wanted to get out of her Lydia persona, she never can," says Kim. "And people start pushing her buttons. They mostly just wanted to hear her say fuck you."

For Lydia, whose expectations for any one project are fleeting, Harry Crews was an opportunity to further appreciate Kim's work in the context of Sonic Youth. "They're under-writers, especially Kim," says Lydia Lunch. "Her writing, like a lot of mine, is so abstract and so basic, she could be saying anything about anything. And in that sense, it's open to interpretation, which is beautiful. There's a difference between leaving something basic and abstract and open to interpretation, and something that's just meaningless."

And while Naked in Garden Hills admirably walks that line, it falls into meaninglessness more often than not; it's recommended for Sonic Youth junkies only. Side projects, however, had begun to play an increasingly important role in the band's interminable quest for new musical ideas.

Sonic Youth's tendency to avoid distortion boxes and the attendant high-tech effects accoutrements of today's standard rock guitarists is less a purist impulse than an urge to keep things simple. Short of the occasional wah-wah pedal or fuzz box, the Sonic Youth sound relies primarily on keeping amplifier volumes turned up to the levels at which they naturally distort.

"It produces an aggressive, violent kind of sound and yet it's got this beautiful thing in it somehow," says Epic Soundtracks, formerly drummer for the British cult band Swell Maps and a good friend of the band's. "It allows them to create a very moving sound that still has a lot of velocity and ferociousness to it."

The same instincts that attract the band to vintage recording equipment and arcane-model guitars are the ones that repel them from the latest in digital frippery. A minimum of clutter is the band's insurance that the sounds it develops are its own and virtually unduplicable. Not that Sonic Youth isn't constantly experimenting with high-tech toys—they're simply employed with restraint, and rarely in the way in which they were intended. (On *Experimental Jet Set, Trash, and No Star*'s "Tokyo Eye," for example, Kim plays a toy beatbox she purchased in Japan through her bass-guitar pickup.) By continually demystifying the processes of writing, recording, and performing, Sonic Youth succeeds in emphasizing its creative ingenuity all the more.

Epic Soundtracks recalls spending time with Sonic Youth in a London studio in October 1988 while the band recorded a "Peel session" for John Peel's legendary BBC taped-live radio show. Rather than recording a few of its own songs, the usual practice, Sonic Youth chose to record four songs by the Fall, the legendarily independent British band. Mark E. Smith, the Fall's phlegmatic leader, had recently taken to knocking his New York contemporaries in interviews, perhaps because Sonic Youth had become the band to which the Fall was most likely to earn comparisons.

Released as a bootleg by the band in 1991 under the title *4 Tunna Brix*, the session features Epic Soundtracks yelling out the chord changes on "My New House." (The other tracks are "Rowche Rumble," "Psycho Mafia," and the Kinks' "Victoria.") "They went in there and listened to the records and worked them out," Soundtracks says. "And when they were putting down the backing tracks, I did the guide vocals. In the end they said, 'We should keep that.' So you can hear my guide vocal going all the way through."

14 | The Middle-Class Whiny Blues

KIM GORDON: ''WE'RE DOING THE WHITE BLUES. WE'RE
WHINY.''
LEE RANALDO: ''YEAH, THE MIDDLE-CLASS WHINY BLUES.''

For a few days in late May 1990, Sonic Youth sat around in the mid-Manhattan offices of Geffen Records. Music journalists were paraded in and out of a generic-looking corporate office, each to spend a precious hour or so interviewing the hippest indie band in the country. It was business as usual for both Geffen and the writers in line, but "press days" constituted new territory for Sonic Youth.

The band, impatient and jittery, paced the room, ate donuts, and picked through piles of complimentary CDs (an added bonus of recording for a major). Already lionized by the music press (except for maybe a few crotchety fanzine publishers), Sonic Youth, by most indicators, ought to have had little to worry about. *Daydream Nation* had been listed at number two in the *Village Voice*'s influential Pazz & Jop Poll. (Public Enemy's It Takes a Nation of Millions to Hold Us Back—also recorded at Greene Street Studios, just before *Daydream*—came in first.) It topped the year-end charts of both *Rockpool* and the *College Music Journal*, two trade journals that monitor radio play and record sales. It also made number one in the U.K. on the NME and *Melody Maker* independent charts. *Rolling Stone*, in its first serious coverage of the group, named Sonic Youth "Hot Band" in its summer "Hot" issue.

And with their signing to DGC, a Geffen "alternative" subsidiary and the subsequent release of *Goo*, the band's seventh album, Sonic Youth had willfully transformed itself into what sat before me on May 23 (I interviewed them for a free-lance piece that never ran)—and so many other journalists since: Four new-era rock musicians just sitting around talking. Media darlings and media manipulators, in true Warholian spirit.

"Does it sound like it cost four times as much to make?" Lee Ranaldo joked, only partly defensively, in response to praise for the album. For a band that had shown up for its first British gig with $65 dollars in its pocket, and once made a video for $20, *Goo*'s $150,000 recording budget was a sticking point.

"It wasn't that we said, 'Let's go out and spend a lot of money,' " Ranaldo said of *Goo*'s recording costs. "We wanted to be conservative, and it just snowballed. It was out of our hands. The engineer was saying, 'We'll do it forty-eight-track, and then this happened and that happened—"

"Well, he suggested that, and we went along with it, and it turned out to be something that—" Steve interrupted.

"Too much time overdubbing that wasn't used," added Kim. "Money doesn't make good records."

For most of my hour, Thurston was on the phone at the other end of the room with an interviewer from the *Boston Phoenix*.

The golden age of independent labels had clearly run its course. ("Punk is something you buy on a T-shirt in the East Village," as Steve put it to one reporter.) Sonic Youth had, like many other bands, become victim to the financial finagling of independent labels. The independent-label network had first expanded by toting its moral imperative: Better music by bands chosen for aesthetic, rather than financial, rewards. But, in retrospect, those claims seemed unrealistically lofty.

Sonic Youth had learned the hard way that commitment to the

music didn't necessarily translate into proper distribution and escalating sales. Sonic Youth had stuck to the independent network until the options had been exhausted. The band had already begun writing and rehearsing the songs for its new album (early on, the band talked about titling it *Blowjob*, a dual reference to a Raymond Pettibon–designed T-shirt and to the band's indie-to-major switch), unsure whether to give it another whirl with a prominent indie, like Chicago's Touch and Go, or to go ahead and sign with a major label.

Sonic Youth had good reasons to approach major-label status with trepidation. Of the few eighties independent-label rock bands to test the mainstream before them, none had fully survived the transition, aesthetically speaking.

The Replacements signed with Sire in 1987; *Pleased to Meet Me*, the resultant album, delivered a decent batch of songs, yet the band's firing of cut-up guitarist Bob Stinson contributed to what turned out to be a senescent collection of songs when compared to the band's previous efforts. Major-label stardom clearly caught the raucous band unawares; over the band's final three albums, they lost both the verve and the inventiveness of the original lineup.

"The Replacements were an enigma to me," Thurston says. "Them signing to a major was no big deal because they were drunkards and you always heard about them playing in punk-rock clubs and locking themselves in the dressing room and doing coke. I would go see them at Folk City and they would come out in dresses, and I'd leave because I thought they were really bad. I wasn't interested in drunken Midwesterners doing covers."

R.E.M., upon leaving I.R.S. Records in 1988 to record *Green* with Warner Bros., shed itself of virtually all its trademark quirks. Gone were Michael Stipe's slurred vocals, Peter Buck's jangly guitar lines, Mike Mills's wandering harmonies, and the band's impressionistic, nonlinear song structures. By the time R.E.M. released *Out of Time*— its platinum-selling, Grammy Award–winning effort—in 1991, the band had staggered far from its original course. "Losing My Religion" and "Shiny Happy People," while catchy enough to garner Top Forty radio airplay, offered little that was new to the realm of tried pop formulas. R.E.M. met with massive success on somebody else's terms.

Having followed the Replacements to Warner Bros., Minneapolis soul mates Hüsker Dü met with a similar fate, producing 1986's credible *Candy Apple Grey*, only to follow it up with the semidisastrous double album *Warehouse: Songs and Stories*. Drummer Grant Hart's departure at the end of 1987 ended the band's foray into the mainstream before it ever picked up steam. Sonic Youth consulted Hüsker Dü leader Bob Mould before making a final decision.

Sonic Youth had entertained offers from the big time for a number of years before ever succumbing. As early as 1985, major labels had expressed interest in the band. Representatives from Warner Bros. and Elektra contacted Homestead Records for copies of *Bad Moon Rising*, having read praise of the album in the *New York Times*. At the time, most thought better of their initial interest once they'd listened to the music.

"It was perfectly obvious to me that at some point the majors would want to get involved," says Paul Smith.

Smith imagined Sonic Youth as the new Grateful Dead, a self-contained operation that expanded its own world with each successive endeavor. For the few years prior to 1990, Smith had been talking to American majors with the idea of turning Blast First into a production company working for a label, with Sonic Youth as its flagship act. Smith essentially wanted to bilk a label in order to fund his operation, a technique that had worked rather well in Britain with Cabaret Voltaire.

But functioning as Sonic Youth's unofficial manager, its agent in the U.K., and its worldwide record label, Smith and Blast First—in both his and the band's opinion—had been wearing too many hats. So when the time came to sign with a major, Paul Smith was left behind.

During a summer 1989 meeting with the band in Smith's New York apartment, ostensibly called to discuss a video project, the young Englishman was told by Bob Lawton—the band's American booking agent and for a brief time its manager—that his services would no longer be required. No one in the band said another word; they stared at the walls to avoid his gaze. The meeting was quickly disbanded. "The leaving was a huge loss to me," Smith recalls. "This band had changed my life, on many levels. To have them to leave would have been bad enough, but the *way* they left—they didn't deal with it at all well." The members of Sonic Youth remember trying to tell Paul for months that he wasn't going to be the band's manager. "He was in huge denial," says Kim.

In the past, Kim had always distrusted Smith's promotion ideas; Lee tended to support Smith up front; Thurston would then give a particular idea a twist that would make it acceptable to everyone. Smith maintains it was Gordon's increasingly opinionated voice within the band that predicated his release. "Kim was becoming more and more radicalized to the view of 'having to deal with a bunch of men,'" Smith opines. "She wanted a greater say. And that obsession that they had with Madonna was very much a stepping stone." Kim counters that some of Smith's views stemmed from the fact that Thurston and Lee were not always honest with him—or, for that matter, with each other.

Gordon embraced Pop Art pioneer Andy Warhol's notion of commercialism as the most evolved fine art. To Smith, Warhol represented an extreme example of commercial exploitation, the American equivalent of Malcolm McLaren, the impish opportunist/ provocateur who "created" the Sex Pistols. (To the band at this point, Smith *was* Malcolm McLaren.)

"We were more into building a relationship with people who could be your friends or were your friends," Steve says.

In retrospect, Gordon's newfangled perceptions of the way rock musicians related to their labels prevailed and served the band quite well indeed: On a major label, with total creative control, Sonic Youth could dramatically enlarge its canvas. Sure, the challenge to stand out would be greater; but the potential for effect would also be more substantial. Sonic Youth remained progressive by continually picking and choosing from the palette of options available and embracing only what appealed to them.

"I don't think we ever really thought that that much was going to change," Kim says. "We hoped we'd get better distribution for our records and get a little more money. But I don't think we saw ourselves as rock stars or as part of that world, because we were still in the ghetto."

"Musically, they had every reason why people should be revered, but it's very rarely just making good music that actually allows you to get through those barriers," Paul Smith says. "It has other things to do with personality and how you're presented." Furthermore, any label that signed Sonic Youth understood that the band would be a magnet for a whole wave of newer bands. Smith expected Dinosaur Jr. would be the first to follow; Seattle's Nirvana, of course, ended up first.

"When the bottom line came down to it in terms of the major-label thing," Smith continues, "Kim had two things to say about it: One, I would never truly understand because I wasn't American; and two, she felt that they were looking to get in with a major label and they wanted to have people around them who would reduce the friction—whereas I was far more of the attitude that the major labels were there to 'use,' in the old punk circumstance of using major labels." The band had become increasingly frustrated with Smith's tendency of alienating potential suitors and his odd habit of disappearing without cause for weeks at a time.

"When you've been working so long outside the mainstream," says Kim, "it becomes more challenging to work within the mainstream. Otherwise you're just talking to your peers. But on the other hand, I don't ever want to be like Urge Overkill [a Chicago indie band that signed to Geffen and hit paydirt in 1993 with its seventies-rock parodies]. To me, they're just making mainstream music. You're still doing the thing. As soon as you're put on an alternative-radio station, you're just like all those other bands."

* * *

The arrangement that Sonic Youth had made with Blast First and Enigma to release *Daydream Nation* in 1989 was cobbled together at the last minute with good intentions and spit. But Enigma—a large-size independent (the Smithereens and Stryper were its biggest sellers) distributed by Capitol Records—proved unable to keep the album in stock and didn't advertise the release to the band's satisfaction.

"Distribution was really screwy and there were always a lot of minor fuck-ups," says Steve. "It seemed like we were always on the phone trying to work out some problem with Enigma. Plus, their packages were always shoddier than the proper, Blast First England editions."

By the time the deal was linked with Geffen (most estimates place the contracted amount at $300,000), though, Sonic Youth had already changed its way of doing business.

After a brief foray with Living Colour's management, the band decided to hire the first real managers of its career, John Silva and Danny Goldberg at Goldberg's Gold Mountain Productions. Goldberg, who is now a vice president at Atlantic Records, came armed with a history not only as a savvy recording-industry figure—he started his career in the 1960s as a music reviewer for *Billboard*, *Rolling Stone*, and the *Village Voice*; he later headed promotion for Led Zeppelin's Atlantic subsidiary, Swan Song—but also as a liberal-minded politico. (Goldberg for a while headed the California branch of the American Civil Liberties Union.)

Most significantly, the band made a ground-breaking decision to sign with a major label. Having met with representatives from Atlantic and A & M, among others, Sonic Youth decided to go with Geffen—home to Guns N' Roses, Whitesnake, and Cher—not because the deal's financial terms were any better than other bidders' but because Geffen offered the band the "complete creative control" clauses it coveted most.

At the time, Geffen was a relatively small major label (a moot point: within months of inking a deal with Sonic Youth, Geffen was bought up by MCA, a corporate behemoth); when the band was delivered to Los Angeles to meet with David Geffen, they found him to be reasonably down-to-earth and approachable. (Not that the band was overly deferential: Later in 1990 Sonic Youth began Sonic Death, the official Sonic Youth fan club; almost immediately, the club began issuing band-sanctioned "bootleg" CDs— the first contained the eight-track demos for Goo. On its back cover: a compromising photograph, taken in the 1970s, of Geffen with onetime girlfriend Cher.)

"When Geffen flew us out there, we thought that was fine," says Steve, "but we were actually pretty sure that we were going to sign with A&M at the time." The band figured it would go to Los Angeles on Geffen's money, meet everybody, and then go hang out with people at A&M as well.

When Gary Gersh—at the time an A&R executive at Geffen— signed Sonic Youth to DGC, he had no idea what kind of impact the decision would make. Gersh, today president of Capitol Records, says, "I was a big fan of EVOL and Sister and knew that they were fiercely independent but wanted to find a way to do something with them." Ray Farrell, the former SST operative, and Mark Kates were two other Geffen employees whose deep appreciation for Sonic Youth helped grease the deal. (Kates later became the band's A&R rep after Gersh left to head Capitol.)

The resounding acclaim that met Daydream Nation upon its release encouraged Gersh to approach the band, because "you could go into a lot of different stores and not find the record." Gersh was convinced that Sonic Youth could continue to make the kinds of albums they had made all along—his main recommendation was to improve the sound quality of the recordings. A bigger production budget and a more professional studio situation, he felt, would automatically bring more listeners to the band.

"I think, in general, the whole thing about big labels and independent labels is bullshit," Gersh says. "I think it's all about people, ultimately."

Geffen was by no means the first major label that Sonic Youth entertained. The band was wined, dined, and slavered over by

Atlantic Records head Ahmet Ertegun; Columbia's (now Sony's) Tommy Mottola, too, summoned Sonic Youth to a meeting. Many industry insiders suspected the band would sign with A&M—then home to the Feelies and Soul Asylum.

"It came very close to us signing with Atlantic, which would have been a nightmare because the people we were talking to all left," Thurston says. "Everybody promised us that we'd be the cornerstone, the new face of the label, but there was no rush to buy an alternative band because there were no successful ones."

While Sonic Youth had always had more than a passing interest in the effluvia of America's mainstream culture, the fascination emanated more from a heightened Warholian perspective than sheerly from face values. In that sense, Sonic Youth was perhaps more prepared than any other American band of its generation to exploit the ironies of making pop art in a consumer culture.

The notion of being a star—territory that Sonic Youth had so eloquently mapped out in songs such as "Starpower," "Marilyn Moore," and in Ciccone Youth—was fleeting. "Her whole life is geared towards being Madonna," Kim Gordon once told a British journalist, trying to explain the pop princess's stardom. "Everything is geared towards the look and the appearance. It's a huge sacrifice, that's why people get so fucked up by it." Of course, it was appealing and fascinating—but in the end, it was simply another filter through which to examine the world. Sonic Youth's battle would be to continue its celebrity field research while perhaps becoming stars themselves. Out-and-out stardom has its privileges but it does not ordinarily take well to those who attempt to betray it.

Not that the band had any intention of abandoning the indie underground. In 1987, Velvet Monkey Don Fleming followed Jad Fair and Half Japanese to New York. He also formed B.A.L.L., a sixties-style garage parody band, with Kramer, Jay Spiegel, and David Licht. When B.A.L.L. went on hiatus after Kramer hurt himself jumping into an audience with nobody to catch him, Fleming decided to form a New York version of the Velvet Monkeys. Don

Fleming, Jay Spiegel, and Malcolm Riviera (now of Gumball) were the band's core; new members included Thurston Moore (on bass and guitar), J Mascis (guitar and drums), and Julia Cafritz (guitar, keyboards, and vocals).

Rake, the resultant album, was the perfect example of the kind of project that still couldn't weather a major label. (It was released on the now-defunct Rough Trade.) Designed as the soundtrack to a nonexistent action movie, *Rake* started as a series of just-for-fun gigs at downtown New York clubs.

After four weeks of playing together, the band spent a few days in Wharton Tiers's Fun City studio laying down nonsensical but hard-rocking songs with jokey names like "We Call It Rock," "Rock the Night," and "Rock Party." The album's front cover features a menacing photo of Fleming "as Rake," flanked by a mollish-looking Julia Cafritz and Daisy Von Furth; the mock marquee on the back cover lists the band members in fake roles: "Thurston Moore as Action Pussy," "Julia Cafritz as Miss Sugarbowl," and "J Mascis as Sweet Dick." It was yet another view of stardom as perceived by people who deep down know stardom, in the end, is kind of silly.

Haphazard, carefree, profane—*Rake* was everything a major label hesitates from banking on. "It was really bizarre to read the reviews for *Rake*," Fleming says. "A lot of people liked it and a lot of people hated it. And the people who hated it seemed to have something built up, like, 'It's supposed to be this—but it sounds like they're just having a party.' Which was the whole point."

Signing with Geffen almost immediately offered Sonic Youth an option it had never before been afforded: a large budget with which to record. But the band was initially reluctant to dive headfirst into the world of slick production values and big-name producers. Nicholas Sansano was again chosen to engineer the proceedings; the services of a producer were, once again, not requested. Sonic Youth chose to spend its advance on the more tangible technical aspects of the album-making process: More money meant the band could record at Sorcerer Sound, a much larger and better-equipped facility than it had ever used before. A forty-eight-track console, actually two twenty-four-track machines hooked together, allowed the band for the first time to record as many overdubs as it wanted to, all in one sitting.

"It was really problematic," says Thurston, "because, technically, it would malfunction a lot. It was harder to record in this huge, massive room. It was an experience and an experiment—but it was fun enough."

J Mascis and Don Fleming helped the band record demos for *Goo* at Waterworks—a tiny, eight-track studio run by Jim Waters on East 14th Street in Manhattan—in November 1989. Mascis remained at Sorcerer Sound throughout the whole recording process—by Thurston's account, "kind of helping out, but watching a lot of TV, of course."

"When we were making the demos of *Goo*, Kim and Thurston were really keen on having Don and J around," says Lee, "both as extended family and as people to have an opinion. And at the time both Steve and I felt a little bit uncomfortable about that, because we'd never made records before where there were other people involved in that way."

Fleming suspects the problems arose from poor planning as much as anything else. "It was never like, 'You're in charge' or 'He's in charge' or whatever," he says. "They ended up spending maybe two days to overdub one song, guitar-wise—which is totally insane."

Although Gary Gersh denies having placed any creative pressures on Sonic Youth to produce a certain kind of album, Nick Sansano says that from the start, the label lacked confidence in the band's ability to make a commercial-sounding album. A listen to the basic tracks calmed Geffen somewhat, but both the label and the band remained leery about Sansano's abilities and insisted on bringing in a name engineer—the band chose Ron Saint Germain, a jazz-percussionist-turned-producer—to execute the final mixes. "When we did the first few mixes," Sansano says, "Gary Gersh didn't like them and the band was wishy-washy on them. I wanted to complete it, I wanted to see it through. I felt that the hammer was over our heads throughout the whole project and at the first sign of weakness, at the first falter, it was going to come down. We lived with that specter.''

The hiring of Saint Germain represented a bridge between two worlds—that of a hits-conscious major label and that of a art-conscious independent band. Although Sonic Youth didn't relate to Saint Germain as a producer, it was satisfied with Saint Germain's impressive résumé—he had worked on the Bad Brains' I Against I, a highly influential reggae-and-hardcore album released on SST in the mid-eighties. Thurston was even more wowed by Saint Germain's early engineering work in the jazz world, which includes five Ornette Coleman albums, three albums with Ronald Shannon Jackson and the Decoding Society, and a well-respected five-disc collection of lost New York jazz called The Wild Flowers.

Geffen was better acquainted with Saint Germain's more recent work—specifically, as an "additional producer" on Agent Provocateur, a late-issue album by Foreigner, the wildly successful corporate rock group, which played the hit-manufacturing game so long its tinny singles sounded as if they were playing through a foot-thick wall of Lucite, no matter what the volume. He also mixed the popular live version of U2's "Bad" that appeared on Wide Awake in America.

In fact, Saint Germain in recent years has gained a reputation for successfully readying album singles for widespread commercial-radio play. Whether it's adding a little echo to the vocal or electronically enhancing the rhythm track, Saint Germain must know something about radio—his remixes of Ashford and Simpson's "Solid as a Rock" and Whitney Houston's "How Will I Know" became mammoth hits.

But what did any of this have to do with Sonic Youth?

"There is no reason why an alternative record has to sound bad to be 'alternative,' says Saint Germain in a gruff voice mirroring the buccaneer-like swagger with which he approaches his craft, "although a lot of people seem to think that that's part of what makes it alternative. I disagree with that entirely."

After a few false starts (the band let him go after relistening to his first mix over three days, then rehired him), Saint Germain was given relatively free rein to sort through the countless guitar and vocal overdubs the band had recorded (and lost track of) with Nick Sansano. Thurston's guitar parts occupied no more than five tracks on any given cut; Lee's however, constituted more than that on some songs. And the fact that the band had placed area microphones in the studio room in an attempt to capture some of the three-dimensionality of its live sound made final remixing all the more difficult and time-consuming.

"We were trying to play live, but it was this ridiculous situation," says Kim, "where if anybody did anything wrong, we'd have to start again from the beginning."

The patchwork process of recording and mixing Goo is apparent in the album's inconsistent sound. The songs themselves, for the most part, meet Sonic Youth standards, yet some finished tracks sound oddly distant.

A few good examples: "My Friend Goo," Kim Gordon's tale of a punk-rock girl with personality, pairs a clunky lyric with an even clunkier mix. Ostensibly the album's centerpiece, it's the rare case of Sonic Youth losing its bearings amid a forest of options. "Tunic (Song for Karen)"—a wry tribute to the late singer Karen Carpenter—originally featured a track of Kim and J Mascis singing Carpenters songs in the background; when its inclusion was voted down, the track was simply lowered to a nearly inaudible level (you can still hear it with a good pair of headphones) rather than removed entirely.

Thurston looks back on the process of recording the eight-track demos with more fondness than he does the album ordeal. "That was a great experience because we just threw everything down," he says. "And those demos are preferable in a way, just because that's the feel that we were into and that's more us. The finished album is what it was—what are you going to do, re-record it?"

Moore laments that the album's sound isn't subtler; he considers the finished product somewhat of a salvage job.

The inclusion of "Mildred Pierce" (one of the first songs Sonic Youth ever wrote) on Goo appears to be the band's reaction against what had become a frustratingly overwrought process. Named after the Joan Crawford film, it's nothing more than a three-chord vamp that leads into a hardcore-inspired maelstrom over which Thurston repeatedly screams the words "Mildred Pierce" at the top of his lungs. Rewarding only in that it urged uninitiated listeners not to take their newfound pop idols too seriously, "Mildred Pierce" provided a clear-cut example of just how far Sonic Youth had come from the out-and-out chaos of Confusion Is Sex and Kill Yr. Idols. Live, it was an amusing punk wipeout; on disc, it's a throwaway. "Scooter and Jinx," the minute-long instrumental track that directly follows, pushes things even farther out—for it, four overlapping tracks were made of Thurston pressing a howling guitar up against his amplifier.

Fortunately, the band's growing pains didn't wholly detract from the album's effect—ultimately, Goo is a triumph. Not surprisingly, a careful listen elicits a compendium of Sonic Youth's favorite styles and subjects. The album's most musically adventurous tracks—"Dirty Boots," "Mary-Christ," "Cinderella's Big Score," "Titanium Exposé"—sound warm and confident, yet radical—even defiant by 1990 major-label standards.

Ranaldo's and Moore's guitar solos on the vaguely heretical "Mary-Christ" sound like braying elephants dueling it to the death. "Dirty Boots" harks back to previous album-opening Sonic Youth cuts, such as "Schizophrenia" and "Teenage Riot." It, too, begins with a carefully delineated guitar arpeggio that lurches into an acid-rock-inspired gait. Another Moore attempt at transposing the quintessential rock-and-roll song into starkly contemporary terms, "Dirty Boots" incorporates grossly outmoded hipster lingo like "jelly roll" and "hi-de-ho" as part of its lyrics. "Disappearer" recalls Sister's fifties sci-fi images of makeshift flying saucers skating through city streets.

"Mote," Lee Ranaldo's lone vocal contribution to *Goo*, takes its lyrical inspiration from "The Eye-mote," a 1959 poem by Sylvia Plath.

A testament to the collective savvy of the band, *Goo* was released with a resolutely controversial bang. Not controversial in the hackneyed classic-rock sense (keep in mind that Guns N' Roses, another Geffen act, had released the proudly sexist and racist *Appetite for Destruction* only months earlier), *Goo* was received well by most critics and fans while still rankling the right kinds of foes.

Early rumors as to the album's content and cover fueled a remarkable amount of advance press. The band reportedly had turned down an offer from Daniel Lanois—who had recently produced breakaway albums for both Peter Gabriel and U2—to produce the album. Then, Geffen balked at the band's choice of a black-and-white drawing by Raymond Pettibon as the album's cover: a cartoon of two fifties hipster types in a car with a caption that read, "I stole my sister's boyfriend. It was all whirlwind, heat, and flash. Within a week we killed my parents and hit the road."

"One night Gary stopped by and took us out to dinner," Steve recalls. "Thurston had mocked up the cover, and Gary's looking at it. And then he says, 'What about if it's like this?'—and he covered up the text."

Critic Dave Marsh reported in the *Village Voice* that *Goo* would be released with a parental advisory sticker, the bane of the recording industry at a time when the Parents' Music Resource Center—an organization that advocates full contents disclosure on rock albums, fronted by Tipper Gore, wife of then Senator (now Vice President) Gore—was at the height of its powers. Fortunately, the band succeeded in skirting the sticker issue. (Even better, *Goo*'s back cover sports a "Smash the PMRC" logo designed by the band.)

Whether the rumors were blown out of proportion or not, *Goo* got Sonic Youth more press attention than the band had ever received previously. Yet unlike most performers in the public eye, Sonic Youth treated interviews as something of an art form. First of all, the band granted an interview to nearly anybody who asked—fanzine editors, cub reporters from local newspapers, syndicated columnists such as Lisa Robinson. Second, the quotes in every article read like remarks from a continuing conversation. Someone once wrote that there weren't a whole lot of original Velvet Underground fans, but every one of those fans went out and started a band. Sonic Youth inspired a corollary: When *Goo* was released, it seemed like every original Sonic Youth fan reviewed it.

"At a certain point it's just more interesting to work within the mainstream," Kim told *Rolling Stone.* "I mean, how much can you shake up the underground? Unless you do what [performance artist] G.G. Allin does—shit onstage and attack women."

It's rock music's contradictory meddling that established it as a cultural force, distinguishing it from its antecedents—on one hand the unlettered, unfettered rawness of blues and country; on the other hand, the calculated bourgeois sophistication of the Tin Pan Alley tradition. Rock music, while certainly a failure as a political force, nonetheless helped change modern culture in drastic ways that no one could have anticipated. The history of rock music has coincided with the true democratization of society. A number of the United States' mushrooming ills are in some way tied to liberating aspects of the sixties' cultural revolution. Recreational drug use turned into crippling addictions and an oppressive international gangster cartel; legalized racial equality predicated deeper race and class resentments; feminism has produced more "victims" than victors; prayers for global peace have been answered by radical increases in gun deaths nationwide. In the name of self-preservation, rock musicians have had to expand their set of tools or else be relegated to the not-so-distant past, the inevitable resting place of all popular music.

For the most part, rock-music listeners eventually grow out of the tastes they formed as adolescents. Either that, or they stop looking ahead for something new or different. And unlike rock's first blush of fans, the teenagers who bought singles by Chuck Berry, Bobby Darin, and Elvis Presley, today's listeners aren't necessarily cowed by their pre-adult obsessions. There has been plenty of rock music made over the last twenty years that addresses adult subject matter, albeit frequently from an attenuated youth's perspective. This kind of half-concealed rock orthodoxy might provide one good explanation for the mitigated successes of—most recently—Lenny Kravitz, the Black Crowes, Pearl Jam, and in the most extreme case, Guns N' Roses. Confronted with the conundrum that is adolescent fury versus adult independence, it's easier for most artists and, as a result, most adult audiences to revert to the musical styles and attitudes that prevailed in the late sixties—i.e., the period when rock music last aspired as a movement to upend the cultural status quo.

Goo, both as a product and as an artistic statement, manages to at least temporarily fill the chasm between "rock as teeny-bopper obsession" and "rock as adult entertainment." "Goo" began as a character in a long-form video by Raymond Pettibon titled Sir Drone, which stars Mike Kelley, Mike Watt, Richard Lee, and Chris Wilder. Subtitled A New Beatles Film About the New Beatles—Love Is God Is Boredom, Sir Drone is the story of a long-haired hippie (Mike Kelley) deciding whether or not to cut his hair in order to become a genuine punk rocker. "My Friend Goo" is Kim's fleshed-out vision of a young "queen of the scene." "Cinderella's Big Score" describes a young woman reacting nastily to a mentally ill friend.

Guitar overdubs for Goo were done at Greene Street Studios, a happenstance that allowed for Chuck D of Public Enemy to drop by. Public Enemy, the hip-hop group generally acknowledged as having propelled rap into the radical sonic realm where it still orbits today, was then at the peak of its powers, working on Fear of a Black Planet, the follow-up to It Takes a Nation of Millions to Hold Us Back. Kim Gordon had imagined a part for a rap star to "Kool Thing," a song inspired by the lack of common ground she had found with rapper L.L. Cool J when she interviewed him for Spin; Nick Sansano provided the necessary introduction to PE's front man.

"Kool Thing" turned out to be one of the first (and last) organically sound rock-rap collaborations. Rather than laboring over the synergistic platitudes that tend to accompany crossover efforts, Sonic Youth kept things quick and simple. Chuck D's improvised part took approximately five minutes to record.

And while "Hey Kool Thing, are you going to liberate us girls from male white corporate oppression?" doesn't sound like a line from a Top 40 hit, a dance beat and a catchy hook won "Kool Thing" the distinction of becoming *Goo*'s first single. A Mylar-besotted video for "Kool Thing," directed by Tamra Davis (*Guncrazy*, CB4), made it into MTV's regular rotation schedule—the song's peculiar celebrity self-referentiality be damned.

Gordon later used the subject of "Kool Thing" as a springboard to discuss a variety of issues with the press. "Why were women such as Jane Fonda and Patty Hearst so into the Black Panther and black-revolutionary movements of the sixties?" she posited to the NME. "I think it was because there was something appealing about wanting to be an anarchist or a terrorist for a woman. . . . I think it is very appealing myself." The ambiguous polemics loosed by the song's lyrics allowed the band to introduce any number of social issues into conversations with journalists.

Both conceptually and imagewise, Kim had become the band's focus. A self-described "pseudo sex symbol," her songs are *Goo*'s most readily topical. In "Tunic (Song for Karen)," Kim imagines herself the late Karen Carpenter, the seventies singer who with her brother Richard had a number of bland but dreamy hit singles. ("I'm in heaven now / I can see you, Richard / Goodbye Hollywood / Hello Janis and Dennis and Elvis and all my brand-new friends.") Gordon used the song, which has a goofy school pageant feel to it (a crude accompanying video by artist Tony Oursler only reinforces that sense), as a means to discuss the cause of Carpenter's death—anorexia. The video for "Kool Thing" even placed a dolled-up Gordon front and center. Amongst friends, she was clearly playing rock star; but to new, younger fans whose primary exposure to the band was through the video's appearance on MTV's "120 Minutes," Gordon was another sexually provocative female lead singer—but one with a mission.

* * *

' ' I f you want to show off, why don't you go on the 'Howard Stern Show'?" a discombobulated Kim Gordon yelled from the Roseland stage. August 10 was a Friday night in 1990, and a big night for Sonic Youth. Roseland, a cavernous, echoey New York dance hall that hosts rock concerts to subsidize its standard ballroom fare, was clearly not the most suitable locale for a band like Sonic Youth. The horde of young male stage divers to whom Gordon's exhortation was directed only fed into Sonic Youth's worst fears—had success spoiled the party?

The antithesis of cool, the Roseland audience acted like it had never been to a rock concert before. Of course, most of the audience were underage teens perhaps drawn to the show by WDRE, the Long Island radio station that sponsored the event. Substantial MTV play and an album as readily available at Woolworth's as it was at Bleecker Bob's had almost instantaneously rendered Sonic Youth a mainstream affair.

Before Geffen, a bad show was nothing more than a minor let-down among devoted fans; now, an off night was a potential career setback. After an hour and ten minutes onstage at Roseland, Kim stormed offstage; the young guys who kept hopping up in front of her and nearly kicking her microphone into her teeth might as well have been drunken frat boys out for a laugh. Instead of an encore, Lee and Thurston stood onstage for ten minutes, mocking the moshers. Would Sonic Youth's self-styled professionalism serve the band well in the larger arena?

If nothing else, larger audiences certainly increased the likelihood that a Sonic Youth performance would make the papers. On December 29, the band shared a bill with Public Enemy at Chicago's Aragon Ballroom. Sonic Youth opened the show to a befuddled audience, composed primarily of hip-hop fans; after an hour-long intermission, Public Enemy dealt out a ferocious ninety-minute set. Outside the ballroom, after the show, a group of protesters rallied against U.S. action in the Persian Gulf. Eighteen people were arrested for yelling obscenities and inciting a riot.

When Sonic Youth subsequently toured Europe, the band invited Babes in Toyland, a raucous all-woman trio from Minneapolis, to open.

In retrospect, it shouldn't come as any surprise that sixties stalwart Neil Young offered Sonic Youth an opening slot on the early-1991 leg of his *Ragged Glory* tour. After spending a good share of the 1980s indulging in a series of genre-hopping, half-successful albums, and publicly embracing Reaganism for his own unclear and eccentric reasons, Young had decided to reaffirm his roots—loud, bone-crunching guitar rock. *Ragged Glory* regrouped Crazy Horse—the renowned backing group with whom Young recorded his most memorable material.

"We were on a list of like twenty acts they were interested in," Thurston says. "Neil wanted some bands that were, well—*interesting*." Oddly divergent names such as Einstürzende Neubauten and Public Enemy reportedly made the short list. Sonic Youth was originally asked to join the tour for a series of West Coast dates, only to find out the band was expected to play third on the bill, opening for the watery sixties throwback act World Party. The band had decided to reject the offer when Young's people came back with a better offer: World Party had dropped out; Sonic Youth could play directly before Neil for the whole three-month tour.

Yet Young's mammoth-size audiences (the tour played 11,000- to 18,000-seat venues such as Madison Square Garden, the Omni in Atlanta, and San Francisco's Cow Palace) were not automatic converts to Sonic Youth's still relatively challenging fare. The crowd was likely to boo throughout Sonic Youth's set; although some, like the one at New Jersey's Brendan Byrne Arena, seemed partially converted to the band's undeniably forceful delivery by the time Young roared onstage. Sonic Youth had never before spent such an extended period on the road. Thurston remembers it ambivalently: "It was interesting, it was fun, it was boring, it was enlightening, it was a drudgery—it was everything."

Onstage his set far overpowered Sonic Youth's (his crew insisted on keeping the opening acts' volume far below Neil's); Sonic Youth almost quit after the first few weeks (a particularly tepid mix ruined the February 4 performance at New York's Madison Square Garden) in protest of its sonic muzzle until a face-to-face meeting with the hoary headliner rectified the matter. And sure enough, as the tour progressed, Young seemed strangely fortified by his esteemed opening act; on some nights he could be caught apparently trying to wrest Sonic Youth–like dissonance from his heavily amplified guitar strings.

Neil didn't socialize much with the band, although he'd occasionally visit the Sonic Youth dressing room to praise the night's version of "Expressway to Yr. Skull," a song he's referred to on occasion as the greatest guitar song ever written. Young's roadies, holdovers from classic rock's dark ages, were less predisposed to what they perceived to be Sonic Youth's art-freak eclecticism. "The Neil Young tour was actually the first time I encountered so-called sexism," Kim later told *Seventeen* magazine. "Every time it was somebody's birthday, there'd be strippers hanging around."

For most of the dates in the South, Sonic Youth played half-hour sets to disinterested crowds who used the band's time onstage as an opportunity to purchase popcorn and Cokes; at some shows, the band went so far as to confiscate chairs from the front rows of the audience and bring the chairs onstage, a gag that perplexed Young's fans but amused the band. Young canceled the tour's Los Angeles dates, one of the main reasons Sonic Youth had stuck things out, when he developed an ear infection.

When I spoke to Young a couple months after the tour (which on many dates also featured the Los Angeles punk band Social Distortion opening for Sonic Youth), he described it as a "fantastic voyage inside a power chord." The typically disingenuous Young, perhaps reluctant to dish out overripe praise to a younger band for whom he had so much respect, explained his affinity with Sonic Youth like this: "I knew if people knew they were there that they'd know, Okay, first of all, he's not going to be doing an acoustic show."

"The Neil Young tour was the first time I really felt like we were suddenly confronting the mainstream," Kim says. "We really had this pretty much redneck, conservative audience. It was interesting because it made me feel like we were performing for the first time. I felt good that we could actually shock people. It made us feel really young."

15 | Wish Fulfillment

''WE'RE THE NEW BEATLES, BUT NOBODY KNOWS IT.''
—THURSTON MOORE TO THE *NEW YORK TIMES*,
JULY 29, 1992

The Seattle scene circa 1991 was hardly unfamiliar territory to Sonic Youth. Not only had the band on occasion performed with Green River in Seattle—the local group that later spawned both Pearl Jam (via Mother Love Bone) and Mudhoney—but along the way had also become friendly with Mudhoney's label, Sub Pop.

Not coincidentally, Sub Pop cofounder Bruce Pavitt, a young graduate of Evergreen State College in Olympia, Washington, began his career as a fanzine publisher. In the mid-eighties, the *Rocket*, a Seattle-based Northwest music paper, ran Pavitt's "Sub Pop U.S.A." column, the February 1985 installment of which began, "As I type this, only eight more days till Sonic Youth! Guitarists Thurston Moore and Lee Ranaldo are *radical* experimenting with dissonant tunings, static, minimal rhythms and slippery chord changes." (Pavitt later included "Kill Yr. Idols" on the *Sub Pop 100* compilation, released in 1986, that launched the Sub Pop label.)

"I remember Bruce coming to New York during the *Sister* period and staying with us," says Thurston. "He was going to move to New York and get involved in the art scene. He just wanted to move somewhere and do something creative and destructive. I also re-member him walking around New York with us for a couple of nights—and deciding against it."

Upon his return to Seattle, Pavitt began releasing singles under the Sub Pop name. *Dry As a Bone*, Green River's 1987 sophomore effort, was the first full-length album Sub Pop issued. Then Pavitt met Jonathan Poneman, a Seattle radio DJ and rock promoter, through Soundgarden's Kim Thayil. The two became quick friends, then partners; Soundgarden's *Screaming Life* became Sub Pop's next album release. By polluting the lean, chattering sound of punk rock with crunching power chords and sinewy guitar solos previously associated primarily with heavy metal, the Sub Pop's Seattle-heavy roster soon developed a sound all its own. It was only a matter of months before Sub Pop became the independent label du jour, the SST of the late eighties and early nineties.

Suzanne Sasic, Sonic Youth's lighting designer, drafted the label for Nirvana's first single, 1988's "Love Buzz" / "Big Cheese." Thurston recalls Sasic describing the new band from small-town Aberdeen, Washington, to him by saying the single "was no 'Touch Me, I'm Sick' "—a reference to the terrific Mudhoney single by which all other Seattle product of the time was judged.

Sonic Youth first got to see Nirvana play in July 1988, at Max-well's in Hoboken, purely by chance: Bruce Pavitt happened to be in town and invited them to the show. "I ended up going right to the front of the stage because they were playing a really long time and they were so good," Thurston says. At the time, Nirvana still boasted its original four-piece lineup: Chris Novoselic on bass, Chad Channing on drums, Jason Everman on guitar, and Kurt Cobain playing guitar and singing.

"They were fucking insane," Moore adds. "They were the first band I saw that really sort of employed Motorhead riffing with a Dinosaur Jr. vibe." J Mascis agreed—he, too, was standing up front, right next to Moore. After a flabbergastingly raucous set, Nirvana spent ten minutes destroying all its equipment. Nirvana was immediately welcomed into the fold.

Thurston went up to Novoselic after the show and wondered aloud what the band was going to use for equipment at its next gig. Novoselic told him they were off to the Pyramid club in "New York City" the next day for the New Music Seminar, not realizing that Manhattan is little more than a five-minute car ride away from Hoboken.

When J Mascis confided in Cobain backstage that Dinosaur Jr. was having lineup problems, the scraggly lead singer pleaded with Mascis to become Nirvana's drummer. (Channing was later replaced by Dave Grohl.) The night after the Pyramid show, Sonic Youth played a show at the Ritz with Mudhoney and Old Skull, a gimmick group comprised of nine-year-olds dressed up as punks.

Less than a year later, Nirvana returned to the Pyramid and played a truly horrendous show. Kim and Thurston had brought Gary Gersh to see the Seattle band; Iggy Pop was also in the audience. "Kurt was wearing a Stooges T-shirt and felt really embarrassed," says Thurston. Cobain felt silly wearing a picture of Iggy on his shirt when his idol was in the audience and the show had been so bad. At the end of the show, the disgruntled Cobain dumped a full pitcher of beer over his amplifier.

The next night Nirvana played another spectacular show at Maxwell's, despite the fact that the band had virtually no money and was at its wit's end. Chris Novoselic had shaved all his hair off, lamenting over the previous night's gig.

Sonic Youth's 1990 tour of the U.S. in support of Goo brought with it a host of opening slots just waiting to be filled. "For every week or two it was easy to ask bands to open up for us that we would like to see," Thurston says. Milwaukee's Die Kruezen, Ann Arbor's Laughing Hyenas, Seattle's Mudhoney—for whichever part of the country the band planned to visit, a favorite up-and-coming local act was corralled into service. Sonic Youth saw this as a way to pay back younger bands—many of whose members had been scene supporters before becoming musicians—for major-label spoils won through years of informal networking.

"It's not that generous," says Steve. "It should be common. You want to be surrounded by people that you like and good people. When we signed to Geffen, the closest band to us on the label was Siouxsie and the Banshees."

For a seven-date West Coast stint in mid-August, Sonic Youth invited Nirvana to be its opening act. But this Nirvana was quite different from the band witnessed back East: For one, the band had been pared down to a trio, with Dale Crover of the Melvins—one of the Seattle bands that first inspired Cobain—on drums. "They were really unhappy with Sub Pop," Thurston says, "because they felt like they weren't getting the attention they deserved, and they would go to a town and nobody would know they were playing. That was their complaint."

Moore suspected that Nirvana's dissatisfaction had at least something to do with a nebulous decision-making process twisted further by the band's skewed sense of reality. Unlike the members of Sonic Youth, who had labored for years in relative obscurity, Nirvana was coming straight from a small-town environment into the "alternative" big time. Yet Moore immediately pegged Nirvana as a band who knew what it wanted: "They wanted total encouragement—and we certainly gave it to them."

Meanwhile, the well-received release of Goo had encouraged major-label A&R executives to start sniffing out newer bands. If Sonic Youth, the most independent-minded of independent bands, could find a comfortable home at a major, they figured, then surely there must be plenty of less idiosyncratic bands ripe for the picking. "They knew they had to sign new bands, because the fucking John Mellencamp records weren't selling so well," Thurston snarls.

Nirvana was definitely one of the bands being looked at. "I remember [Geffen's] Gary Gersh saying, 'I might be interested in Nirvana,'" Thurston admits. "And I said, 'That's good, because they're really great.'" Sonic Youth subsequently agreed to relay Gersh's favorable nod to Nirvana. In the end, Nirvana not only ended up signing with Geffen but also decided to take on Gold Mountain's John Silva as its manager.

Despite the fact that Sonic Youth witnessed at its inception what millions of music listeners later rushed to in droves, Thurston doesn't have any grand theories as to the mammoth success of *Nevermind*, Nirvana's first Geffen release: "Things led up to them being in the right place at the right time with the right record." Industry eyes were already peeled for an accessible formulation of all the things held dear by the twenty-something generation—disaffectedness, domestic rage, dysfunctional upbringings, and, of course, harmonic resolve. In many people's minds, it was simply a matter of sighting the right prey.

A few days before embarking on a European festival tour that lasted August 19 through September 1, Thurston called filmmaker Dave Markey and invited him to trail along. A mere twenty-eight years old, Markey had long ago made his mark on the underground film circuit with Super-8 cult classics *Desperate Teenage Lovedolls* (1984) and *Lovedolls Superstar* (1986), both of which chronicle the rise of a make-believe all-female punk band called the Lovedolls. On the strengths of the *Lovedolls* films, and a documentary he shot of Black Flag's final tour, Sonic Youth had hired Markey to shoot videos for "Mildred Piece" and "Cinderella's Big Score." This time around, Sonic Youth bankrolled Markey; the end result was a 95-minute tour diary seditiously titled *1991: The Year Punk Broke*.

For two weeks, a lineup that included Dinosaur Jr., Babes in Toyland, Gumball, Nirvana, and Sonic Youth played outdoor venues in Dublin, Stuttgart, Rotterdam, and Reading, among others. The film itself is most notable historically for its documentation of the members of Nirvana in a pre-*Nevermind* state, acting far goofier than their post-success selves. The opening sequence features Kim Gordon and Kurt Cobain performing a silly interpretive dance to an impromptu tone poem courtesy of Thurston Moore; another highlight is Kim applying makeup, lipstick and all, to Kurt backstage.

A near parody of every rock documentary from the Rolling Stones' *Cocksucker Blues* to Madonna's *Truth or Dare*, *The Year Punk Broke* deflates airs by focusing on banal touring rituals in lieu of rock-and-roll excess: Instead of Mick Jagger being fellated on camera,

Punk Broke has Steve Shelley putting in his contact lenses. Most significantly, 1991: The Year Punk Broke emphasizes the role Sonic Youth had come to play among its peers—that of unwitting grandparents. Always magnanimous and ineffably well-adjusted (when Kurt Cobain would fall offstage mid-song, Thurston would more than likely be the one to pull him from the pit), Sonic Youth made even the punkiest Young Turks seem palatable to larger and larger audiences. After all, if Sonic Youth—still the most musically radical group in the pack—could rev up massive crowds, maybe the underground wasn't so underground anymore.

Back in the U.S., matters weren't as risky as they seemed anyway. By the time Nevermind was released in September 1991, the first Lollapalooza festival—a kind of alternative-music three-ring circus organized by Perry Farrell of Jane's Addiction—had already completed its successful summer run. Lollapalooza, billed as a multicultural, socially conscious alternative to the summer's more mainstream affairs, featured Jane's Addiction, the Butthole Surfers, Siouxsie and the Banshees, Living Colour, Nine Inch Nails, Ice-T, and the Rollins Band—all traveling together and playing full-day concerts in front of scores of young fans. Attendance figures for the first Lollapalooza tour proved better than for many of 1991's highly touted pop-music excursions—tours by established performers such as David Lee Roth, Whitney Houston, the Doobie Brothers, Huey Lewis and the News, and Steve Winwood were financial disasters. Even Guns N' Roses' much-ballyhooed comeback tour, a "sure thing," fell short of its promoters' expectations.

Unlike in the early eighties, though, when the mainstream recording industry had virtually ignored the small but steady stream of discerning young listeners being drawn to hardcore without a smidgen of promotion, the recession-battered major labels of 1991 were prepared to exploit absolutely anything if they thought it might unearth a new source of revenue. Labels in the sixties had ably latched on to the psychedelic counterculture in casually insidious ways, such as by inserting token negative references to "the Man" (the establishment) into ad copy; in the same way, the unambiguous success of Lollapalooza's left-leaning lineup made it relatively easy for the majors to commit to a grass-roots movement. The joke among older, jaded commercial-radio programmers had been that the term "alternative" referred to bands that didn't sell and thus didn't merit airplay. Lollapalooza, and the subsequent success of Nirvana's Nevermind, proved the old guard's assumptions flat-out wrong.

Many figures in the independent-label world would eventually reap benefits from Nevermind's wildfire sales (it went to number one on the Billboard album chart a few months after its release and eventually sold over nine million units); one of the first was a mild-mannered, devoted independent producer named Butch Vig.

Vig, a Wisconsin native, first entered the music world as a rock drummer. While studying film at the University of Wisconsin at Madison in the late seventies, he and fellow student Steve Marker recorded local bands in Marker's basement on a four-track tape machine. Vig's band, Spooner, was one of the first bands documented.

After Vig and Marker decided to stick things out in Madison rather than chase pipe dreams in Hollywood, in 1983 the two took out loans, purchased an eight-track, and began making records in earnest with the best acts in Madison's then-fertile local scene—Mecht Mensch, Tar Babies, Killdozer. Smart Studios, as it became known, slowly but surely acquired production work from top independents such as Touch and Go (Killdozer, Die Kreuzen, Laughing Hyenas) and Twin Tone. "Back then we used the slash-and-burn approach," Vig says. "You'd come in and record all the tracks in a day, you'd finish the vocals on the second day, and then mix everything on the third day and send the tape off." With modest profits made over the years, Vig and Marker upgraded the studio, first to sixteen-track, then to twenty-four-track.

Even though most of the bands Vig recorded then were hard-core-inspired thrash bands, his tastes tended more toward melodic Beatles-influenced pop (Spooner's music was more new wave than punk). Accordingly, Vig's early work earned him a reputation for squeezing superior sound out of cheap equipment and a limited budget. In 1990, Sub Pop hired Vig to produce discs by two up-and-coming Seattle bands—the Fluid's *Glue* EP and Tad's *8-Way Santa*.

When Sub Pop's Jonathan Poneman sent Nirvana to Vig, the producer had never heard them before. Vig listened to *Bleach*, Nirvana's first album, only a week before the band arrived to record. "A lot of the punky stuff I thought was kind of cool, but I especially liked the more pop song on there, 'About a Girl,' " says Vig. Nirvana recorded a few tracks at Smart Studios for a new Sub Pop album, which—once the band negotiated with Geffen—ended up as demos for *Nevermind*.

Although *Nevermind* took only five weeks to record, Vig subjected Nirvana to a rigorous recording process that the band resisted every step of the way. "I had to figure out ways to motivate them to want to keep doing stuff again," he says. "I wanted to use things in the studio—like doubling guitars, dropping in guitars here and there—subtle production techniques to make the band sound a little larger than life, without necessarily making them sound un-natural."

Vig's knack for keeping catchy hooks and melodic phrases at the forefront without sacrificing a band's live-performance power made the impossible possible for Nirvana: By the start of 1992, phenomenal sales for *Nevermind* compelled even Top 40 radio stations to play "Smells Like Teen Spirit," the album's catchy yet coarse first single.

Vig had first met Sonic Youth when the band came through Madison on the *Daydream Nation* tour in 1989. "I went with Dan Hobson from Killdozer and hung out," he says. "They seemed real distracted. I met Kim and Thurston and they were at some bar upstairs from the club they were playing at—this was pre-show—and I don't think they seemed like they were in a very happy mood to talk." The brief meeting left Vig with the impression of Sonic

Youth as a recherché band too cool for its own good. The two parties might never have met again were it not for their mutual relationships with Gary Gersh and Gold Mountain. It was those crossed paths that allowed Vig's name to be tossed about when Sonic Youth began its search for a producer to stanch the creative wounds sustained while making *Goo*.

Vig's second meeting with Sonic Youth took on quite a different tenor. "We were eating over in Little Italy with him when we met," Thurston recalls. "And I had just run into Tom Verlaine [of Television] who said, 'You should check out Magic Shop studios, I think it would be perfect for you guys. It's an old board, it's somewhat tube-driven.' So when we met Butch, I said, 'Oh, by the way, round the corner there's this studio Tom Verlaine told me about.' We just walked over there, knocked on the door, looked at it and said, 'We'll take it.' "

"When I first came by Kim and Thurston's apartment, Thurston said, 'I want our record to sound just like this'—and he pulled out this Mecht Mensch record I did in 1983 that sounds terrible," says Vig. "There were maybe only five hundred copies made—and he had one. And he put it on and played it really loud, with a shit-eating grin, going, 'It *has* to sound just like this, this is a fucking amazing record.' And I'm thinking, Oh no, what have I gotten myself into?"

Not surprisingly, it was Vig's work with seminal eighties bands like Killdozer and Die Kreuzen, rather than his nineties work with Nirvana, that sealed the match. The band also took on *Nevermind*'s mixer, Andy Wallace, despite widely reported, after-the-fact complaints from Kurt Cobain that Wallace had burnished the punk edges off Nirvana's DGC debut. (On *Dirty*, Steve avers that Wallace mixed in an additional sample with each drum beat to give it more *oomph*—a kind of augmenting Sonic Youth hadn't used before and hasn't since.)

"They weren't really around—they just got the final mixes [for *Nevermind*] and okayed them," Thurston says of Nirvana's dissatisfaction. "We were. We would go in after a couple hours of mixing a song and then spend another six hours finalizing with Butch and Andy Wallace."

Dirty was recorded during five weeks in early 1992 on a budget similar to that of Goo's. Gone, however, were the self-doubts that marred the production of the previous effort. Vig's methodical work habits and even temperament encouraged the band to be itself and record in a more spontaneous manner. At first bewildered by the band's unorthodox song structures and off-kilter harmonics, Vig soon enough devised ways to clarify Sonic Youth's trademark sound. "It was little difficult for me to figure out their tunings," he says. "I'd look at what Lee was playing and what Thurston was playing and what Kim was playing and go, I can't quite figure out what's going on in this section. Sometimes, indeed, one of the guitars maybe was a little out of tune, which made the tunings sound even stranger than they normally are.

"'One of the things that's interesting about how they play is that there are certain sections where they have definite arrangements and they're playing certain parts," Vig continues. "But they're not necessarily always locked into playing them exactly the same way, so there's a little bit of this intuitive kind of jam thing going on. Which makes takes interesting, because if they do two or three takes, they're not always going to be exactly the same."

Sonic Youth recorded a whopping eighteen tracks during the Dirty sessions, perhaps a testimony to the level of comfort the band had achieved in the studio. By recording at a slower tape speed, 15 ips rather than 30 ips, Vig was able to retain more dramatic low-end definition, giving the tracks a fuller, meatier sound. The able producer quickly came to realize that no matter how loud or sweeping the band's arrangements became, at each song's heart was a bit of pure sonic inspiration.

"It doesn't necessarily have to be a pretty, melodic kind of thing," Vig says. "It could be a bass groove or a back-and-forth rhythm on a guitar or something that works with a kick-and-snare pattern. I do try to make everything sound as focused as it can, too.

It can sound kind of weird or fucked-up, but it can still sound good, whatever good means."

Focused and feral, Dirty's core is the six songs on the album that deal overtly with broad social issues. The band's pitch of Daydream Nation as its "political album" had been largely a diversionary tactic culled from the fact that it was recorded during a presidential election year; only on Dirty did Sonic Youth begin to look outward without a drab of self-consciousness.

"Swimsuit Issue" is Kim's follow-up to gender-related songs such as "Tunic (Song for Karen)" and "Kool Thing." Ostensibly a jab at Sports Illustrated's "swimsuit issue," the yearly volume of the sportsweekly that features photos of scantily clad models instead of sports stories, the song also makes not-so-thinly-veiled references to a sexual harassment incident involving an high-ranking executive at Geffen that made the rounds in recording industry circles. Having never worked in a typical office situation herself only seemed to make Kim all the more capable of mustering the appropriate amount of outrage for the status quo.

Increasingly, Kim's mere presence as a woman with controlling interest in one of the past decade's most cutting-edge rock bands had upped her currency as an icon above and beyond the confines of the alternative rock world. Gordon in some ways had become the aesthetic inverse of another, much more famous female pop star—Madonna. But unlike Madonna, who early in her career substituted a confrontational persona and a keen business sense for a bona fide artistic temperament, Kim seemed from the very start to put the texture of her art before any commercial value her smoldering sexual image might win her.

"Kim has this intense gaze," Butch Vig says. "She's very open and she's not afraid to question what you're doing or make a comment, and she doesn't shy away from her opinions."

In the lyrics Kim contributed to Dirty (she sings all six of the songs she wrote), she reasserted her status as artist first and woman second (or equally). When the rest of the band joked that the instrumental track for "Drunken Butterfly" sounded like a song by

Heart, the woman-led band that gummed up early-eighties rock radio with a cluster of cloying pop hits, Kim responded by appropriating innocuous lyric fragments from Heart songs and stringing them together for her song's lyrics.

Gordon—who during the countless interview sessions for *Dirty* took to stating that women make the best anarchists—had become the band's most snarled element. New songs like "Orange Rolls, Angel's Spit" and "Créme Brûlèe" had no hope of being mistaken for straightforward pop songs. On the cryptically titled "Orange Rolls," Kim voice is reduced to an adenoidal scream that she delivers with teeth clenched. Exploring the realm of nonmelodic vocal timbres is nothing new for men—legions of heavy-metal outfits have barked their way through whole careers—but previous to Kim Gordon, women in rock were more likely to find a vocal style and stick with it than to play with the different, dark personas implied by shifting deliveries. (*Pretty on the Inside*, the 1991 debut of the Los Angeles band Hole—coproduced by Kim Gordon and Don Fleming and fronted by Kurt Cobain's spouse-to-be Courtney Love—was one of the first albums to further Kim's radical precepts.)

Meanwhile, Thurston had become the post-*Nevermind* alternative world's elder statesman and premier recidivist punk rocker. "Chapel Hill" imagines Republican senator Jesse Helms foisted into the slam-dancing pit at Cat's Cradle in Chapel Hill, North Carolina, whose audiences were some of the first in the Deep South to receive Sonic Youth with open arms.

"Youth Against Fascism" made an even better case for squaring banner political sentiments with a distrust for easy solutions. By setting provocative sentiment (one verse begins, "Yeah, the President sucks / He's a war-pig fuck"; another joyously proclaims, "I believe Anita Hill") against a simple three-chord vamp and then grafting on a deflating refrain ("It's the song I hate"), Moore simultaneously knocks dirty politics and preachy folk singers. (Fugazi's Ian MacKaye happened to be in New York and agreed to add a noise-guitar cameo to the track before the lyrics were written—lyrics that arguably attack the very kind of grandstanding that is his band's stock-in-trade.)

According to Butch Vig, "Youth Against Fascism" almost didn't make it to the album. "They had played it, but I don't think they were seriously thinking of putting it on the album," he says. Vig had heard a version of it on a live tape the band had played for him and suggested they record it. "All Thurston was singing was, 'I hate this song / This is the song I hate,' kind of facetiously, I think, because he really wasn't into it," Vig recalls. "I was like, 'You've got to write some lyrics to this song, this is really cool.' People would come by the studio and I would put that track on and play it really loud."

"Nic Fit" is an even more overt tribute to the hardcore scene of the early eighties. Originally recorded by the Untouchables, a Dischord band that included Alec MacKaye, Ian's brother, "Nic Fit" was a superfast, angry diatribe against smoking, written by a bunch of angry kids who didn't smoke. On Dirty, it still is. It took some prodding from Vig to convince the band to keep it on the album. "I wanted to use it on a B-side somewhere," Thurston says. "I wish I had sang the words instead of just shouting. The way it is it just sounds kind of stupid to me."

Of the fifteen tracks that made the final cut, "Theresa's Soundworld"—a grand, bathyal wave of sound—is Vig's favorite. "There was this calm in the studio, the lights were down real low, it was late at night," he recalls. "They'd done several takes on it, and all of a sudden they did that one and the hair on the back of my neck stood up."

Both "100%" and "JC" concern the brutal fatal shooting of Joe Cole, Henry Rollins's Los Angeles roommate and a close friend of the band's. (He can be seen in the crude video Thurston made for "My Friend Goo," included on the commercially available Goo video reel.)

Lee's one contribution to Dirty is "Wish Fulfillment," a song that almost didn't make the album, due to a standoff. "There were a couple of songs that Lee brought in and we cut one of them out because we had to cut something, and he wanted to use both of them," Thurston says, hinting at rumors that Lee briefly threatened to leave the band. "The band started more as a center for me to sing songs in, and Kim as well, and as it went along he would bring in things here and there but the bulk of it was me and/or Kim."

"Sugar Kane" and "Purr" are arguably Dirty's most overt stabs at pop-hit songwriting. Both have easily digestible lyrical conceits—"Sugar Kane"—the name under which Marilyn Monroe used to check into hotels—explores the desire men have to protect women; "Purr" toys with cat imagery. And both stand as brilliant codas to the band's quest for incorporating No Wave's experimentation into conventional song configurations.

Sonic Youth had invited Mike Kelley to produce cover art for the Master-Dik EP back in 1987, but the Los Angeles artist was unable to finish it in time to meet the band's deadline. Both parties hoped the future held another opportunity to collaborate.

By 1992 Mike Kelley had obtained status in the high-stakes commercial art world—a status his art itself, like Sonic Youth's, had never by any means courted. (He had an NEA grant revoked in the wake of U.S. Senator Jesse Helms's much-publicized artist witch-burning campaign of 1990; in November 1993, New York's Whitney Museum of American Art launched a well-publicized Mike Kelley mid-career retrospective.)

As far back as 1986, Kelley had fashioned works of art from tattered handmade stuffed animals he found at yard sales. "The first ones that I did were a reaction to the rise of commodity art in the art world," Kelley says. "For the first things I did I collected homemade things, not specifically dolls or stuffed animals, but anything that was homemade—like afghans."

Soon he only collected stuffed toys. For Kelley, these crafts items represented the ultimate in "anti-art" art. The worth of these objects was intrinsic to the number of hours someone had spent assembling them; they in fact existed as commodities in the "psychological economy," in Kelley's lexicon.

"I thought that by accumulating large amounts of them that they would have this quality of being more amounts of gift-giving than you could ever repay," he says. "You would become kind of an emotional indentured servant." In 1987 Kelley constructed a wall tapestry by sewing together stuffed animals from his collection and titled it *More Love Hours Than Can Ever Be Repaid*.

"When kids play with stuffed animals, or even when adults look at them, they see them as kind of generic human beings, so you don't really notice the oddness of their shape," Kelley says, "because they're really just stand-ins for human forms." Obsessed with why the misshapen toys looked the way they did, Kelley imagined their pasts. "They represented adult fantasies that were then projected onto children," he explains. "But they really have nothing to do with childhood, because generally people see dolls and stuffed animals as being symbols of childhood. But they're not—they're really adult constructions."

In reaction to successful New York artists, like Haim Steinbach and Jeff Koons, whose art frequently hinges upon the inherent appeal of store-bought objects, Kelley sought to reject the notion that fresh art demanded, literally, brand-new materials. "It didn't have to be a brand-new, store-bought thing," Kelley says. "It didn't have to have that allure of being new. It could be an old, fucked-up thing and still do the same thing."

For a 1991 installation called *Craft Morphology Flow Chart*, Kelley exhibited photo portraits of some of the stuffed animals alongside the actual dolls displayed on tables. He also photographed color headshots of the dolls for a project published in *21st Century*, a Canadian arts journal. Kelley included a photo of himself at seventeen, when he was a senior in high school, among the series of stuffed animal portraits. "There's nothing heavy about it," Kelley assures. "It's really simple: There are these things that people think of as symbols of youth, and then there's this picture of me when I was young. And they don't look very good together."

When Kim Gordon called Kelley in 1992 and explained that Sonic Youth was interested in using some of his work on the cover of a new album, Kelley directed the band to the issue of 21st Century. "I also wanted them to incorporate this other picture of [a] naked man and woman," he says. "Generally, in their stuff they keep away from any kind of rock negativity, like the kind of stuff you find in heavy metal." Kelley felt that positioning what appeared to be a photo of some adult act of perversion (depicting performance artists Bob Flanagan and Sherry Rose, naked, wiping their incontinent behinds with stuffed animals; it appears only in the Dirty limited edition package, slightly obscured by the amber CD tray) alongside the relatively innocuous portraits of stuffed animals would satirize the "evil rock" aesthetic. "The kind of deviance you normally see on rock album covers is more sexual," says Kelley. "But this is more infantile."

Sonic Youth ran with Kelley's lead and named the album Dirty, a mocking reference not only to the grubby stuffed animals and the prurient nature of the inlaid photo, but also to the so-called "grunge" aesthetic that the mainstream press latched on to in the wake of Nirvana's success.

Even while Dirty was still in production, industry insiders were predicting immediate Top Ten status for Sonic Youth upon its release. The band remained more skeptical. In the end, the album sold over 300,000 copies, more than any previous Sonic Youth album but nowhere near the upper echelons of underground-turned-mainstream sales reached by R.E.M., the Red Hot Chili Peppers, and Nirvana.

And while Dirty's moderate success was hardly a disappointment to the band, Thurston admits, "We were sort of maybe looking forward to the insanity of the Nirvana thing happening—but it didn't happen."

In the wake of Dirty, an album the band was infinitely more content with than Goo, Moore began to shy away from the "professional punk" world that formed in Nevermind's wake. "I was drawn more toward what was going on in the last couple of years with bands like Sebadoh [Lou Barlow's post–Dinosaur Jr. band] who were doing records in their basement and doing seven-inches a lot," he says. "I was more interested in going to Pier Platters [in Hoboken] and just buying a dozen singles a week that were just done by all these little basement bands. That, to me, was the best music of the last few years." It was the band's collective response to the newest grass-roots movement that inspired an even sparer approach in recording Dirty's follow-up.

16 | Chaos Is the Future

''THE MAJORS STILL SUCK. BUT THE THING IS, AN INDIE CAN SUCK JUST AS BAD. BANDS NOW ARE MORE LIKELY TO HAVE AN ATTITUDE THAT SUCCESS IS MEASURED BY THE QUALITY OF THE MUSIC. SO AT LEAST, THAT ATTITUDE WAS BORN OF THE WHOLE INDIE MOVEMENT.''

—DON FLEMING

Mike D of the Beastie Boys remembers New York in the early 1980s as a place and time wherein hip-hop and noise rock were the only exciting games in town. "And once hardcore fell off," he says, "all that was left then was hip-hop." When the Beastie Boys switched from hardcore to hip-hop, they lost nearly all interest in what they had decided was the spent rock scene. "We kind of thought of Sonic Youth as 'art-core'—and I can only say that, at the time, I didn't embrace it."

To the generation of music fans that came of age in the eighties, guitar rock died in 1980. "That was the whole John Lydon thing with Public Image Ltd.," Mike D says. "He was on Tom Snyder's 'Tomorrow' show saying like, 'Rock and roll is dead—it ended with the Sex Pistols.' And I totally believed it." It wasn't till later on, when *Daydream Nation* was released, that Mike D once again entertained the idea that cutting-edge music could be played on electric guitars.

"The Beastie Boys are in such a different world," says Thurston. "They became superfamous really young, when their first album came out. Then they moved to California. They missed the rise of indie rock. I think they were sort of aware of it, but at the same time didn't follow it; they didn't really get into the world of it—spending years getting in vans and going cross-country and playing at little clubs and seeing little bands sprout up and just feeling the vibe."

Yet the Beastie Boys established themselves as mavericks in much the same way that Sonic Youth did. Not only were they not African-American, which automatically created a hip-hop credibility problem, but they were also exploring musical styles that in 1985 extended well beyond the technological pale. "*Licensed to Ill* was pre-sampling," says Mike D "We had to use tape loops because there wasn't any real easy or available sampling technology." To this day, few hip-hop acts have continued down the path beaten by the Beastie Boys. Thurston says, "I think people today look at our two bands as having a relationship because they're both somewhat experimental in their respective genres."

By most estimates, Public Enemy's *It Takes a Nation of Millions to Hold Us Back* and Sonic Youth's *Daydream Nation* were the two most influential albums released out of New York in 1988. Mike D was bowled over by the brilliant noise collage Public Enemy devised using the absolute newest computer sampling technology available. But at the same time, Sonic Youth also suddenly commanded the attention of discerning ears. "You can really make a case—it's not even a stretch—as to the significance of them both coming out of the same studio at around the same time," Mike D says.

In 1989 the Beastie Boys released *Paul's Boutique*, the group's experimental breakthrough (and first commercial misstep), and thus became members of the elite club of popular musicians willing to trade in their listeners' expectations for greater creative freedom. Sonic Youth sought to test its commercial viability by signing to Geffen around the same time the Beastie Boys began retreating from the image that had made them millions. (They were also dropped by Def Jam and signed by Tim Carr, then an A&R rep at Capitol.)

When Mike D married Tamra Davis, feature-film director (*Guncrazy*, CB4) and creator of the videos for "Dirty Boots" and "Kool Thing," it seemed only to further strengthen the creative bond between the two bands.

After making *Paul's Boutique*, the Beastie Boys began wondering where to go next. "We felt, ourselves, that we were burnt out on sampling," says Mike D "We'd spent so many nights till five and six in the morning, meticulously sampling everything. We took that to a limit and now wondered, What now?"

Only the work of a guitar band as inventive as Sonic Youth could have convinced a bunch of hip-hop diehards like the Beastie Boys to switch back. The Beastie Boys decided for the first time since hitting it big to pick up basic rock instruments once again—electric guitars, real drums. "It was just kind of like, 'Okay, let's try this,' " says Mike D *Check Your Head*, the Beastie Boys' 1993 album, featured the band playing real guitars and drums. And even with the album's muddy, no-fi sound, the hour's-worth of funk-punk hybrid sold millions.

And while Mike D has no great love for *The Whitey Album*, Sonic Youth's most ambitious (if half-hearted) attempt at hip-hop, he praises the impulse behind it. "They kind of had the right idea," he says. "It actually surprises me that more people haven't pursued that route."

Whichever of the two groups more closely represents the future of popular music (though one suspects the answer lies somewhere in between, or else nowhere near either), both Sonic Youth and the Beastie Boys believe downsizing is the first step. "One definite thing we have in common with those guys," says Mike D, "is that when we're listening to new records, shit that's done on a four-track always sounds the best to us. I kind of expect some kids to completely broadside all of us with some completely homemade combination of it all."

"I remember telling Gary Gersh [before Gersh left Geffen in 1993 to become president of Capitol] that I wanted to make a record that was really quick and not get so involved in making a great major-label record," Thurston says of *Experimental Jet Set, Trash, and No Star.* "And when I called Butch about this one, I said, 'Look, we want to go into Sear Sound and just work two weeks, get the tracks down, mix really quick, and get the hell out of there.' " The band even went so far as to keep some of the "roughs"—the tracks recorded before mixing in the studio, ostensibly as a guide—on the final tape.

After mixing the tracks at Sound on Sound, a more modern, computer-run facility, the band decided to return to Sear Sound and run the digital mixes back through the vintage board to regain some sonic fuzz. While at Sound on Sound, Butch Vig and engineer John Siket would find notes on the mixing board instructing them not to touch anything that would drastically alter the sound of the album.

In the minds of many performers who reached creative pinnacles in the midst of the eighties independent-music scene, limited distribution makes good music even more prized. "Is the music private or public? Does it sound good on the street?" Kim wonders. "As soon as Nirvana became big, I couldn't possibly listen to the record at home anymore. I didn't need to; it was all around me. It no longer fulfilled that need for a private obsession."

"It's always been hard to even get my records distributed to the people who want them," says Lydia Lunch. "But that design of obsoletion—I dig that concept. I dig that if you want to know what I've done and you want to really know about all the formats I've created, you have got to search."

The very manner in which Sonic Youth pursues certain musical directions over others draws into question what makes a great pop-music group. "Oftentimes, we write songs where someone will say, 'Gee, you should've put this part in a couple of more times,' " says Lee. " 'Starfield Road' on the new record is like that. It's got a really abstract section and then it's got a really catchy section that only happens once. It's really bizarre."

Most musicians who have recently won "creative control"

clauses in their freshly inked major-label contracts admit that such stipulations are no guarantee. Even Sonic Youth is expected to answer to the bottom line.

"The problem that a lot of people have is that they expect that whatever kind of music they're doing is going to be popular," says Steve Albini. "People need to come to grips with the fact that certain types of music are not going to be popular and successful. And doing them as a livelihood is not necessarily a realistic expectation."

Pavement—a guitar band on Gerard Cosloy's Matador label hailed for its power and innovation—opened six shows for Sonic Youth during the summer of 1992. Mark Ibold, Pavement's thirty-one-year-old bass player and a longtime acquaintance of Sonic Youth's says, "They've always been supportive of more unknown bands and brought them on tour with them. We were a band that a lot of people hadn't really heard—but that *they* had heard and liked."

"Through the eighties, we and other bands built up a whole vocabulary that now—it's almost like it's all folk music," says Kim. "You take the new vocabulary, and depending what your sources are, you come up with your sound, like Sebadoh, like Pavement. And it's natural."

Of course, the inevitable accusations of creative co-option that Sonic Youth's inviting Pavement to again share a bill, this time in Europe, brought upon the lesser known band were not necessarily welcome. "I can see some comparisons," says Ibold, "but I don't think that anyone in Pavement is nearly as talented a musician as the musicians in that band. They're highly developed technically and they're really good at producing unusual sounds. Our band is more of a pop band."

If nothing else, Sonic Youth's notion of aesthetic persistence alone will outlive the band. The band's ideas on what makes pop product fly remain resolutely ahead of their time. The very point at which Sonic Youth elevates a new sound, structure, or lyrical conceit to the level of innovation is, more often than not, the same point at which the band pops a hole in the conceit by making a joke of it. Of course, deflating concept at this juncture only makes it more resistant to attack at higher altitudes. That firebrand-in-slacker's-clothing guise influences new post-postpunk groups all the time.

"Sonic Youth is the most influential band in American popular music of the last decade," says Gary Gersh. "The underground scene and how all of these bands want to learn how to grow and have careers independently has been forged by Sonic Youth. There would be a very different underground scene if they didn't exist. That's why every single one of those bands talks to them and wants to open for them and wants to tour with them and wants to learn from them."

"One of the most valuable things we've learned from them, we've learned just from the way we've been treated by them on tours," Mark Ibold confirms. "They're very supportive. One of the problems in rock—especially in indie rock, where you wouldn't think it would happen—is that there's a lot of sneering, bad attitude between bands. Sonic Youth are into having fun and making jokes about other bands, but really they have a very good attitude."

"They brought a lot of bands to the attention of the world, really, because of an attitude that they had," says Don Fleming. "An attitude about being involved in their local scene, which is now sort of a national scene. They expanded what they used to do probably just here in New York to bands across the country."

All four members of Sonic Youth put their beliefs into practice by keeping their respective ears to the street. Thurston seems forever scouting New York's clubs for new talent for both Ecstatic Peace, his own label and repository for rock and jazz obscurata, and for Geffen. Sonic Youth has a rare A&R agreement with its label, which has so far allowed the band to sign Cell and St. Johnny, two New York–area acts, to DGC. "It's a very loose arrangement," says Geffen's Ray Farrell. "Thurston can do whatever he wants. Sonic Youth—but it's essentially Thurston—can bring things to the label in an A&R capacity and put them out either under the Ecstatic Peace banner or on DGC and they will be given credit for that, in terms of points."

Smells Like Records, Steve's self-financed singles label, recently released basement-issue singles by Sentridoh (an even grungier offshoot of Sebadoh), Jad Fair, and Blonde Redhead.

Early in 1993, three members of Sonic Youth toured Tokyo and Osaka together—but not as Sonic Youth. Mosquito (a now-defunct band Steve Shelley formed with Jad Fair and his old friend Tim Foljahn, from the Spastic Rhythm Tarts) and Free Kitten (a radical trash-blues band that includes Kim, Julie Cafritz, formerly of Pussy Galore, Yoshimi from the Boredoms, and Mark Ibold, bassist for Pavement) played on a double bill. Thurston opened each show alone, performing early versions of "Tokyo Eye," "Skink," and "Screaming Skull" with only a guitar.

"The whole punk-rock thing with us—on one hand it's tongue-in-cheek," Kim says. "But it also indicates the kind of experiences that we had, that we saw, that marked us. There are aspects of it that we identify with, but not really so much the structure. For us, it's more about the free aspect and not wanting to be homogenized."

Perhaps it's the band's unflagging curiosity that allows it to forge ahead where so many others lost interest. "I've been in New York with them and they'll catch a show virtually every night," says Epic Soundtracks. "They're very interested, where maybe a lot of people who have been in the business or whatever you want to call it for that long might be a bit jaded. But they seem to keep the enthusiasm up."

Back in 1991 Thurston convinced punk pioneer Richard Hell to join him, Steve Shelley, and Don Fleming in Waterworks studio to record two obscure covers: "The Plug," by Unnatural Axe, a seventies Boston punk band, and "Christian Rat Attack," by Stickmen with Rayguns, a mid-eighties Texas outfit. "Thurston had been talking to Richard Hell on the phone for a couple of years, on and off," says Don Fleming. "He really just wanted, again, to line up some sort of a weekend project." An impromptu half-hour in-the-studio rendition of "You Gotta Lose," an old Hell song, went so well that Thurston decided to press three seven-inch singles and package them in one sleeve. Thus the first release from Dim Stars—formerly a fake band name Thurston had used in early Ecstatic Peace ads—included "The Plug," "Christian Rat Attack," the newly written "Dim Star Theme," and four sides of "You Gotta Lose."

For Hell, one of New York punk's most brilliant (and some would say, squandered) natural talents, the decade between *Destiny Street*, the final Voidoids album, and the Dim Stars project had provided him with a much-needed respite from the recording industry. Having been gypped out of royalties, and subsumed by a nagging heroin addiction, Hell decided to restrict his formidable energies to the realms of poetry and spoken-word performance. Only something as positive and as informal as the first weekend of Dim Stars recording could have renewed Hell's faith in his musical powers. "Suddenly Richard really wanted to do an album, but he wouldn't go in any other studio," says Fleming. "He said that it was the first time he had ever been to a studio where it wasn't complete chaos."

Dim Stars, the full-length effort that resulted—comprised of lyrics by Hell—turned out to be a fitting trophy for all the parties involved. Robert Quine, formerly the Voidoids' guitarist, played on a few tracks: Jad Fair appears, squawking on a saxophone during a cover of T. Rex's "Rip Off." Songs such as "She Wants to Die" and "Stop Breaking Down" are arguably some Hell's finest, and the performances captured on tape are easily some of the loosest he's ever recorded. As if to flaunt the power of the project's indie-powered dynamo, the fourteen-song collection was released on six different labels around the world: Caroline Records in the U.S., New Rose in France, Paperhouse in England, City Slang in Germany, Au Go Go in Australia, and Alpha in Japan.

Unfortunately the album's afterglow was a bit marred. "In his

own way, [Richard] was old-school about the way to do things,''
says Steve. ''In all my work with Sonic Youth and any other band,
we've almost always split publishing equally amongst everyone
who plays. Richard comes from the old school, where the singer
not only writes the words but he's also contributing a melody—
and so he's due fifty percent and everybody else divides the other
fifty percent.'' Although the band's loose live performances
augured a promising touring career, a mutual reluctance to face
future squabbling over royalties suggests Dim Stars are never again
to convene.

Undaunted, Thurston recently indulged his increasing obsession
with avant-garde jazz by recording half an album's worth of guitar-
drums duets with William Hooker. (The other half of the album,
titled Shamballa, features Hooker collaborating with guitarist Elliot
Sharp.)

Kim looks forward to playing more six-string guitar (rather than
bass) with Free Kitten. Unlike Harry Crews, the band she and Lydia
Lunch briefly formed in 1991, Free Kitten has had time to develop.
''Free Kitten is an outlet for a certain kind of trashy blues that I
like,'' Kim says. ''Since 'Brother James' it's always been in the back
of my mind.''

Call Now—a Free Kitten EP they produced with Don Fleming,
which includes songs such as ''Platinumb'' and ''Skinny Butt''—
was released on Ecstatic Peace in 1992. ''It sort of bothered me that,
musically, Harry Crews could have been stronger,'' she says. ''Free
Kitten is a completely different thing because Julie and I are best
friends. With Lydia, even though I liked her and we were friends,
I never really felt that close to her.''

In fall 1993 the Breeders, a group headed by former Pixies
bassist Kim Deal, asked Kim Gordon to direct a few music videos
for their Last Splash album. ''They felt stupid doing videos, kind of
nerdy,'' says Kim Gordon. ''They said they thought because I was
so cool that if I directed the videos it would be okay. I like Kim

Deal. She's nutty, but I admire her perseverance—she perseveres and she gets what she wants."

Nothing, it seems, can phase Sonic Youth's creative momentum. They have contributed more tracks to performer-tribute albums than any other band alive; in the past year they have participated in album projects to support AIDS research and Greenpeace, among other admirable causes. Sonic Youth even paired up with the marijuana-and-wisecracks hip-hop group Cypress Hill to record "I Love You Mary Jane," one of a series of alternative–hip-hop collaborations that appeared on the soundtrack to the movie *Judgment Night*.

''Sonic Youth early on did what none of those other bands of their day did: They figured out how to tour," says Tim Carr. "They went and fucking played every Podunk place between here and L.A. twenty times between 1982 and 1985. And then another twenty times between 1985 and 1988. So by the time they got signed to Geffen, they had friends everywhere. Every single person that was going to matter, Sonic Youth had been the underground railroad that had connected them."

Most stops on that underground railroad continue to display signs of life, whether or not the post-Nirvana alternative industry acknowledges their worth. "In the last few years any number of bands has blown my mind to the same exact extent that my mind was being blown in the mid-eighties," says Steve Albini. "It's just that in addition to those records there are a ridiculous number of fluff, crap, unlistenable, mediocre, pap mainstream records as well. And because there has been a perceived shift in the marketplace, they're all competing for attention in the same stores."

It's ironic that the state of mind that Sonic Youth helped create— the same one that later made bands like Nirvana, Pearl Jam, Soul Asylum, and Smashing Pumpkins rich—also threatens its livelihood. There's a new bottom line: If alternative bands can sell millions, goes the precept, shouldn't Sonic Youth be selling millions?

"Nobody cared about Nirvana until they sold a million records," Kim points out. "They weren't written about in a critical way—only in fanzines, like, 'This is a good record.' And then suddenly, when it sold millions, people started taking everything so seriously. Sure, there's that whole other level, where rock and roll exists semiotically in the culture—that they have achieved. But lyrically, nobody cared, say, that Kurt hated macho men."

It's difficult to imagine the last decade and half of popular music having taken the course it did without Sonic Youth. Sonic Youth's top-to-bottom overhaul of its medium by no means made them a household name. But few musicians or people who make their living off music who have come to appreciate the band's work remain unchanged. The mere fact that Sonic Youth remains constantly at work, forever eliminating pop-music permutations, makes any new band's job all the more difficult. "Every record we do, it's harder to do the next one," Kim laments, "because you don't want to repeat yourself."

"There's always the possibility that the next record's going to come out and that everyone in general is going to say, 'Oh, we know this,'" says Steve. "Not that we set out, every record that we make, to make the most extreme record at the time. I think we're just setting out to record ten songs. And at this point, they can be different enough that one can be mellow, or one can be traditional even—but that's just this time. Next time, it's going to be different."

''We're in a period right now where the record companies don't know exactly what they can sell," Mike Kelley says. "So they're willing to let people do something a little more open. That's how it was in the late sixties—they didn't know how to market the stuff so they just let people do what they wanted to do."

Lydia Lunch is less optimistic. She no longer performs with bands, having eschewed the music world for spoken word, for the simple reason that she believes the format is no longer conducive to communicating shocking ideas. "At the time I got started, music was the most convenient format and there was so much to fight against," says Lunch. "Now no one is fighting against the music that already exists—they're all wanting a piece of it. That's what's driven me away from clubs, away from live music, and away from alternative music. The only thing I listen to basically is rap—they're the only ones that are saying anything. When you get someone like 2-Pac [Tupac Shakur], who is twenty-two or twenty-three and saying all these incredibly heavy social statements in a way that's fresh and seductive, evocative, and hard-core—there's nothing like that in the white community. Spoiled white kids, who wants to hear about it?"

The future of popular music (how many units does one need to sell these days in order to qualify as pop?), one suspects, lies somewhere at a smaller scale—in some sealed-off recess where it's been allowed to grow undarkened by the close scrutiny of product-hungry A&R executives. More affordable and user-friendly technologies, everything from portable four-track recorders to lap-top computers, suggest that the next big thing will involve some digital analog hybrid.

"In the late eighties, some people decided we were wearing out our welcome," says Thurston. "We'd get write-ups in fanzines that would say, What's the point? There are so many bands that are influenced by you that are refining and taking your ideas down a fresher avenue. Our response was, Well, we're not trying to do anything except maintain a band."

Fortunately for the band, most new Sonic Youth fans are kids—a good indicator of the band's lasting cachet on cool. Kim and Thurston suspect that some in the band's younger audience have little idea that some members of their favorite group are their parents' age. Though teenage girls do occasionally approach Kim after shows and tell her they wish she were their mother.

Kim's brash, independent image seems to have been a primary inspiration for a loosely allied network of bands, many from Olympia, Washington, that call themselves "riot grrrls." The hard-rocking groups—with names like Bikini Kill, Bratmobile, and

Huggy Bear (from England)—are committed to the indie-label ethic. (Most record for the Olympia label Kill Rock Stars.)

That Lee Ranaldo coproduced *Fontanelle*, the second album from Babes in Toyland—a Minneapolis trio that also furthers the notion that women can form uncompromising rock bands without pandering to male stereotypes—is also worth noting. In fact, whether you're talking about Britain's "dream pop" bands (My Bloody Valentine, Ride), San Diego's hard but humorous alternative scene (Truman's Water, Rocket from the Crypt), or the buzz-pop revolution (Superchunk, Pavement, Sebadoh), Sonic Youth remains a necessary underground reference point—practically a raison d'être for the many smart young bands who still believe there's merit in music made with electric guitars.

Yes, for Sonic Youth, the future doesn't seem as uncertain as it used to be. Lee is still publishing Sonic Youth tour diaries—the latest appeared in the June/July 1993 issue of *Raygun*. But he also had a letter published in the *New York Times* last December arguing in favor of the New York City public-school system (in which his nine-year-old son Cody is currently enrolled as a pupil).

"[Sonic Youth] will fit in as people who dug up the ground, built a platform, and will be acknowledged by some and conveniently ignored by others," says Greil Marcus, who has kept listening to the band over the years. "But it seems really dubious to me that they're ever going to be able to enter into the mass consciousness—I mean, they're a very bohemian band in their ambitions and their view of the world.

"They've never had the pop sense, the fan's soul—maybe Thurston does, but I don't think Kim does—that animated Kurt Cobain at his best," Marcus says. "On the other hand, if you look at that movie 1991: *The Year Punk Broke*, onstage they're fabulous."

But was Nirvana's unfettered success the end of the era ushered in by groups like Sonic Youth, or the beginning of another? "It's both," says Don Fleming. "I don't think that what they did is even going to be the most influential thing that happens." One suspects

Kurt Cobain's suicide in April 1994 will end up serving, in some way, as (at least) a symbolic end.

Regardless of what the future holds for Sonic Youth—greater sales and more exposure, or dwindling sales and a slow fade back into obscurity—one can rest assured that unearthing fresh creative outlets will remain a band priority. Even as you read this, Kim, Thurston, Lee, and Steve are most likely off in different directions, in search of some hard-to-find secondhand record store, bookstore, art gallery, or concert venue, driven once again by that insatiable thirst for something that strays even just a slight bit from the norm.

And, alas, new musical inspiration might be just a concert experience away. "When I saw the first Royal Trux gig and it was just the two of them playing, I was like, Wow, you really don't need a whole band," Kim says. "That's why Free Kitten's first gig was just Julie and me on guitars."

"We're going to get more involved in just putting live music down ourselves in the studio, because a lot of the new record was written that way," says Thurston, predicting the future. "I can't ever really see us breaking up. I can imagine us kind of fragmented but still vital as a recording unit."

Lee agrees. "You have four different opinions, like the four corners of a square. And rather than one opinion asserting itself and saying this is how it's going to be, something slowly gets mutated and molded until everybody is happy with it."

Sure, rock is dead. But judging from Sonic Youth's upcoming schedule, you'd never know it. "Every time I go someplace," says Thurston, "even now, like Australia, anywhere; before I arrive, I don't care—but once I'm there, all of a sudden I just become totally ensconced in the whole local music scene. It's really a drag."

Discography

While this discography aims to please completists, omissions are inevitable. The members of Sonic Youth, together and individually, have recorded for so many different labels it remains nearly impossible to track every release. (Even the band occasionally loses sight of an obscure one.) Also note that Sonic Youth has released a series of "bootleg" albums themselves, mostly through the Sonic Death fan club.

LP = vinyl album
EP = extended-play vinyl disc
CS = cassette
CD = compact disc

ALBUMS

Sonic Youth
The Burning Spear / I Dreamed I Dream / She Is Not Alone / I
Don't Want to Push It / The Good and the Bad
1982   12″ EP/CS on Neutral (Neutral 001, UK)
1982   12″ EP/CS on Zensor (ND 01, UK)
1987   12″ EP/CS/CD reissued on SST (SST097, US)

Confusion Is Sex
(She's in a) Bad Mood / Protect Me You / Freezer Burn / I Wanna
Be Your Dog / Shaking Hell / Inhuman / The World Looks Red /
Confusion Is Next / Making the Nature Scene / Lee Is Free
1983   LP/CS on Neutral (Neutral Nine, UK)
1983   LP/CS on Zensor (ND 02, Germany)
1987   LP/CS/CD reissued on SST (SST096, US)

Kill Yr. Idols
Protect Me You / Shaking Hell (1+2) / Kill Yr. Idols / Brother
James / Early American
1983   12″ EP on Zensor (Zensor 10, UK)

Sonic Death
Live tracks from 1981 to 1983.
1983   CS Ecstatic Peace (E#2)
1988   CS/CD SST/Ecstatic Peace (SST181, US)
1988   CS/CD Blast First (BFFP32, UK)

Bad Moon Rising
Intro / Brave Men Run / Society Is a Hole / I Love Her All the Time /
Ghost Bitch / I'm Insane / Justice Is Might / Death Valley '69
1985   LP/CS on Homestead (HMS016, US)
1985   LP/CS on Blast First (BFFP1, UK)
1987   LP on Au Go Go (ANDA66, Australia)

Intro / Brave Men Run / Society Is a Hole / I Love Her All the Time /
Ghost Bitch / I'm Insane / Justice Is Might / Death Valley '69 /
Satan Is Boring / Flower / Halloween / Echo Canyon
1987   CD on Blast First (BFFP1CD)

Death Valley '69
Death Valley '69 / I Dreamed I Dream / Inhuman / Brother James /
Satan Is Boring
1985   12″ EP on Homestead (HMS021, US)
1985   12″ EP on Blast First (BFFP2, UK)

EVOL
Tom Violence / Shadow of a Doubt / Starpower / In the Kingdom
#19 / Green Light / Death to Our Friends / Secret Girls / Marilyn
Moore / Expressway to Yr. Skull
1986   LP/CS on SST (SST059, US)
1986   LP/CS on Blast First (BFFP4, UK)
1987   LP on Au Go Go (ANDA67, Australia)
Tom Violence / Shadow of a Doubt / Starpower / In the Kingdom
#19 / Green Light / Death to our Friends / Secret Girls / Marilyn
Moore / Expressway to Yr. Skull / Bubblegum
1986   CD on SST (SST CD 059, US)
1986   CD on Blast First (BFFP4, UK)

Sister
Schizophrenia / (I Got a) Catholic Block / Beauty Lies in the Eye /
Stereo Sanctity / Pipeline/Kill Time / Tuff Gnarl / PCH / Hot Wire
My Heart / Kotton Krown / White Kross
1987   LP/CS on SST (SST134, US)
1987   LP/CS on Blast First (BFFP20, UK)
1987   LP on Au Go Go (ANDA60, Australia)
Schizophrenia / Catholic Block / Beauty Lies in the Eye / Stereo
Sanctity / Pipeline/Kill Time / Tuff Gnarl / Pacific Coast Highway /
Hot Wire My Heart / Cotton Crown / White Cross / Master-Dik

1987   CD on SST (SST CD 134, US)
1987   CD on Blast First (BFFP20CD, UK)

Master-Dik

Master-Dik / Beat on the Brat / Under the Influence of the Jesus and Mary Chain [live on Suisse radio, July 87] / Ticket to Ride / Master-Dik [version] / Introducing the Stars / Ringo/He's on Fire/Florida Oil Drums/Westminster Chimes / Chinese Jam / Vibrato / Guitar Lick / Funky Fresh / Our Backyard / Traffick

1987   EP on SST (SST155, US)
1987   EP on Blast First (BFFP26t, UK)

Daydream Nation

Teenage Riot / Silver Rocket / The Sprawl / 'Cross the Breeze / Eric's Trip / Total Trash / Hey Joni / Providence / Candle / Rain King / Kissability / Trilogy: a) The Wonder; b) Hyperstation; z) Eliminator Jr.

1988   2×LP/CS/CD Enigma (75403-02, US)
1988   2×LP/CS/CD Blast First (BFFP34, UK)
1988   CD on BMG Compact Disc (D-201076, US)
1988   2×LP on Au Go Go (ANDA90, Australia)
1992   CS/CD rerelease on Blast First/Mute in U.S. (BFFP 34 CD, UK)
1993   CD reissue on DGC (DGCD-24515, US)

Goo

Dirty Boots / Tunic (Song for Karen) / Mary-Christ / Kool Thing / Mote / My Friend Goo / Disappearer / Mildred Pierce / Cinderella's Big Score / Scooter and Jinx / Titanium Exposé

1990   LP/CS/CD on DGC (24297-D2, US)

Dirty

100% / Swimsuit Issue / Theresa's Sound-world / Drunken Butterfly / Shoot / Wish Fulfillment / Sugar Kane / Orange Rolls, Angel's Spit / Youth Against Fascism / Nic Fit / On the Strip / Chapel Hill / JC / Stalker [LP-only bonus track] / Purr / Créme Brûlèe

1992   2×LP/CS/CD on DGC (DGC/DGCC/DGCD-24485, DGCD-24493, US)

1992   CD on DGC (MVCG-92 [DGCD-24495], Japan)

Experimental Jet Set, Trash and No Star
Winner's Blues / Bull in the Heather / Starfield Road / Skink / Screaming Skull / Self-Obsessed and Sexxee / Bone / Androgynous Mind / Quest for the Cup / Waist / Doctor's Orders / Tokyo Eye / In the Mind of the Bourgeois Reader / Sweet Shine
1994   LP/CS/CD on DGC (DGCC/D-24632)

SINGLES AND EPS

Making the Nature Scene
Making the Nature Scene / I Killed Christgau with My Big Fucking Dick
1983   7″ single on Forced Exposure (FE-001, US)

Death Valley '69
Death Valley '69 / Brave Men Run
1984   7″ single on Iridescence (I-12, UK)

Flower/Halloween
Flower / Halloween
1985   12″ single on Homestead (HMS047, US)
1985   12″ single on Blast First (BFFP3, UK)

Flower
Flower [Anti Fuckword Radio Edit] / Rewolf [Special Natas Mix]
1985   7″ single on Blast First (7BFFP3)

Halloween II
Halloween / [B-side hand-etched by Savage Pencil]
1985   12″ single on Blast First (BFFP3, UK)

Starpower
Starpower [edit] / Bubblegum
1986   7″ on Blast First (BFFP7, UK)
Starpower [edit] / Bubblegum / Expressway to Yr. Skull [edit]
1986   12″ EP/CS on SST (SST080, US)
1986   12″ on Blast First (BFFP7, UK)
1990   CD3/CD5 on SST (SST080CD, US)

I Wanna Be Your Dog
I Wanna Be Your Dog [with Iggy Pop] / Sister
1987   7″ single bootleg

Silver Rocket
Silver Rocket / You Pose You Lose / Non-Metal Dude Wearing
Metal Tee
1988   7″ single on Forced Exposure (FE-012 on vinyl, FE-014 on
       cover, US)

Teenage Riot
Teenage Riot [one-sided flexidisc]
1988   7″ flexidisc by *The Catalogue* (CAT064, UK)

Providence
Providence [stereo] / Providence [mono]
1989   7″ single on Blast First (BFFP48, UK)

Candle
Candle [edit] / Intro / Hey Joni / Flower / Ghost Bitch / Conversation
1989   12″ EP on Enigma/Blast First (EPRO-193, UK)

Halloween/Touch Me I'm Sick [Mudhoney/Sonic Youth split single]
Halloween / Touch Me I'm Sick
[Each band covers the other's song.]
1989   7″ single on Sub Pop (SP26)
1989   12″ single on Blast First (BFFP46)

1990   12″ single on Sub Pop/Tupelo (SP26-2)
1990   12″ single on Glitterhouse (GR 56, Germany)

Kool Thing
Kool Thing / That's All I Know (Right Now)
1990   EP on DGC (24297-D2/D4G, US)
Kool Thing / Kool Thing [8-track demo version]
1990   12″ single promo on DGC (PRO-A-4123, US)
Kool Thing
1990   CD5 promo on DGC (PRO-CD-4123, US)
Kool Thing / That's All I Know (Right Now) / Dirty Boots [Rock-and-Roll Heaven Version] / Kool Thing [8-track demo version]
1990   EP/CD on Geffen (GEF 81cd-7599-21616-2, Germany)

Disappearer
Disappearer [edit] / Disappearer [8-track demo version] / That's All I Know (Right Now) / Dirty Boots [8-track demo version/long version]
1990   12″ EP/CD5 on DGC (24297-D2/21623-2, US)
Disappearer [edit] / Disappearer [LP version] / Disappearer [8-track demo version]
1990   12″/CD5 single promo on DGC (PRO-A-4172/PRO-CD-4172, US)

Dirty Boots
Dirty Boots [edit] / White Kross [live] / Eric's Trip [live] / Cinderella's Big Score [live] / Dirty Boots [live] / The Bedroom [live and previously unreleased]
1990   12″ EP/CD on DGC (DGCDS-21634, US)

Personality Crisis
Personality Crisis / Dirty Boots [8-track demo short version]
1991   7″ in *Sassy* (DGC 7-19664-dj, US)

100%
100% / Créme Brûlèe / Genetic / Hendrix Necro
1992   CD5 on DGC (DGCDM-21735, US)
1992   12″ on DGC (DGCT11, US)
1992   10″ on DGC (DGCV11, US)
100% / Créme Brûlèe
1992   7″ on DGC (DGCS11)

Youth Against Fascism
Youth Against Fascism [Clean Version] / Youth Against Fascism
[Album Version]
1992   7″ promo on DGC
Youth Against Fascism [clean-ex mix] / Purr [from the Mark
Goodier BBC program] / Youth Against Fascism [LP version]
1992   7″/10″ on DGC
Youth Against Fascism [clean-ex mix] / Purr [Mark Goodier ses-
sion version] / The Destroyed Room [previously unreleased] /
Youth Against Fascism [LP version]
1992   CD5 on DGC (GFSTD 26, France)
1992   CD5 on DGC (GED 21756, Germany)

Sugar Kane
Sugar Kane [edit] / The Destroyed Room / Purr [acoustic/Mark
Goodier version] / The End of the End of the Ugly
1993   CD5 on DGC (DGCDM-21818, US)

Drunken Butterfly
Drunken Butterfly / Stalker (LP vers.) / Tamra
1993   CD on Geffen

Whores Moaning: Oz '93 Tour Edition
Sugar Kane [edit] / Personality Crisis / The End of the End of the
Ugly / It Is My Body / Tamara
1993   12″/CD on Geffen (GEFDM 21783, Australia)

TV Shit [Sonic Youth with Yamatsuka Eye]
Movements 1–4
1994   LP on Ecstatic Peace

CICCONE YOUTH

Tuff Titty Rap
Burnin' Up / Tuff Titty Rap / Into the Groovey
1986   7″ single on New Alliance (NAR030, US)
1986   12″ single on New Alliance/SST (NAR030, US)
1988   12″ single on Blast First/Mute (BFFP 8T, UK)

Into the Groovey
Into the Groovey / Tuff Titty Rap
1988   12″ EP on Enigma

The Whitey Album
Needle-Gun / [silence] / G-Force / Platoon II / MacBeth / Me &
Jill / Hendrix Cosby / Burnin' Up [orig. demo] / Hi! Everybody! /
Children of Satan/Third Fig / Two Cool Rock Chicks Listening
to Neu / Addicted to Love / Moby-Dik / March of the Ciccone
Robots / Making the Nature Scene / Tuff Titty Rap / Into the
Groovey / Macbeth [instrumental version, Blast First CD release
only]
1988   LP/CS/CD on Enigma/Blast First (7 75402-1)
1988   LP/CS/CD on Blast First (BFFP28)

PROMOTIONAL INTERVIEW RELEASES

Sister Interview Disc
The Sister Concept / Schizophrenia / Sonic Song Structure &
Method / The Forthcoming Vids / Tuff Gnarl / Da Noo Yark Scene /
Food Favorites / Sonic Signoff
1987   LP on Blast First (CHAT1, UK)

Sonic Youth Interview Soundsheet
1990   flexidisc single on DGC (EV-106-610-00-1 ST, US)

DIM STARS [RICHARD HELL, THURSTON MOORE, STEVE SHELLEY, AND DON FLEMING]

Dim Stars
The Plug & Dim Star / Christian Rat Attack / You Gotta Lose (Pt. 1) / You Gotta Lose (Pt. 2) / You Gotta Lose (Pt. 3) / You Gotta Lose (Pt. 4)
1991   3×7″ single on Ecstatic Peace (E#11) distributed by Forced Exposure

3 New Songs, Richard Hell
The Night Is Coming On / Baby Huey (Baby Do You Wanna Dance?) / Frank Sinatra
[Richard Hell, Thurston Moore, Steve Shelley, and Don Fleming]
1992   7″ on Overground (Over 24)

Dim Stars
She Wants to Die / All My Witches Come True / Memo to Marty / Monkey / Natchez Burning / Stop Breakin' Down / Baby Huey (Do You Wanna Dance) / The Night Is Coming On / Downtown at Dawn / Try This / Incense Is the Essence / Weird Forest / Stray Cat Generation / Rip Off [CD bonus: Dim Star Theme]
1992   CD on Caroline (1724-2)
1992   LP on Paperhouse (paplp 014)
1992   LP in Germany on EFA (04902-08)
1992   City Slang (LC 6853)
1992   CD on New Rose (Rose290CD)

SONIC YOUTH APPEARANCES ON COMPILATION ALBUMS

Just Another Asshole, Number 5
Shift [Lee Ranaldo] / The Fucking Youth of Today [Thurston Moore] / untitled [Kim Gordon and Miranda] / Faspeedelay Bop [Glenn Branca and Lee Ranaldo]
1981   LP on Just Another Asshole (No. 5)

Noise Fest
untitled track
1982   Cassette on Zg Music Number 5 (C-82)

Who You Staring At, Glenn Branca and John Giorno
Lee Ranaldo and Thurston Moore play guitars on "Bad Smells."
1982   LP on Giorno Poetry Systems Institute (GPS025)

Symphony No. 1 (Tonal Plexus), Glenn Branca
Thurston Moore and Lee Ranaldo play guitars; Ann DeMarinis plays keyboard and percussion; Richard Edson plays trumpet. Ranaldo produced.
1983   CS on ROIR (A125)
1991   2×LP/CD on Danceteria (DAN LP 081/DAN CD 081)

Symphony No. 3 (Gloria), Glenn Branca
Lee Ranaldo and Thurston Moore play guitars.
1983   LP on Les Disques du Crepuscule (TWI 151, Belgium)
1983   LP on Base (Italy)
1983   LP on Neutral (N4, U.S.)

Speed Trials
"Dig This!"
1984   LP/CS on Homestead (HMS011)

You Bet We've Got Something Against You
"World Looks Red" [Recorded live at the Hammersmith Palais, March 1985.]
1985   LP on Cathexis Recordings/Pleasantly Surprised (PS014)

A Diamond Hidden in the Mouth of a Corpse
"Halloween"
1985   LP on Giorno Poetry Systems (GPS 035)

Chemical Imbalance #4
"Marilyn Moore"
1986   7″ single compilation on Chemical Imbalance (CI04)

Impact [auto edit]
"I Love Her All the Time"
[Recorded live at the Hammersmith Palais, April 28, 1985.]
1986   12″ on Audio Instant (INST 2)

Communicate Live at the James Poly
"Kill Yr. Idols" [live]
1985   2×LP on Thames Poly Student Union (TPSU 0001, UK)

Sub Pop 100
"Kill Yr. Idols"
1986   LP/CS compilation on Sub Pop (SP10)

EMMA Presenteert
"Brother James"
1986   2×LP on M.A. Draje (001TM4)

Hits $ Corruption
"World Looks Red"
1986   LP on HAC (HAC 1)

Lovedolls Superstar soundtrack
"Hallowed Be Thy Name"
1986   LP/CS/CD on SST (SST062)

NME's Hat-trick
"White Kross" [unreleased live version from Florida 1986]
Feb. 1987   7″ flexi single with NME magazine (GIV-5)

Mini Plot
"I Am Right" [Goofy Mix]
1988   CD3 on SST (SST CD 234)

Sgt. Pepper Knew My Father [Childline benefit]
"Within You Without You"
1988   LP/CS/CD on NME Presents (NME PEP LP1000/NME PEP
        CD100/NME PEP MC 100)

Good Feeling
"(I Got a) Catholic Block" [live]
1988   LP on 53rd and 3rd (AGAS3)

Gigantic!
"Teenage Riot" [special video mix]
1989   CS compilation on Melody Maker (MM RTD 001)

Melting Plot
"I Am Right"
1989   LP/CA/CD compilation on SST (SST249)

The Bridge
"Computer Age"
1989   LP/CS/CD compilation on Caroline (1374/KAR002)

Every Band Has a Shonen Knife Who Loves Them
"Burning Farm"
1989   2×LP/CS/CD compilation on Gasatanka/Giant (GRI6032-
1/GRI6036-2)

Nothing Short of Total War (Part One)
"Come and Smash Me Said the Boy with the Magic Penis," "He's
on Fire," and "Magic Wand," Sonic Youth; "Scratchy Heart," Lee
Ranaldo; "****," Ciccone Youth
1989   LP/CS/CD compilation on Blast First (BFFP13, UK)

Devil's Jukebox
"Come and Smash Me Said the Boy with the Magic Penis" and
"Magic Wand," Sonic Youth; "****," Ciccone Youth
1989   10×7" box set on Blast First (BFDJ1-10, UK)

Pump Up the Volume: Music from the Original Motion Picture Soundtrack
"Titanium Exposé"
1990   LP/CS/CD on MCA (MCA-8039/MCAC 8039/MCAD-
8039)

Fast 'N' Bulbous: A Tribute to Captain Beefheart
"Electricity"
1990   LP/CS/CD on Imaginary (ILLUSION 002 LP/CD)

DK Pulser number 1
"Su nioj" [instrumental]
1990   CD3 compilation on DK Pulser, no number available
1992   CD5 compilation on Danceteria (DK1CD1)

Vera Groningen: Beauty in the Underworld
"Broken Eye" [Recorded live at Vera Groningen (a club in the
Netherlands) on June 11, 1987.]
1990   LP on VERA (001)

Never Mind the Mainstream: The Best of MTV's "120 Minutes" Volume 1
"Kool Thing"
1991   CS/CD compilation on Rhino (R4 70545/R2 70545)

Sub Pop June/July Singles Club Single
"Is It My Body"
1991   7" single on Sub Pop (SP121)

Guitarrorists
"Blues for Space Girl" [Thurston alone] / "Kitten" [Kim alone] /
"Here" [Lee alone]
1991   CD on No. 6 (KAR 009-2), distributed by Caroline

Outlaw Blues: A Tribute to Bob Dylan
"Sitting on a Barbed-Wire Fence," Kim Gordon, Thurston Moore,
and Epic Soundtracks; "Mama You've Been on My Mind," Lee
Ranaldo
1992   CD on Imaginary (ILLCD 014)

Fortune Cookie Prize: A Tribute to Beat Happening
"Black Candy," Kim Gordon, Thurston Moore, and Epic Soundtracks
1992   LP/CD compilation on Simple Machines (CD007)

Burning Leaves: The Third Fall of DGC
"Stalker"
1992   promo CD on DGC

Smiles, Vibes, and Harmony: A Tribute to Brian Wilson
"I Know There's an Answer"
1990   LP/CS/CD on DeMilo Records (DM0004-1/DM0004-4/
        DM0004-2)

Freedom of Choice: Yesterday's New Wave Hits As Performed by Today's Stars
[Planned Parenthood benefit]
"Ça Plane Pour Moi"

1992   2×LP/CS/CD on Caroline (Carol 1715-2)
1992   2×LP/CD on City Slang (City Slang 026, Europe)

Judgment Night: Music from the Motion Picture
"I Love You Mary Jane," Sonic Youth and Cypress Hill
1993   CS/CD compilation on Immortal/epic soundtrax (EK 57144)

No Alternative [AIDS research benefit; Sonic Youth track on cassette format only]
"Burning Spear"
1993   CS compilation on Arista (07822-18737-4)

Alternative NRG [Greenpeace benefit]
"JC"
1994   CS/CD on Hollywood (HR-61449-2)

THURSTON MOORE

The Coachmen, *Failure to Thrive*
Thurston's Song / Girls Are Short / Household Word / Radical Lifestyle / Stay in My Room
1979   LP/CD on New Alliance (NAR035/NAR CD 035, US)

Lydia Lunch, *In Limbo*
Plays bass. Lunch and Moore cowrote "I Wish . . . I Wish," "Friday Afternoon," "1000 Lies," and "What Did You Do."
1984   LP/CS on Doublevision (DVR 5, UK)
1986   LP on WidowSpeak (WSP19)

Lydia Lunch, *Honeymoon in Red*
Cowrote and plays guitar on "So Your Heart"; plays guitar on "Three Kings."
1988   LP/CS/CD on WidowSpeak (WSP12/WSP12 CD)

Lydia Lunch and Thurston Moore, *The Crumb*
"The Crumb" [Sings.]
1988   EP on WidowSpeak [WSP13]

The End of Music (*As We Know It*)
"European Son"
1988   CS compilation on ROIR (A156)
1991   CD compilation on Danceteria

Velvet Monkeys, *Rake*
We Call It Rock / She's Not a Girl / The Ballad of "Rake" /
Something's in the Air / Velvet Monkey Theme Song / Rock the
Night / Harmonica Hell House / Love to Give / 7 Angels / Rock
Party / Velvet Monkey Theme [Assassin Mix]—[CD only]
[Plays bass and guitar. Cowrote "The Ballad of 'Rake,' " "Rock the
Night," and "Love to Give."]
1990   LP/CD on Rough Trade (RUS 102-1/ROUGH CD 159)

Borbetomagus, *Barefoot in the Head*
All Doors Look Alike / Tanned Moon / On the Phrase "Ass Backwards" / The Date / Reduced Loaf / Concerning the Sun as a Cool
Solid
Plays guitar.
1990   LP on Forced Exposure (FE-015, US)
1991   CD on Shock

William Hooker, *Shamballa: Duets With Thurston Moore and Elliot Sharp*
Plays guitar with drummer Hooker on "Sirius Part 1: Wheels" and
"Sirius Part 2: Wings."
1993   CD on Knitting Factory Works (KFW 151)

Shonen Knife, *Rock Animals*
Plays guitar.
1994   CS/CD on Virgin

LEE RANALDO

Plus Instruments, "Special Agreement"

1980   7" single on Plurex (0011)

Glenn Branca, *The Ascension*
Lesson No. 2 / The Spectacular Commodity / Structure / Light
Field (In Consonance) / The Ascension
Plays guitars.
1981   LP on 99 Records (99-001)

Plus Instruments
1982   LP on Kremlin (KR005)

No Age: A Compilation of SST Instrumental Music
"Florida Flower"
1987   CD compilation on SST (SST CD 102)

From Here → Infinity
Time Stands Still / Destruction Site / Ouroboron / Slo Drone /
New Groove Loop / Florida Flower / Hard Left / Fuzz / Locusts
to Mary / Lathe Speaks / The Resolution / Sav X / The Open End
1987   LP/CS on SST (SST113)
1987   LP/CS/CD on Blast First (BFFP9)
Time Stands Still / Destruction Site / Ouroboron / New Groove
Loop / Florida Flower / Hard Left / Fuzz / Locusts to Mary (X2) /
Lathe Speaks / The Resolution / King's Ogg
1987   CD on SST (SST CD 113)

Kleg, *Zing*
Producer.
1991   CD on Barooni (Bar 006)

Melt [compilation]
"Drift 4"
1992   CD on Works in Progress (WIP002)

Bullets Wrapped in Sugar
"Deva, Spain: Fragments" [free with Bananafish magazine]
1992   compilation 7" on Stomach Ache (SA002)

Babes in Toyland, Fontanelle
Coproduced with Kat Bjelland.
1992   LP/CS/CD on Reprise (9 26998-2)

You Am I, Coprolalia
Producer.
1993   CD on Ra (4509925502, Australia)

You Am I, Sound As Ever
Producer.
1993   CD on Ra

Deity Guns, Trans Lines Appointment
Producer.
1993   CD on Big Cat (ABB47)

Caged/Uncaged: John Cage Venice Biennale Tribute [compilation]
"329 Overtones for John Cage"
1993   CD on Artis (CRSCD 097)

America the Beautiful [10th anniversary compilation]
"How Much Needs Crushing?"
1994   2×CD on RRRecords (CD-14)

Scriptures of the Golden Eternity
Two solos live at Knitting Factory (1989).
1994   CD on Father Yod

KIM GORDON

Harry Crews, *Naked in Garden Hills*
Man Hates a Man / Distopia / Gospel Singer / Knockout Artist /
(She's in a) Bad Mood / The Way Out / Bringing Me Down /
Car / S.O.S.
1990   LP/CS/CD on LSR (WSP24/WSP24CD)
1990   LP/CS/CD on Blast First (BFFP38)

Mirror/Dash (Thurston Moore and Kim Gordon)
"Electric Pen" / "Gum"
1992   7" on Ecstatic Peace (E#12)

Free Kitten, *Call Now*
Platinumb / Smack / Falling Backwards / Oneness / Dick / Skinny
Butt
1992   EP on Ecstatic Peace (E#22)
1992   CD on Time Bomb (CD-05, Japan)

Free Kitten, *Straight Up*
Platinumb / Smack / Falling Backwards / Oneness / Dick / Skinny
Butt
1992   10"/CD on Pearl Necklace (PN-1, Australia)

Free Kitten, *Yoshimi vs. Mascis* [Free Kitten/Mosquito split single]
1992   7" on Time Bomb (09, Japan)

Die Haut, *Head On*
"Intoxication" [Sings.]
1992   LP/CD on What's So Funny About . . . (SF 122)

Hole, *Pretty on the Inside*
Coproduced with Don Fleming.
1992   LP/CS/CD on Caroline

Free Kitten [picture disc]
"Oh Bondage Up Yours!" / "1, 2, 3"
1993   7″ on Sympathy for the Record Industry (256)

Free Kitten
"John Starks Blues" / "Guilty Pleasures"
1993   7″ on In the Red (015)

Free Kitten
"Platinumb"

Lollapalooza '93 [promotional item]
1993   CD on Sony (CSK 5256)

Yoshimi [featuring Kim and Julie Cafritz]
"Speaker" / "Tuna Power"
1993   7″ on Ecstatic Peace (E#31)

Free Kitten
"Cleopatra" / "Loose Lips"
1993   7″ on SOS (01)

STEVE SHELLEY

Lucky Sperms, *I Am the Man* [with Mike Watt]
Walking the Cow / Tomorrow Never Knows / Glass Onion
1991   7″ on Ecstatic Peace (E#15)

Nikki Sudden
Whiskey Priest / Venetian Rags
Plays drums.
1991   7″ on Singles Only (SOL-228-7)

Mosquito
Down / Pretty Lil' Thing / Fat Man Walks / Oh No, Oh Yes, Oh No
1992   7″ on ERL (ERL009)

Sentridoh, Losercore [with Lou Barlow on Shelley's own label]
Losercore / Really Insane
1992   7″ on Smells Like Records (SLR-68)

Mosquito, Time Was
Mothership Singapore / Erl Duke / Automatic Vaudeville / Blues Implosion / Time Was / In the Night (Drive My Car) / (The Legend of) Seven Skulls / The Sound of This Song I Love / Walking Pneumonia / Night of Manhood / Hot Corn Girl / Don't See Twin Peaks the Movie / Gum Shoe / Frodown O King Cacha / Evilthing Catcher / Gentleman's Tan / Joey Davison / McGurk's Suicide Hill / Beneath the Invisible / Wake Up Wake Up Wake Up
1993   CD on Au Go Go (ANDA 162CD, Australia)

Mosquito, U.F.O. Catcher
Blood and Thunder / Leslie Is No Name for a Cowboy / Leslie West / Leslie Nielsen / Early Grunge / Dry Bones / Haywagon / Martin Denny / Four-Button Man / Daddy, That's Me / It Cut / Happy-man / Funky Got a Function / Book of God / Ragpicker's Den / Bayonne Trailerpark / Sandwichmen / The Hard Walk / Swamp Angel / Gashouse / Shad Belly
1993   CD on Time Bomb (Bomb CD-13, Japan)

OTHER APPEARANCES

Jad Fair and Kramer, Roll Out the Barrel
Kim and Thurston make guest appearances.
1988   Shimmy-Disc 012

Moe Tucker, *Life in Exile After Abdication*
Chase [Kim Gordon on bass, Lee Ranaldo on guitar, and Thurston Moore on guitar] / Pale Blue Eyes [Kim Gordon on bass and backing vocals] / Bo Diddley [Kim Gordon on bass and backing vocals; Steve Shelley on drums] / Talk So Mean [Kim Gordon on bass]
1989   LP/CS on 50 Skidillion Watts (MOE 7-1)

The Ex, *Joggers and Smoggers*
Thurston Moore and Lee Ranaldo perform on "Gentlemen" and "Tightly Stretched."
1989   2×LP/2×CD on Ex (EX 040/041, Ex040/041D)
1989   2×CD on Fist Puppet, Holland (Fist 005-CD)

William S. Burroughs, *Dead City Radio*
Spoken-word LP. Sonic Youth performs on "William's Welcome," "Dr. Benway's House," and "The Lord's Prayer."
1990   LP/CS/CD on Island (Island 422-846 264-2, US)

Epic Soundtracks, *Rise Above*
Lee plays guitar on "Fallen Down" and Kim Gordon sings backup on "Big Apple Graveyard."
1993   CD on Bar/None (AHAON-0029-2)

SONIC YOUTH TRIBUTE ALBUM

Gioventul Sonica: 11 Young Bands Play Sonic Youth's Songs
Star Fuckers, "Death Valley '69" / Killbrains, "Tunic" / Redrum, "Silver Rocket" / Third from the Sun, "White Cross" / Headspring, "Catholic Block" / Neumann, "Stereo Sanctity" / Welcome Idots, "Starpower" / Subterranean Dining Rooms, "Mote" / Carnival of Fools, "Shadow of Doubt" / Saint Luka, "Teenage Riot" / Pagan Easter, "Kill Yr. Idols/Kool Thing/Shakin' Hell"
1991   Electric Eye (EEHSLP020)

''OFFICIAL'' BOOTLEG RELEASES

Walls Have Ears
C.B. / Green Love / Brother James / Kill Yr. Idols / "Mad" Groove /
I Love Her All The Time / Expressway to Yr. Skull / Spahn Ranch
Dance / Blood on Brighton Beach / Burning Spear / Death Valley
'69 / Speed Jamc / Ghost Bitch / The World Looks Red / The
Word (E.V.O.L.) / Brother Jam-Z / Killed & Kicked Off
1986   2 LPs on Not Records (NOT 1 [BUT 2], UK)

Goo Demos
Tunic / Number One / Titanium Exposé / Dirty Boots / Corky /
My Friend Goo / Bookstore / Animals / DU2 / Blow Job? / Lee
#2 / Dirty Boots [single edit]
1990   LP
1991   CD from Sonic Death Fan Club (SD 1301)

4 Tunna Brix
Rowche Rumble / Psycho Mafia / My New House / Victoria
1991   EP on Goofin' Records (SD-SP 10)

Hold That Tiger
Intro / Schizophrenia / Tom Violence / White Kross / Kotton
Krown / Stereo Sanctity / Brother James / Pipeline/Kill Time /
Catholic Block / Tuff Gnarl / Death Valley '69 / Beauty Lies in the
Eye / Expressway to Yr. Skull / Pacific Coast Highway / Encore:
Loadmouth / I Don't Wanna Walk Around with You / Today Yr.
Love Tomorrow the World / Beat on the Brat
1991   LP on Goofin' Records (SD-SP 20)

Live at the Continental Club
Tom Violence / Shadow of a Doubt / Starpower / Secret Girls /
Death to Our Friends / Green Light / Kill Yr. Idols / Ghost Bitch /
Expressway [cut] / World Looks Red / Confusion (indeed)
1992   CD from Sonic Death Fan Club (SD 13002)

Shaking Hell
"Shaking Hell" [live] / "Little Jammy Thing"
1992   7" single (SCONC 020, Italy) with *Sonic Life* booklet

BOOTLEG RELEASES

Killer Kills All
Intro by Iggy Pop [Detroit 1974] / I Wanna Be Yr. Dog [live with
Iggy Pop 1987] / White Kross [live 1987] / (I Got a) Catholic
Block [live 1987] / Kill Yr. Idols [live 1987] / I Love Her All the
Time [live 1985] / World Looks Red [live 1985] / New Speedway
Boogie [1987 radio special] / Death Valley '69 [Flaming Lips with
Thurston Moore, 1987] / Silver Rocket [Videomix 1989] / The
Bridge [Lee Ranaldo studio track 1985] / Fucking Youth Today
[Thurston Moore studio track 1982] / Within You Without You
[BBC studio, 1986] / The Closet [original by Teenage Jesus & the
Jerks; Harry Crews, live Hamburg 1988] / European Son [original
by Velvet Underground; Thurston Moore studio track 1988] /
Brother James [live 1985]
1989   LP (GEMA-LC8214, Germany)

Moo
Tunic / Number One / Titanium Exposé / Dirty Boots / My Pal
Goo / Bookstore / Animal Song / Du II / Blow Job / Notorious
Rockin' Lee
1990   CD on Handmade (Germany)

Anarchy on St. Mary's Place
Halloween / Death Valley '69 / Intro / Brave Men Run / Madonna /
I Love Her All the Time / Ghost Bitch / I'm Insane / Instrumental /
Brother James / Kill Yr. Idols [Piano] / Flower / Express Way to
Yr. Skull
1991   CD on Youth (YTH-082, Germany)

Blow Job
Tunic / Number One / Titanium Exposé / Dirty Boots I / Dirty Boots II / Corky / My Friend Goo / Bookstore / Animal Song / Dull / Mildred Pierce / Notorious Rockin' Lee
1991   CD on Youth (YTH-086, Germany)

Live in Vienna 1989
Silver Rocket / The Wonder / Hyperstation / Eric's Trip / Candle / Kissability / The Sprawl / Teenage Riot / Hey Joni / White Cross / Eliminator Jr.
1991   CD on Oblivion (OR CD 9105, Italy)

The Mira Tapes
Mote / Song for Karen / Dirty Boots / Chapel Hill / I Love Her All the Time / Mary Christ / Kool Thing / Expressway (for Patti Smith) / Spot'ssz Christ
1992   CD on Wombat Tontraeger (Germany)

Happiness Is a Warm Gun . . .
Personality Crisis [New York Dolls] / Dirty Boots [demo] / Is It My Body? [Alice Cooper] / Flower [Anti Fuckword Radio Edit] / I Wanna Be Your Dog [with Iggy Pop] / Song for Karen [live, Hamburg] / Computer Song [Neil Young] / Burning Farm [Shonen Knife] / Gum / Electric Pen / Disappearer [demo] / That's All I Know / White Cross / Sister [The Town & Country, June 4, 1987] / Rewolf [Special Natas Mix] / It's an Interview / My Friend Goo [Hamburg] / Cinderella's Big Score [Hamburg
1992   CD on Bad Fuck

The Social Power Performance
Social Power [Lee Ranaldo] / The Wonder / Hyperstation / Eric's Trip / Confusion Is Next / (She's in a) Bad Mood / Brother James / Kill Yr. Idols / The Burning Spear
1992   CD on Blue Knights (BKR 05)

Warpower
Teenage Riot [live, Hamburg 1989] / Starpower [live, Baton Rouge 1986]
1989   7″ single (Germany)

Speak No Evol
Corporate Ghost / Ruben's Beard / Major Label Chicken Feed / Clippers
1989   7″ single on Maida Vale Studio (UK)

John Peel Session #2
Clippers / Rubin's Beard / Corporate Ghost / Major Label Chicken Feed
1990   7″ single

Kooler Thing
Bookstore (Mote) / Lee #2 / Dirty Boots
1990   7″ single (US)

Personality Crisis
Personality Crisis / Disappear / Beat on the Brat / Red Vinyl
1990   7″ single

All Fall Down
Psycho Mafia / Rowche Rumble / My New House
1991   7″ single (US)

Bad Mood
Making the Nature Scene / World Looks Red / Bad Mood / Brother James / Kill Your Idols
1991   2×7″ singles

VIDEOS

Put Blood in the Music
Directed by Charles Atlas, 57 minutes, approximately 24 of which are devoted to Sonic Youth.
1989   Vision Productions

Goo
Dirty Boots / Tunic (Song for Karen) / Mary-Christ / Kool Thing / Mote / My Friend Goo / Disappearer / Mildred Pierce / Cinderella's Big Score / Scooter and Jinx / Titanium Exposé
1991   VHS on DGC (DGCV-39508)

1991: The Year Punk Broke
Directed by Dave Markey
Sonic Youth live: Schizophrenia / Brother James / Teenage Riot / Dirty Boots / I Love Her All the Time / Mote / Kool Thing / Expressway to Yr. Skull
1992   VHS on DGC (DGCV-39518)

Gila Monster Jamboree
1992   Sonic Death Fan Club (SD13005)

Sonic Death Fan Club
Box 6179
Hoboken, New Jersey 07030